CHASING UTOPIA

CHASING UTOPIA

The Future of the Kibbutz in a Divided Israel

by David Leach

For Jenny
and our own
children of the dream

Contents

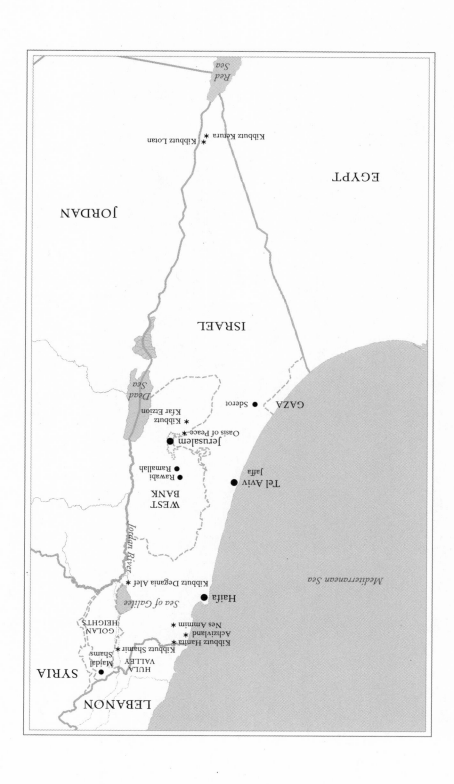

It Is Dangerous to Read Facebook

These things only are impersonal:
insomnia, land mines, and long hours of work.
Everything else is ours or not ours,
divided like the world
inside and outside the skin.

—Susan Tichy, "Volunteers"

Another summer. Another war.

Like tinder in a dry valley, it rarely takes much spark to set Israel and its neighbours alight. In the hot months of 2014, Gaza catches fire again. The world watches it burn. As the violence spikes, I can't avert my eyes from the headlines that call to mind the lines from "It Is Dangerous to Read Newspapers," an early poem by Margaret Atwood: *Each time I hit a key / on my electric typewriter, / speaking of peaceful trees / another village explodes.* Decades later, it's not any safer to read blogs or Facebook updates, browse Twitter feeds or YouTube channels. My TV, laptop and smartphone scroll a digital tickertape of bomb strikes and body counts, punctuated by diatribes and denunciations from friends and strangers. Most people, like myself, have no real stake in this Middle East feud other than our own curdled sense of outrage. *We need* to have an opinion, though, because the bloody stalemate between the state of Israel and the stateless Palestinian people has become the political litmus test of our age. Who you support says who you are—politically, personally. In a land claimed by two peoples, only one story can be heard at a time.

In the summer of 2014, the catalyst and the conflict prove especially gruesome. Three Jewish pupils, studying at an Orthodox *yeshiva* in the occupied West Bank, disappear while hitchhiking. Eighteen days later, Israeli authorities find the boys' bodies under a pile of stones. The army sweeps through Palestinian villages in search of the killers, while Israeli politicians blame the military wing of Hamas, the Islamic Resistance Movement. Right-wing Jewish settlers burn an Arab boy to death. Palestinian militants from Hamas renew a campaign of lobbing crude rockets from the coastal enclave of Gaza deeper into Israeli territory. The Israeli Air Force responds with missile strikes. Airlines divert international flights. Israel musters tanks, artillery and tens of thousands of reserve soldiers for a ground assault. Generals dub the new military operation "Protective Edge," which sounds like a high-tech shaving device but is far, far bloodier. Images of shattered schools and apartment blocks in Gaza proliferate across the Internet. Anti-war protests turn violent in Paris and other European cities. When Israeli peaceniks march in Tel Aviv, right-wing thugs shout, "Death to leftists! Death to Arabs!" Hamas militants emerge from hand-dug tunnels near border kibbutzes and kill several IDF soldiers. Israeli commanders tell residents in Gaza to abandon neighbourhoods targeted as missile caches and Hamas command centres. More than 2,000 Palestinians, many women and children, die in a month-long storm of concrete and shrapnel.

I live thousands of miles away, along the Pacific shoulder of North America, on an island as lush and placid as Gaza and southern Israel are dry and volatile. And yet I am drawn into a debate in which rhetoric flees from all reason. Torrents of angry words and numbing images cascade down my screens. *Israel is an apartheid state of baby killers and war criminals! Gaza is ruled by Jew-hating Islamo-fascists who martyr their children as human shields!* #GazaUnderAttack and #StandWithIsrael compete for clicks from armchair slacktivists like myself. My sympathies ping-pong between the Israelis I know, threatened by rocket fire and terror tunnels, and the horror show broadcast from the bombed-out, body-strewn streets of Gaza. I don't recognize the Israel where I once lived, the country to which I have returned several times. I can't hear the voices of the people, Jews and Palestinians alike, who spoke to me of hope and reconciliation.

In the weeks after the ceasefire, the Israel Defense Forces and Hamas will pull back to the heavily armed no-man's land of mutual antipathy that divides Israelis and Palestinians. Politicians and pundits will proclaim victory. The Internet will assign blame. Both sides will mourn their dead. And I will be left to wonder, *What happened to the original vision of this nation?* The Israel I know began more than a hundred years ago with twelve pioneers on the shores of the Jordan River. It began with a naive faith that these young dreamers could break ground and build a peaceable society for the long-exiled Jewish people and share the land of Palestine with their Arab neighbours. It began in the hope that, by living as equals, they could inspire the rest of the world to throw off the shackles of envy and overcome our long-held tribal hatreds. It began with the kibbutz.

PART ONE
Who Killed the Kibbutz?

Anyone who has never lived on a kibbutz doesn't understand the first thing about it. It's impossible to understand from the outside and this whole investigation of yours is pointless.

—Batya Gur, *Murder on a Kibbutz: A Communal Case*

— CHAPTER I —

Ghetto Life in the Finger of Galilee

Every child is born utopian. Our urge to create new worlds kicks in as soon as we can lift a block or wield a crayon. We build towers as precarious as Babel. We design tiny cities, guided by the divine laws of Lego or Fisher-Price—and now *Minecraft*. We imagine societies with leaders and followers, heroes and villains, histories and intrigues. Our instincts to build worlds and tell stories are entwined, a double helix of human creativity. Overshadowed by an adult society we can't quite understand, let alone control, we build microcosms over which we *can* rule.

Like most kids, I was obsessed with building worlds. Growing up, I engineered neighbourhoods for legless, bullet-headed toy figurines and played grade-school Jane Jacobs in my parents' basement. An old Kodachrome photo reveals a boy in a blond bowl cut, ever the good Catholic, arranging his Star Wars action figures on tiny wooden pews so they can attend Sunday Mass; in *my* galaxy far, far away, Boba Fett the bounty hunter needed to attend confession. My oddest obsession

was the Maginot Line. At 11 or 12, I read about France's military fortifications in an illustrated history text. Built in the 1930s to withstand a
German assault, the Maginot Line became a Second World War footnote when the Nazis did an end run through Belgium on their blitzkrieg
to Paris. I didn't care if the Maginot Line worked. To my young eyes,
it was a marvel of design, an entire world carved beneath the surface
of the earth. I was fascinated by the architecture, the cross-sections of
underground chambers, tunnels and armaments—a subterranean network for a strategically inept nation of mole people. I filled notebooks
with Maginot renovations and populated my corridors with bustling
stick men.

Lewis Mumford, the American social critic and urban historian,
called our instinct toward city-making a "will-to-utopia." "It is our
utopias that make the world tolerable to us," he wrote in 1922. "The
cities and mansions that people dream of are those in which they finally
live." In *The Story of Utopias*, Mumford distinguishes between different
types. Our childhood visions of alternate realities satisfy what he calls
the "utopia of escape." In fantasy worlds, the human mind finds temporary respite from the drudgery and pain of daily life. A science-fiction
novel. A postcard of a tropical beach on a cubicle wall. A Disneyland of
the mind. Utopia as a flight from reality, a return to innocence.

One of the first urban scholars, Mumford was less interested in
utopia as escapism than in "utopias of reconstruction"—utopia as an
ambitious social-engineering project; utopia as a blueprint for a better
life; utopia as a cure. The utopia of reconstruction, he explains, is "a
vision of a reconstituted environment which is better adapted to the
nature and aims of the human beings who dwell within it."

When I first read those lines, I thought, *That sounds like the kibbutz.*
The pioneers of Israel's kibbutz movement had chased a vision of
a new life and a better world. Their utopias of reconstruction didn't
remain on the page, like Plato's Republic. Instead, they etched their

schemes into the rough earth, one settlement at a time, until an archipel-ago of communities stretched from the northern mountains to the Red Sea. Every wall they erected, every garden they sowed, every pathway they paved reflected a model society based on a communal way of life. "We shape our buildings," Winston Churchill once wrote, "and after-wards our buildings shape us." If you create the perfect village, in other words, the village will perfect you in turn.

That was the dream. But a blueprint for paradise is one thing. Making the vision a reality tends to be messier.

—

When people ask why, at the age of 20, I dropped out of university to live on a commune in Israel, I reply, "Look at my wrist." There you can read a faded map of my past, a thin white scar that runs as straight as the Jordan River. It's all that remains, aside from the odd arthritic pang, of what I like to call my "old college football injury."

Which is true to a point. Fact: I fractured my right wrist in a scrim-mage during my first semester of university. A little macho-deflating context: I'd been playing *touch* football. In the snow. With journalism students.

Still, that bad break meant deferred exams and months in a cast and, after the tiny bone refused to heal, a screw and a bone graft. More time in a cast nixed plans to join my hometown high school sweetheart on a tree-planting contract in northern Alberta. She promised she would only be gone for a month and vowed to write every day. This was the summer of 1988, a more innocent and disconnected era: pre-satellite phone, pre-email, pre-Facebook and Skype. Our relationship would live or die on the wings of Canada Post.

I worked a temp job filing accident reports for the city's transpor-tation department. At home, I taught my left hand to type soppy love letters to a remote P.O. box in the boreal forest. I kept mailing these letters, even when the replies diminished and then stopped.

In the wilderness, my hometown high school sweetheart had soured on our saccharine suburban dreams and traded up for someone new. He was, I would learn, ten years my senior, a veteran tree planter from the west coast and, worse, an artist. He had a thing for dinosaurs and topless chorus girls that he depicted in canvas collages slopped together from airplane glue, marbles and dismembered Barbie dolls. He had once been a heroin junkie but now only drank till his eyeballs went yellow. How could I compete?

I considered pulling a Lancelot, stealing my parents' Malibu Classic and driving across the continent to win her back. My friends talked me down from that fantasy. "Dude," they told me, "get over her."

It wasn't so easy. I had a broken heart, an aching wrist and enough money for tuition or trans-Atlantic airfare. I chose Door #2 and bought an open plane ticket to Tel Aviv.

Why Israel? A friend had backpacked around the Mediterranean and told me about something called a kibbutz. "What's that?" I asked. A kibbutz, I learned, was a cooperative farming village where backpackers could swap manual labour in fields or factories for room and board. Israel had hundreds of kibbutzes, from the grassy foothills of Mt. Hermon to the desert valley that led to the Red Sea; many had established the borders of what would become, in 1948, the Jewish state. Kibbutzes could be as small as 80 members or as large as 2,000. They ran collective economies, often described as "the purest form of communism in the Western world," uncorrupted by the police-state bureaucracies that ruled Russia, China and Cuba. Every year, thousands of young travellers passed through the gates of the frontier farms and lived together briefly, and intensely, as volunteers. By the late 1980s, volunteering on a kibbutz had reached a peak of popularity; the 1985 film *Not Quite Paradise*—a hammy romantic-comedy by the British director of *Educating Rita* and *The Spy Who Loved Me*—dramatized the clash of cultures between rough-edged Israeli kibbutzniks and over-sexed, hard-drinking backpackers.

I'd never been political, and if all I'd wanted was a rural sabbatical, my prairie uncles could have put me to work on their wheat farm. The kibbutz, however, promised an exotic land filled with history, adventure and camaraderie, far from my own romantic failures. I'd been raised on Sunday school stories, too, and still had a fascination with the ancient geographical names of the Bible: *Gethsemane, Golgotha, Galilee.* In Hebrew, David meant "beloved." That seemed a good sign, too. And it was a chance to live, however briefly, like a true utopian.

My friends threw a going-away party. Or rather they invited me to drop by the same parent-free townhouse where, every Friday night for the past three years, we gathered in the basement to shotgun six-packs of beer, watch a VHS bootleg of *The Breakfast Club* and renew the great Ally-Sheedy-versus-Molly-Ringwald debate that had paralyzed a gen-eration. When I arrived, they presented me with a handcrafted goodbye gift: a joint the size of a baby's arm. Sadly, they knew as much about street drugs as they did about contemporary cinema. The fat wand of loose tobacco was so parsimoniously seeded with rat turds of low-grade suburban hash that it was less a monster joint than the *representation* of a monster joint, a dim Platonic shadow of a mega-doobie. It didn't matter: they had only rolled it for the placebo effect. As the evening grew hazier, a high-school acquaintance interrogated my motives for dropping out of school to live in Israel. "Why are you throwing away your life—" he shouted, inches from my face "—for a *girl?*"

I passed around an address book for postcards I knew I would never write. Days later, in the airport departure zone, an Israeli secu-rity agent from El Al Airlines scattered the contents of my backpack across a steel table. My mother had sewn a red maple leaf into the top corner of the pack; the fabric talisman was meant to confer diplomatic immunity upon all young Canadians abroad, mostly by proving you weren't American. Now on public display, the net worth of my newly transient life ranged from the pretentious (a paperback copy of James Joyce's *Ulysses*) to the pathetic (long bandoliers of Trojan condoms; hope, amongst other things, sprang eternal). But the agent's suspicion was piqued by my address book.

He pointed to an open page. "Who is Massoud Falsometer?"

I blanked. I'd never heard the name. What was it doing in my book? Then I recognized the handwriting. Under the letter *F*, a friend had scribbled an Arabic-sounding pen name.

I explained to the skeptical agent that, honestly, I didn't know a Mr. Falsometer. That, no, he hadn't given me any "packages" to transport. That, in fact, he probably didn't exist. That the person who had entered the address was a Kyle from Quebec, not a Massoud from the Middle East. That the name was a gag. ("Falsometer, get it?") A joke at my expense.

The agent's glare darkened. "What kind of joke is that?"

Good question. How could I explain to this dour gatekeeper the emotionally stunted rituals of the North American male? I barely understood them myself.

I'd tried to leave early from my going-away party. But the host wouldn't let me escape. He grappled me in a sumo hold and demanded I stay. I resisted. He resisted back. Robert Bly and *Iron John* were still two years off, so this is what passed for a man-hug in the late-'80s. We caromed off kitchen counters and through the screen door and down the back steps and into the small yard of his absentee parents. We scrummed, laughing mirthlessly, until I felt too tired to care. We staggered backwards and crashed through the sliding metal doors of a garden shed. There we lay, panting, limbs tangled amid corroded rakes and pruning shears. Our fraternal farewell consummated in blood, my friend dusted off his jeans and left me sprawled in the dark.

At least, I thought—pinned in the broken embrace of a hard-ware-store cabana, hypnotized by the vertiginous dance of the autumn stars above me—*at least*, I knew, *wherever I was going couldn't be any more fucked up than where I was leaving.*

Of course, even about this, I was so very wrong.

—

"Are you Jewish?"

I've fielded that question since running away to the kibbutz. My blond crewcut and boiled-ham pigmentation suggest *my* people weren't chosen by anyone other than sunscreen marketers. I grew up Catholic and lapsed a few years before leaving for Israel. My knowledge of the Promised Land got fuzzy after the first century A.D. In my mind, Jerusalem didn't extend beyond the walls of the Old City; Bethlehem and Nazareth were the other metropolises, while sandalled disciples netted fish from the Sea of Galilee to go with their loaves. The Holy Land had likely been touched up since its Biblical heyday, but I didn't have a precise image in my head.

I had serious homework to do. Before I left, I arranged a letter of introduction from the Jewish Community Centre. The coordinator set me in front of a *Welcome to Israel!* VHS tape and gave me a few brochures that showcased a romantic image of kibbutz life. Swarthy men and women bent over shovels in orchards and cotton fields, shaded by white sun hats and kerchiefs, sleeves rolled on proletari-at-blue work shirts. Muscled legs stretched short-shorts that would make Kareem Abdul-Jabbar blush. Kibbutzniks, I learned, were the native-born descendants of pioneers who had left Eastern Europe for Palestine in the early 20th century, inspired by the utopian dreams of socialism and Zionism, the conjoined philosophies of Karl Marx and Theodor Herzl. They'd been promised "a land without a people for a people without a land"—a sales pitch that turned out to be only half-true. In the epic of the kibbutz, the first pioneers had abandoned Europe's stifling and persecuted Jewish *shtetls* to live in secular communes. They governed their relations by direct democracy and absolute economic equality. Everyone shared everything, from their profits to their boots. Everyone voted on everything, no matter how minor—and the majority ruled. Together, the young idealists built a nation out of swamp and rock. They settled the frontier and defended its future borders. They were Hebrew Marlboro Men with Marxist leanings.

The kibbutz was most famous for the "children's house" in which kids were raised collectively, separated from their parents except for pre-dinner visits of an hour or two. In co-ed groups, they studied and played, ate and slept, all under the care of the *metapelet* or "nanny." The communal childcare system freed women to contribute fully to the economic, political and social life of the kibbutz while also teaching children the spirit of collective enterprise. Throughout the 1960s and 1970s, psychologists studied Israel's experiment in communal child-raising; in 1969, Bruno Bettelheim published *The Children of the Dream*, in which he concludes the kibbutz "clearly reached its own goal: to create a radically new personality in a single generation."

By 1988, kibbutz brochures played down these socialist experiments. Communism wasn't a big draw for backpackers. Most volunteers came to Israel instead for the lusty promise, as one volunteer coordinator told me, of "sun, sand and sex." The brochures had air-brushed away mentions of wars and terrorism, but I couldn't ignore the headlines: the West Bank and Gaza, captured by Israel in the Six-Day War of 1967, had erupted in clashes between Palestinian youths and the Israeli army. Thrown rocks versus rubber bullets. Molotov cocktails against live rounds. The protesters called the uprising an *intifada*, or "throwing off" in Arabic. I was walking into the thick of it.

9

After finishing the paperwork, the JCC coordinator asked for a favour. Could I deliver a care package for a friend in Israel? He gave me three hefty plastic bottles, stout as table lamps, filled with Head & Shoulders, at least according to the labels. "You can't get it over there," he said with a shrug. I left Canada in a late-October snowstorm and arrived in Israel to waves of heat shimmering off the tarmac. I disembarked, grabbed my backpack, stepped through the airport's sliding doors and felt the thick air chest-bump me. A corridor of faces barked greetings and thrust hand-scrawled cardboard signs. My dry eyes blinked, but the lettering refused to snap into focus until I realized, *It's all Hebrew to me now.*

By the time I reached Tel Aviv, I'd sweated through my T-shirt under the weight of the contraband shampoo. Scooters and *sherut* minibuses honked in the low canyons of dirty white buildings. Soldiers and street hawkers, businessmen and beach-goers flooded the sidewalks. Young women strolled together in olive army uniforms with Uzis slung like Gucci bags over their arms. I felt a clammy light-headedness, a jet-lagged dislocation, as I stepped out of the sun into the low-lit cloister of the kibbutz office.

I presented the introduction letter to the head of the volunteer department. He asked me to show my visa. Then he studied a list of kibbutzes looking for volunteers. "Where do you want to go?" It sounded like a philosophical query. "The north, the centre or the south?"

I stared at a map on the wall. Tel Aviv was in the middle, and I could feel myself dissolving in its heat. The south—and the expanse of the Negev Desert—would be hotter. My eyes drifted upwards till I spotted the cool blue bulb of the Sea of Galilee.

"The north," I replied.

"*Shamir,*" he declared.

His finger traced a route up from Tel Aviv, past Haifa, and skirted the western shore of the Sea of Galilee, where I expected it to stop, but it then climbed the thin line of the Jordan River into a funnel of land near the top of the country. An inch or two below its edge, I noticed *Shamir* in small script and the bolder-faced names of its neighbours: *Lebanon*, *Syria*, *Golan*. That evening, I caught a bus for Kiryat Shmona, the nearest town to the kibbutz. As we drove into the dusk, young soldiers dozed in nearby seats, nestled like lovers against their rifles. By heading north, I realized, I had dodged the heat but not the fire.

—

A second bus dropped me at Kibbutz Shamir in the dark. I was issued a room in a tin-roofed cabin and fell into a distracted slumber on a thin slab of foam. High-pitched cries outside my door haunted my first sleep, like a serenade of gremlins. (Mongooses, I learned.) Eight hours later, I rolled off the cot, threw open the door and confronted a vista that remains embedded in my memory. A smudge of red and yellow spread across a gently serrated ridge, the rest of the valley in shadow. The sun seemed about to launch from behind these western mountains until the light exploded over my shoulder instead, leaping off the high ground to the east. It wouldn't be the last time this land fooled my senses. The warming air burned off the hovering mist and revealed the tributaries that fed the Jordan River. I discerned orthogonal irrigation pools and fishponds, a patchwork of orchards and fields. I heard birdsong, a tractor's engine coughing to life. That first dawn, Kibbutz Shamir delivered its promise of a pastoral escape from my troubles back home. I was hooked.

Ami, the kibbutz's volunteer coordinator, arrived in an electric cart. My new boss was in his thirties but looked older. He was shorter than me by a foot and walked with a high-kneed march, his large puppet's head topped with a swoop of thinning blond hair. He suffered from a genetic condition that accelerated his body's aging—that was the rumour. Ami gave a tour of the kibbutz. A ring road formed a wobbly ovoid on the slopes of the valley, with sidewalks spoking into a central hub, a common kibbutz design. On the westernmost downslope was the volunteers' district, better known as the Upper and Lower Ghetto, with three long bungalows that each housed four rooms, a few smaller duplexes, a concrete bunker for communal showers and bathrooms and a small cabin with a TV, fridge, card table and sagging sofa. To the north were the swimming pool, sports hall and apiary. To the south, the industrial district contained two factories, the chicken sheds and cattle barns. On the high ground to the east, kibbutzniks lived in tree-shaded pocket neighbourhoods of connected bungalows. Ami and I followed a path into the core of the kibbutz—cars were shared by members and kept to the ring road. We passed the volunteers' pub, the small general store, the main office with a pay phone on its outdoor wall, the children's house and finally the centre of the entire community: the dining hall and industrial kitchen. Here, members ate, danced and voted in a shared space.

As we walked, Ami retold the history of his home, both kibbutz and country. A handful of young pioneers, mostly from Romania, had founded the kibbutz in 1944. They were Marxists, members of a socialist youth group demanding a challenge, so they were sent to land purchased in the cartographic extrusion known as the Finger of Galilee; the kibbutz occupied the final knuckle. They named their new home Shamir, "The Rock" in Hebrew, after the great chunks of limestone they had to clear before they could lay foundations or till fields. It felt like a true frontier. "We are right on the edge of the Golan Heights," Ami said, gesturing at the slope to the east. I didn't grasp the significance.

Even after Israel's independence and the armistice of 1949, he explained, the Syrian army had shelled Shamir from the high ground of the Golan; border soldiers took potshots from their outposts at kibbutzniks in the fields. Everything changed in 1967 with the pre-emptive attack of the Six-Day War. The Israel Defense Forces (IDF) overran Syrian positions and pushed across the Heights until Israel occupied roughly 1,200 square kilometres of strategic high ground. (To the south, the IDF captured the West Bank and the Gaza Strip, which collectively became known as the Occupied Territories.) In 1981, the Israeli parliament extended Israeli law and administration through the Golan, an act of quasi-annexation unrecognized by the international community. The UN has maintained a peacekeeping force in the Golan since 1974. The capture of the Heights, said Ami, made life on his kibbutz more peaceful. Most men on the kibbutz, he told me, had fought in one or more of Israel's six major wars. And yet Ami could see both sides, the long view, the road beyond the conflict. That, too, was the philosophy of the kibbutz movement, one of the nation's most progressive political forces. "If we want peace with the Arabs," Ami said, "Israel will have to give up some of the Territories." It would prove to be a hard promise to fulfill.

—

After Ami's primer, my political education took a backseat to the routines and rotation of kibbutz work. I had to earn my three meals a day, my nights on a foam mattress in a bare cabin, my weekly ration of toiletries and cigarettes, the 30 shekels a month added to my bar tab. Shamir had roughly 500 members, a mid-sized kibbutz. No task was too menial for a kibbutznik—and certainly not for a volunteer. Everyone pitched in for the common good. Managers of work branches requested extra hands, and Ami assigned volunteers to different jobs on a weekly cycle: the kitchen, the communal daycare, the old-age home, the chicken run, the cattle sheds, the optical or the fabric factory, the vegetable or flower gardens, the cotton fields, the apple, kiwi or avocado orchards in the valley.

At any one time, Shamir hosted 15 to 30 foreign volunteers or "vol-lies." We lived together (and slept together) in our warren of crude cabins with beige walls and tin roofs. We ate together and gossiped (mostly in English) in the noisy main dining room with a huge wall hanging that read (also in English): *We Are All One Woven Humanity*. From my first meal to my last beer, I was surrounded by a Babel of languages I'd rarely heard before: Hebrew, of course, but also Dutch, German, Spanish, Danish, Portuguese, Arabic, Afrikaans, as well as global variations of spoken English nearly as puzzling. The volunteer ghetto felt like a student-run United Nations with more booze and less corruption. I became fluent in no single foreign tongue but learned to curse and flirt in several. A quarter-century later, I can recite the lyrics to a Swedish drinking song and whisper, *"Ska vi älska?"*—"Shall we make love?"—an essential kibbutz skill.

My first assignment was to operate the industrial dishwashing machine, a steam-spouting dragon's mouth with a conveyor-belt tongue into which diners fed plates, cutlery and trays after every meal. It was a smelly, noisy, messy job—and one assigned to every kibbutznik as a reminder to stay humble. I scrubbed the huge steel pots and pans and climbed into the dragon's belly to extract a loose fork jamming its mechanism. A week later, I graduated to kitchen duty, running chores for Yaffa, the diminutive and vocal head cook, a chihuahua in an apron, who barked, *"Yalla! Yalla!"*—"Hurry! Hurry!"—as we hustled hot food to the hungry workers in the dining room. Afterwards, I pulled on thick elbow-length rubber gloves like a hazmat worker's, walked into an industrial oven as tall as a phone booth stucco'd with a week's worth of carbonized meat sauces, and slopped its blackened walls with an acidic brown jelly that ate quickly through my apron and jeans and then, more slowly, through my skin.

I welcomed my reassignment to the orchards, where I earned the nickname "Monkey Man" by shimmying up the high branches to retrieve avocados. Autumn gave way to winter; mornings dawned cold and rainy—no sun, no sand, not nearly enough sex—and the summer-browned valley turned green again. Snow descended the ski slopes of Mt. Hermon to the north. I shuffled between the optical factory and fieldwork. We dug irrigation trenches in the mud of the apple orchards, pruned the bare limbs of kiwi trees and burned stubble from the cotton harvest until the leaping flames singed the hair from our forearms, and our faces turned coal-miner black with soot. At shift's end, I returned to the volunteer ghetto with my work clothes and canvas boots scuffed and torn, my body aching, ravenous, bruised and often bloodied—and more alive than I'd felt in years.

It wasn't all work. Tuesday nights, the sports hall screened subtitled Hollywood hits, foreign movies and Israeli films. We played basketball, floor hockey and Ping-Pong, or gathered in the common room to holler at the heroes and villains of American wrestling on Jordanian TV. We signed up for Hebrew lessons and took out English books from the kibbutz library; I devoured Israeli military history and indulged a brief obsession, common to angsty young men, with the "philosophy" of Ayn Rand, reading *The Virtue of Selfishness* on a socialist commune. Friday nights, kibbutzniks swapped blue work uniforms for pressed shirts, while volunteers got dolled up from the collection of flared slacks and paisley blouses left behind by generations of backpackers. The kibbutz reunited in the dining room for Shabbat dinner and the weekly miracle in which industrial urns of tap water instead dispensed gallons of cheap white wine. At the Friday night meal, we saw the whole kibbutz—and they saw us. Families who lived on the far side of Shamir; middle-aged bosses from the orchards and factories; and greying seniors, hunched over their trays, who glanced skeptically at the table of loud volunteers refilling jugs of wine. Later, the Volly Bar swelled with a rowdy mix of young backpackers and kibbutzniks—many just finished their three years of mandatory army service—all shouting over the tinny stereo.

Past midnight, we scrawled our names and nationalities and bar-room boasts across the rainbow mural of the bunker's back wall. Then we staggered into an old grain elevator that kibbutzniks had turned into a disco and danced until our knees ached. Saturday mornings, we slept off hangovers and idled on the shaded porches of our cabins. Afternoons, we played soccer with kibbutzniks or rugby against tattooed British soccer hooligans from another kibbutz in the valley.

Aside from a handful of Orthodox communities, kibbutzes were largely secular institutions. There was no synagogue on Shamir, and I never saw a *kippa* on any man's head. But kibbutzes adapted traditional Jewish holidays into a seasonal cycle of community gatherings: the harvest festivals of Sukkot and Shavu'ot; Yom Kippur, with its tart memory of the surprise attack in 1973 by the armies of Egypt and Syria; Channukah, Purim and Passover—celebrations of Jewish uprisings and exoduses. For Christmas, kibbutzniks surprised volunteers with a pig to roast from an Arab butcher in Nazareth; kosher laws made it illegal for Israeli Jews to raise pigs. A bearded British expat kibbutznik named Johnny dressed as Santa on Christmas Eve and let us perch on his lap as we exchanged gifts—I got a box of Earl Grey and a styrofoam toy glider—and sang off-key (and off-colour) carols into the night. For the Super Bowl, I joined the two others who cared about American football and watched the 49ers beat the Bengals.

I fell into the rhythms of volunteer life. I gossiped around the volunteers' table in the dining room: who was mad at whom, who had slept with whom, who was leaving—and who might be arriving. I savoured the casual encounters with foreign friends and Israeli acquaintances as I walked the quiet grounds of the car-free inner campus or jogged its ring road to sweat off the beer and cigarettes. The work was hard but broken up by camaraderie, as kibbutzniks and volunteers cracked jokes over tea breaks. I felt part of a community, even if my tenure was temporary. I could ignore the dangers beyond the fences, the troubles we read about in the morning paper—most of the time.

One week, though, I was assigned to clean the bomb shelters. Why now? Was there a threat they weren't telling us about? The shelters were scattered across the kibbutz and looked like concrete phone booths with steel doors, ventilation pipes and stone steps that descended into the dark. I found one shelter half-flooded and uninhabitable; in another, a teenaged punk band had cleared the cots and added a drum kit for a jam studio.

I knew the kibbutz had been touched by tragedy. In 1974, four Palestinian terrorists had crossed from Lebanon, armed with guns, grenades, explosives, a map with several potential targets, including Shamir, and leaflets demanding the release of a hundred Palestinian prisoners. The ultimate goal was the dining hall, where a dawn attack might capture dozens of hostages. "We love death," read a note carried by one militant, "as you love life." On the morning of June 13, 1974, the gunmen crept into the kibbutz near the bee house but were spotted by two members—one was grazed by a bullet as he retreated to warn others. Kibbutzniks rushed from breakfast with the weapons they brought to work each day, and Uzi Tsur, a paratrooper, shot and killed two of the intruders. The remaining terrorists exchanged fire with kibbutz members and died in a siege of the apiary after the army arrived, when the entire building exploded. By then, the Palestinians had killed three women: two kibbutzniks, including a pregnant mother, and Judi Sinton, a 18-year-old volunteer from New Zealand. The deaths made headlines in Israel as well as New Zealand and led the evening news in the United States; President Nixon was visiting the Middle East and the attack may have been an attempt to overshadow his diplomacy. "The terrorists have demonstrated their suicidal determination to attract attention to the Palestinian cause," observed a CBS reporter, at the "honey-producing village" of Shamir, after interviewing Defence Minister Shimon Peres near the burnt-out remains of the bee house. "The commandos who took part in the raid," noted a writer for *Time* magazine, "were dressed in the headbands and cloaks that many young Western hippies wear when they stop to work at such kibbutzim."

Fifteen years later, the attack loomed large in the mythology of Shamir. Ami told me the story on my first day. My friend Yoav had been a young boy in the children's house sprayed with bullets; his father, an artist, heard the warning in the dining room and photographed the fire-fight and aftermath. On the kibbutz, we walked past the sculpture built by the grieving husband of the young mother killed by the terrorists. Any one of us could be next—that was the message. We were visitors in a divided land. And we needed to choose sides.

—

Twice a year, kibbutz leaders relieved volunteers of work duties for a five-day road trip to the Red Sea resort of Eilat and back again. We would sleep outdoors and in hostels. We would stop at tourist highlights: the Dead Sea, the Ein Gedi nature reserve, the citadel of Masada, the Old City of Jerusalem, the Bedouin market in Be'er Sheva. The autumn trip rewarded volunteers for harvesting the cotton and apples, the avocados and kiwis. The cargo space of an old yellow school bus was filled with sleeping bags, potato chips and instant soup, sacks of vegetables and rattling cases of cheap Israeli beer. Our chaperones packed guns. Heading south, down the Jordan Valley, our bus approached Jericho, the oldest surviving city in the world and a flashpoint in a modern conflict. In Israel, voters were heading to the polls in the ugly autumn election of 1988. The political rancour centered on how to contain the Palestinian uprising. The right-wing Likud Party advocated military suppression of the stone-throwing protesters. The centre-left Labor Party sought concessions in exchange for peace. Days before the balloting, an act of violence inflamed the nation.

On a Sunday evening, a public bus with nearly two dozen passengers approached Jericho and the driver slowed to avoid boulders strewn across the highway. Suddenly, two gasoline-filled bottles smashed the rear window, and the bus erupted into flame. Passengers scrambled for exits or clawed through broken glass. A 26-year-old mother and her three children died in the attack, and a soldier succumbed to smoke inhalation. The attack provoked national outrage. The army imposed a curfew on Jericho until three Palestinians confessed, and then soldiers destroyed their families' houses and bulldozed orchards they'd used as cover for the attack. "This tragedy," lamented a Labor Party official, "couldn't have come at a worse time."

Our volunteer expedition passed Jericho a week after the incident. At checkpoints, our laughter dimmed as hard-eyed IDF officers stared into our windows before we accelerated onto the highway again. I realized how little I knew about this land beyond the rural isolation of the kibbutz.

A day later, we stopped at the Bedouin market in the desert city of Be'er Sheva and posed for photographs beside the camels. I haggled badly to buy a souvenir *keffiyeh*, a checkered Arab scarf with a tasseled headband, and looped it around my brow in an attempt at Mideast chic. A Bedouin man spotted me and ran beside our bus, pointing at the pale foreigner in the headgear of the PLO leader, as he laughed and chanted, "Ar-a-*fat!* Ar-a-*fat!* Ar-a-*fat!*" At Yad Vashem, we moved in silence through the memorials and physical remnants of the Holocaust, the bodies turned to ash, the bureaucratic paperwork of the Final Solution. An exhibition titled *6,000,001* reminded us that the unfathomable depth of the Nazis' slaughter was the sum of individual human lives snuffed out one by one. In a Jerusalem ice cream store, one of our chaperones sat transfixed by a documentary about the Holocaust on a small black-and-white TV while the younger guide flirted with an Australian volunteer. "How they must fear another explosion of hatred toward the

Jews like in Nazi Germany," I wrote in my diary. "The life of a Jew, an Israeli even more, must be a wary existence, knowing that should he let his guard down, his entire race may be extinguished from the face of the globe, by the newly risen Hitler, by the pressure of Arab hatred, by the apathy of the world."

We descended into the Old City's crowded and shadowy arcades. Narrow shopfronts displayed racks of tourist T-shirts, bootleg cassette tapes, handmade jewellery, oddly shaped fruits and vegetables I couldn't identify. The throaty calls of shopkeepers and Arabic music pumped through ghetto blasters echoed down corridors filled with the tangy smells of Turkish coffee and grilled meat. The ancient area code has a reputation for short-circuiting the imagination. Psychologists label it the Jerusalem Syndrome, a psychosis (or "spiritual intoxication") that overcomes visitors with delusions of saintly revelation in this crossroads of major faiths. "Jerusalem sadness" is how novelist Arthur Koestler describes his first trip to the Old City. "The angry face of Yahweh is brooding over hot rocks," he wrote, "which have seen more holy murder, rape and plunder than any other place on earth." Amos Oz, who grew up in the city, is more blunt: "Jerusalem is an old nymphomaniac who squeezes lover after lover to death before shrugging him off her with a yawn, a black widow who devours her mates while they are still penetrating her." Ouch.

On our visit, we watched gaggles of Christian pilgrims, mostly European, imitate their saviour's final journey down the Via Dolorosa, clutching rosaries as men dragged thick wooden crosses. Some had training wheels, which seemed like cheating on the "Way of Pain." Ultra-Orthodox boys dashed up stone stairs, a blur of black and white, side curls bouncing behind their ears. Faith ebbed and flowed through the stone labyrinth that joined the Christian, Muslim, Armenian and Jewish quarters. Every step down the city's cobbled streets pitched me back a century. Time came unmoored, only to be jerked back to earth by a stern Haredi Jew who wagged a finger at Mandy, a British volunteer with a zoned-out smiley face on her T-shirt and the words *Shit Happens!*

"*Not* in the Holy City!" he chastened.

We laughed like kids caught smoking by the school janitor. Looking back, I feel a pang of shame at our blithe youth, how we snapped photos of devotees deep in prayer at the Western Wall or the Church of the Holy Sepulchre, how we gawked like visitors in a zoo at the accoutrements and genuflections of faiths we would never understand.

Shit *did* happen in the Holy City, though. It happened all the time. On this trip, the city was tense with rumours the PLO might announce Palestinian statehood. Squads of Israeli soldiers rushed down alleyways, rifles to chests, and demanded ID papers from Arab men. In a jewellery shop in the Christian Quarter, I haggled over a necklace for my hometown high school ex-sweetheart until the proprietor glanced at his watch and grew anxious. Yasser Arafat had called a half-day strike and if the shopkeeper kept his doors open past noon, he could face the wrath of PLO enforcers. We sealed the deal, and he slammed the shutters.

I entered the grounds of the Temple Mount, site of the Dome of the Rock and Al-Aqsa Mosque, the Noble Sanctuary of the Muslim faith and landing pad for the prophet Muhammad's angel-guided "night journey" from Mecca to Jerusalem. The walls supporting the golden dome were mosaicked in sea blue and turquoise and a vibrant turtle green, a fractal network of tiles with stylized Koranic scripture scrolling across the upper panels. A middle-aged Arab guide talked me through the history as I stood in torn Reeboks and army-surplus pants, a shoulder-length blond mullet feathering out of a Labatt Blue ballcap, the very incarnation of the ugly North American. We looked down into a stone-walled backyard, where a scrum of boys was playing. I turned my attention back to the guide and—*ʒiiing!*—a rock, thrown with the force and precision of a split-finger fastball, struck me in the back of the cap. My eyes watered with pain as the guide scolded the boys in Arabic. Only later did I think of the perfect novelty T-shirt: *I Got Stoned at the Dome of the Rock!* At the time, all that ran through my aching head was *What the hell am I doing here?*

———

I had planned to work on a kibbutz for a month or two and move on. I wanted to explore the Middle East and the Mediterranean. See the world. But Shamir seduced me into prolonging my stay—and so did my fellow volunteers. I fell in and out of love. I hitchhiked up and down the country. I returned to Jerusalem as often as I could. Eight months later, as summer approached, Ami learned of my past as a lifeguard and offered a position at the kibbutz pool. It would be an easy job compared to polishing lenses in the optical factory or pulling rocks from the cotton fields. Some volunteers had stuck around for a year or longer. A few barstool conversations had blossomed into kibbutz marriages. Israel would always be a dangerous place but life was good in the Hula Valley.

I considered a career as the poolside hero in a socialist utopia. And then I declined.

It was time to go home.

CHAPTER 2

Between the Hammer and the Anvil

On May 26, 2009, Yossi Schneiberg walked into the administration offices of Kibbutz Ramat HaKovesh. Now in his sixties, he had been a maintenance worker for much of his adult life at the community of 400 members, 21 kilometres northeast of Tel Aviv and minutes from the fenced-off border of the Palestinian West Bank. He had complained to his wife and friends about changes within the kibbutz. Decisions by hired managers—*outsiders*—were eroding his sense of belonging and security in his longtime home. He had struggled, without success, to find affordable housing for one of his adult children. Nobody would listen. Recently, the municipal directors of Ramat HaKovesh had informed Schneiberg his job would be reclassified at a reduced salary. Today, they would meet to set the lower wage.

Schneiberg planned to argue against the decision. When he arrived, he was told the appointment had been postponed. He grew agitated. He shouted at staff and was escorted from the office by the director of community life. Outside, Schneiberg and his escort stepped beyond the shade of a low awning and into the midday sun. Schneiberg drew a pistol from his pocket, fired point blank and wounded the director. The shot echoed across the quiet grounds. Then he lifted the pistol to his own head and squeezed the trigger.

In Israel, the shooting/suicide symbolized a discontent deeper than mere workplace rage. Yossi Schneiberg's final act of protest bloodied a collective enterprise that was meant to resolve the tensions between employers and employees. Schneiberg's home, like Shamir, was part of Israel's renowned experiment in direct democracy, communal living and absolute equality. Where the founding generation had put into practice Karl Marx's bumper-sticker promise that, one day, we would live according to the principle: "From each according to his ability, to each according to his need."

That spring, the kibbutz movement was planning festivities for its centennial—and I was preparing for my return to Israel. The following year, 270 kibbutzim would celebrate the 1910 founding of Degania, the original kibbutz, on the banks of the Jordan River. More than 100,000 kibbutzniks would memorialize the movement's role in the history of modern Israel. How pioneers had drained the swamps and tilled the fields of colonial Palestine during the waning years of Ottoman rule and the British Mandate that followed. How they'd established and defended the borders of the new Jewish state. How they'd coaxed the deserts to bloom after the 1948 War of Independence and fed a nation of refugees. How they'd nurtured politicians and diplomats, generals and pilots, authors and musicians.

Kibbutz members had much to be proud of. But they'd once held grander ambitions. Their leaders and philosophers had imagined Israel remade as a collective paradise for an evolved human species—*Homo kibbutznik*—in which citizens of a modern Hebrew nation and its Arab neighbours toiled in peace. The spirit of this model society would spread from nation to nation, across oceans and continents, until the entire world lived in harmony as one giant kibbutz.

They're still waiting.

To insiders, the bloody showdown on Yossi Schneiberg's kibbutz seemed inevitable. The shooting only made public the social, economic and political tensions that pulled at the sleepy rural enclaves. "Another such incident is only a matter of time," the directors of other kibbutzes warned in an open letter. "There have been more than a few attempted murders and attempts to inflict physical harm . . . and they occur daily on almost every kibbutz. We stand every day on the front and between the hammer and the anvil."

———

After one final toga party, I'd said goodbye to friends on Kibbutz Shamir in the late spring of 1989, backpacked through Egypt with my British girlfriend for a few weeks, recovered from a bad case of Mummy Tummy and then crossed the Atlantic again. I assumed I'd return to the kibbutz one day. But I didn't. I wasn't Jewish. I didn't have family in Israel. Most volunteers returned home. Many of my Israeli friends left the kibbutz, too. We had postcards and aerograms, not Facebook, to stay connected. And so we didn't. Twenty years later, I was lurching into middle age. I had become a journalist and a teacher, with a wife, two kids, an incontinent dog and a mortgage. I'd moved to the west coast of Canada, far from the desert haze and ancient feuds of the Middle East. I had kept my old journals and photos, but with every move, my kibbutz keepsakes sank deeper into unopened boxes and undisturbed memories.

Today, the Internet lets us Google-stalk our past with a single click. One afternoon, I typed in *Shamir*. The first few hits nearly pitched me off my chair. I'd expected a sunrise photo of the Hula Valley, cotton workers in the fields, maybe a shot of the swimming pool or a blog from old volunteers. Instead I saw a photo from Wall Street—yes, *that* Wall Street—with a video display announcing *NASDAQ welcomes Shamir Optical Industry Ltd.* Another photo of kibbutzniks, in business suits, clapping as they rang the bell to end the day of trading. Behind them hung the trademark of Shamir Optical, a stylized Superman *S* in an oval like a dragon's eyeball. A few years earlier, in 2005, the lens factory had gone public and sold a quarter of the company on the NASDAQ. I could call my broker and buy a piece of my old kibbutz.

An Israeli initial public offering wasn't news. In the past two decades, the country had become "Start-Up Nation." A national economy built on socialism, unionism and cooperatives (plus American military aid) had turned into an incubator for high-tech innovation and digital entrepreneurs (plus American military aid). With a population of only seven million, Israel boasted the third-most companies on NASDAQ, after the U.S. and China. Still, it was odd for an agrarian commune founded by Marxists to be competing with the greyhounds of global capital. And Shamir was *my* kibbutz. I had worked the lens-polishing machines in the factory that was now the toast of Wall Street. If I'd stayed as a lifeguard, maybe I'd be a millionaire, too.

It made me wonder what had become of the kibbutzniks I once knew and worked with. And how had Shamir changed? Between the terrorist attack in 1974 and the NASDAQ launch in 2005, the sleepy village hadn't made headlines. Israel, on the other hand, couldn't keep out of the news. The First Intifada gave way to the First Gulf War and then to the high hopes of the Oslo Accords, the near-peace with the Palestinians. Followed by despair: the assassination of Prime Minister Yitzhak Rabin. The suicide attacks of the Second Intifada. Rockets and reprisals in Lebanon and Gaza. The nuclear threat from Iran. The election of Hamas. 9/11. The rightward drift of Israeli politics.

Shamir, I soon learned, was not the only kibbutz to change in the years since I'd lived there. Throughout Israel, economic privatization had reshaped the kibbutz movement. A few communities got rich; many more fell into debt. Nearly all had been forced to shed their ideals of radical sharing. The kibbutz movement, it seemed, was giving up its collective dream of transforming Israel—and the world—into an Eden of equals. Then, when I read the news of the shooting/suicide, I realized the kibbutz might be in worse condition than I'd thought. A snake had entered its garden; perhaps it had always been there.

I had wanted to return to Israel. Finally, I had an excuse. Before it faded into history, I needed to know what the kibbutz meant to the nation—and to me. I wanted to understand how its bold utopian spirit had taken flight and if that original willingness to experiment with new ways of living still existed. Did the kibbutz have anything left to say about the search for peace in the Middle East? I'd met former volunteers on my travels and we all felt an immediate affinity through our tales of kibbutz life, so I knew I wasn't the only visitor who had been altered by my kibbutz experiences. But I'd never stopped to consider how or why. Until now.

—

I'd boarded a connecting flight from Toronto to Zurich and settled into my exit-row seat when I saw her striding from the front of the plane. She stood six-feet-plus but looked nearly seven as she negotiated the narrow aisle and industrial broadloom atop open-toed high heels that seemed designed by a skyscraper architect with an S&M foot fetish. Her blade-nailed hands juggled a boarding pass, an over-stuffed micropurse, a crumpled pack of Marlboro Lights, an iPhone and a Starbucks über grande about to blow its lid. She wore a death-black barely there Barbarella outfit through which her taut bronze skin shone like an ice-dancing trophy. Up from her tanning-bed toes, a filigree of tattooed thorns and vines and subcutaneous script made a calligraphic journey past a thin ankle, along a bare leg and vanished under a miniskirt, cinched by a belt of headbanger studs. The tattooed words reappeared above her thin waist and climaxed at her throat. I tried to decipher the biker mottos hieroglyphed on the vellum of her skin: *So Wild . . . So Fast . . . So Young . . . So . . .* What?

My chin jerked up. I wasn't staring. Honest.

Tattoorella plopped into the seat beside mine and fidgeted with a tangled headphone cord until she noticed me. "I'm Julia," she said, leaning in. "Where ya going?" Her assumption: Nobody goes *to* Zurich, just *through* Zurich. She was right.

"Tel Aviv."

"Me, too!" she exclaimed. "For the Gay Pride Parade?"

"No," I admitted. My schlubby, middle-aged-dad travel-wear didn't exactly scream *Fab-ulous!* I explained I was returning to Israel for the first time in 20 years to visit the kibbutz where I'd lived. Julia looked bewildered, as though I'd confessed I was a Civil War reenactor or a Mormon missionary. She told me she worked as a waitress at a high-end men's club in Toronto and liked to visit friends in Tel Aviv. Since 2005, the bus bombings and terrorist attacks of the Second Intifada had dwindled, and Tel Aviv promoted itself as the queer capital of the Middle East—a bit like boasting you served the best falafel in Antarctica. Good-looking party kids talked about the White City in the same tones as South Beach and Ibiza, Berlin and Goa, while activists complained Israel's PR machine used the city's gay-positive image to "pink-wash" the treatment of Palestinians.

"Watch for me!" said Julia. "I'll be dancing on one of the floats!"

In 1988, on my original flight to Israel, I'd squeezed into a middle seat between a pair of dour and stout middle-aged men in woolly beards and thick black suits: ultra-wide and ultra-Orthodox Jews. When dinner arrived, they complained to the steward that the in-flight meals hadn't been declared kosher by the *right* rabbi, a technicality that puzzled a famished *goy* like me. I felt like I'd stepped into a Borscht Belt joke: "Two rabbis and a *gentile* get on a plane . . ." Twenty years later, I was retracing a trip I'd made as a broken-hearted bachelor. This time, I was travelling in the company of a strip-club waitress with her carnal desires inked across her skin. But now I had a wife, two toddlers and a barber who sheared me like an accountant. Just my luck: one journey had been written by Woody Allen, the other by *Penthouse Letters*. But the plots were out of order.

Julia interrupted any Mile-High fantasies to prep me for landing. "Ah, man, that place is so fuckin' crazy! Have you seen the way they drive? Absolutely fuckin' nuts! I don't know if they have a death wish or what. And everybody—I mean *everybody* there is, like, right in your face all the time. And talkin' a million miles a minute. Un-*fuckin'*-real!"

———

On my connecting flight from Zurich to Tel Aviv, my neighbour was a compact and unsmiling businessman on the downslope of the middle-age bell curve. We sat in silence for an hour before he told me he lived in the port town of Ashdod and dealt in metal recycling. I told him I hadn't visited his country in 20 years.

The Recycler from Ashdod looked puzzled. "When you were a boy?"

I smiled. The plane tilted toward Ben Gurion International. I remembered a rinky-dink airport. It had undergone major renovations.

"The airport change," my seatmate explained. "Israel change."

Clusters of glass towers reached skyward. Car-clogged highways clover-leafed below us.

"What has changed the most?"

The Recycler thought for a moment. "Everything change."

I told him I'd lived on a kibbutz now listed on the NASDAQ.

"Kibbutz lose a lot of money."

I assumed he meant the recent global financial meltdown. "We all did," I joked.

"But kibbutz . . ." He paused. We felt our ears pop as Tel Aviv loomed. "Kibbutz no longer kibbutz."

—

Volunteers once provided kibbutzes with free labour—untrained and sometimes unreliable. In return, the kibbutz supplied a get-your-nails-dirty introduction to Israeli life. By 1988, when I arrived, hundreds of thousands of volunteers had done time on a kibbutz. We gravitated to Israel for different reasons. Many of us wanted a gap year after high school or between university terms. Some were on a mission to "find themselves," searching for a wandering epiphany. More than a few were running away from something or someone back home: a broken heart, a broken home, a flunked degree, a failed career, a rap sheet or arrest warrant, a stigma or trauma only revealed under duress. The kibbutz didn't ask too many questions. I had come to Shamir for a mix of purposes: a break from my studies, a broken heart, a chance to figure out what I wanted from adult life.

Others volunteered for more specific reasons. A young beekeeper from Argentina apprenticed in Shamir's apiary. A Dutch triathlete winter-trained with an Israeli athlete. Volunteers came to Israel because of cultural or political motivations, too. North American Jews wanted to learn Hebrew. Danes arrived as "righteous gentiles," in honour of their nation's rescue of the small population of Danish Jews during the Holocaust. Swedish groups came, too, to drink heavily, far from their over-taxed Nordic home, and to tease the Danes. ("They talk like they have a potato in their mouths," a Swede complained to me.)

The kibbutz always attracted young idealists. In 1926, the

Hungarian-born author Arthur Koestler, inspired by the promise of Zionism, travelled from Vienna to Haifa by horse cart to a kibbutz in the Jezreel Valley. The young writer planned to stay for a year and then go into politics. The reality of pioneer life in Palestine, however, didn't match his utopian vision. "I found myself in a rather dismal and slum-like oasis in the wilderness consisting of wooden huts surrounded by dreary vegetable plots," he recalled. "The huts were not the log cabins made familiar by illustrations of the American pioneering age, but ram-shackle dwellings in which only the poorest in Europe would live, as an alternative to the discarded railway carriage." A concrete cowshed and the communal children's quarters were the only permanent buildings. "I don't know what I had imagined the settlement would look like, but not like this."

Koestler proved useless at removing stones from the fields and picking fruits, and the general assembly of kibbutzniks rejected him as unsuited to pioneer life. Both disappointed and relieved, the author walked for three days, with dysentery, back to Haifa. He later wrote a heroic account of kibbutz life in his novel *Thieves in the Night* and an indictment of Soviet communism in *Darkness at Noon*. "I had gone to Palestine as a young enthusiast," Koestler admitted. "I had found reality, an extremely complex reality which attracted and repelled me." I could understand his mixed reaction. I'd lived on a kibbutz that was far from ramshackle and was now spinning off stock-market dividends faster than members could spend them. I was probably a more reliable stone-mover and fruit-picker than Koestler, too. But the Jewish state remained an enigma. There was much to admire in Israel. And yet only patriots and propagandists could ignore its often-violent complexities. Kibbutz life, I felt, offered a critical view of that tension between light and dark.

The young Noam Chomsky was also drawn to the kibbutz's anar-chistic politics and its vision of Palestine as a binational state for Arabs and Jews. In 1953, he and his wife stayed for six weeks on a kibbutz near Haifa, a test run for immigration, and found a "functioning and very successful libertarian community." Chomsky admired the simple life and intellectual discussions on the kibbutz and planned to return, but a research position at MIT kept him in the U.S. The kibbutz lost a bookish fieldworker; the world gained a linguist who revolutionized our understanding of language acquisition—and who became a staunch critic of Israel's occupation of the Palestinian territories. "The kibbutzim came closer to the anarchist ideal than any other attempt that lasted for more than a very brief moment before destruction, or that was on anything like a similar scale," recalled Chomsky, years later. "But they were embedded in a more general context that was highly corrosive." Bernie Sanders, America's best-known socialist and 2016 Democratic presidential candidate, also volunteered on a kibbutz in the early 1960s and remains a proponent of two neighbouring states for the Jewish and Palestinian peoples.

In 1967, Israel's manpower mustered for war, and the kibbutz movement swung open its gates to volunteers en masse. Adventure-seeking hippies soon joined patriotic Jews from the Diaspora, including several who went on to greater fame. "I dreamt we'd all be working out in the fields like pioneers, singing away," said actress Sigourney Weaver, part of the first wave. "We were stuck in the kitchen." One morning, the potato-peeling machine erupted in a shower of spud shrapnel, and cockroaches swarmed the windfall. "It was one explosion after another," the star of *Ghostbusters* and *Aliens* recalled. "It should have put me off science fiction forever." The British actor Bob Hoskins, a volunteer in 1967, loved the physical work, the romance of rural life, and wanted to join the kibbutz, except for one hitch: "They said to me, 'You gotta join the army,' and I said, 'But I'm not Jewish,' and they said, 'It don't matter.' So I left." In 1971, a 17-year-old Jerry Seinfeld endured two months on a kibbutz near the northern Mediterranean coast on a get-to-know-Israel summer program. He hated it. "Nice Jewish boys from

Long Island don't like to get up at six in the morning to pick bananas," he recalled. "All summer long I found ways to get out of work."

Simon Le Bon, future singer of Duran Duran, stayed for three months in Kibbutz Gvulot, in 1979, where he wrote his first songs; his dorm bed was preserved as a shrine for fans of the dreamy-eyed New Wave icon. "It's what kids in the 1970s used to do when they didn't have enough money to go on holiday," he recalled, 35 years later. "It really opened my eyes. I saw a different life, a different world. The kibbutz was one of the most formative experiences of my life."

———

The volunteer office of the kibbutz movement had relocated to the basement of a hotel a block from the beach. Three middle-aged women sat behind desks, swigging coffee, fielding phone calls, flipping file folders. One was telling a forlorn female backpacker from Sweden that no kibbutzes needed volunteers. Not one. Could she come back next week? Capitalism, ironically, had killed the need for free labour. The director waved me into her office and asked why I was here. I explained I was a former volunteer.

"I know the kibbutz definitely affected me," I said, "and I want to—"

"What did it do for you?" she asked.

·"What did it do for *me*?"

"Yes, I want to know."

"Well, it gave me a sense of—"

"You are Jewish?"

"No, I'm not." I waited for another interruption. "It's just a different way of living. A different sense of priorities." My face flushed as I tried to articulate how the kibbutz had infiltrated my imagination. "I knew very little about Israel at the time, and they taught us a lot about that history and culture."

She nodded. "Most of the volunteers go home and become ambassadors for Israel," she said. "The new Israel is not like in the television and in the newspaper—all the time bombs and attacks. That it's not safe to come to Israel. Volunteers see another view of Israel because they feel it's not a place that's all danger. They see that many people want peace." Ex-volunteers in Europe, she told me, often became diplomats and politicians. "They can give something back to Israel because they know the problem. They have another view."

"We get a very narrow view of Israel," I agreed.

"We know what the media are like," she said. I hadn't told her I was a journalist.

I wondered—and worried—if the volunteer movement was simply a propaganda tool of Israel's foreign office. Between the beer bongs and fieldwork, had I been indoctrinated by subliminal Zionist messages and sent home as a sleeper agent to blindly praise the Jewish state? In Israel, the Hebrew word *hasbara*—or "explaining"—has the split connotation: either proud public diplomacy or devious spin doctoring. It all depends on your political slant. For decades, the kibbutz had played a starring role in the image-making of the nation. Volunteers spread the myth. Kibbutzniks took us into their homes. And we returned to tell their stories to the world.

—

On Shamir, most volunteers didn't disturb the equilibrium of the ghetto. A romance might flourish. A minor rivalry might flare. Nothing serious. Volunteers came. Volunteers left. We scrawled our names and our nations on the walls of the bar and then hefted our backpacks home and were soon forgotten. Rarely did a fresh arrival upset the dynamics of our boozy, over-sexed enclave of international itinerants. Except for Wolf. I'll always remember him. I wonder if every kibbutz had its own Wolf.

He appeared in late November, a month after I'd arrived. We could tell the new German volunteer was different: he was in his *thirties*! Most kibbutzes didn't accept volunteers over the age of 35, even as free labour. At 32, Wolf was on the edge of eligibility. He was an imposing presence, with a broad-shouldered swagger and thick biceps sporting blurry tattoos inked by army buddies in a drunken stupor. His biography came wrapped in myth and mystery. He was from West Germany and had volunteered on a nearby kibbutz years earlier. He had married and then separated from a kibbutznik and still had a daughter in Denmark. Wolf was returning to Israel under fuzzy legal circumstances, a refugee of sorts, after going AWOL from the army and getting hassled by the police for knowing a member of the Baader-Meinhof Gang, the left-wing terrorist outfit. I'm not sure now which stories he told us and which we simply invented.

To Wolf, our frat-house follies paled beside the bacchanalian revelries he had enjoyed during the Golden Age of volunteer life. He seemed disappointed, like a racing stallion with high expectations for retirement life as a stud, by the meagre sexual prospects in the volunteer ghetto. "I vish there vere more female volunteers to stalk," he lamented. Wolf's English was tinged with a German accent softened, in all but its *W*s, by years in Denmark. It contained quirks of diction that had as much to do with his personality as his vocabulary. Surely, he meant something other than *stalk*? "Vhen vee vere volunteers," he continued, "vee vould have *org*-ees every veekend!" The way he pronounced *orgies*, so that it rhymed with *corgis*, made the act sound especially lewd.

"Really?" we asked. "Orgies?"

"*Ja,*" Wolf confirmed. A nostalgic distance filled his dark eyes. "And vhen it vas your birthday, they vould send two girls to your room for the night."

Who was in charge of this arrangement? The volunteer coordinator? Wolf himself? Was it like our weekly supply of cigarettes and toiletries? We forgot to ask. If anybody could restore the ritual of the birthday threesome, it would be our new German guest. Wolf began to act as our unelected social organizer.

"Vherever I go," he explained, "I like to make the parties."

From his tone it was clear that when he "made the parties," we were expected to attend and most certainly have fun. Drinking was tolerated on Shamir, but drugs were verboten and a cause for deportation. It didn't take long for Wolf, however, to secure a supply line of Lebanese hash. On weekends he turned his small room into a pop-up nightclub using the Port-a-Party he'd brought in his luggage: a Sony ghetto blaster with dual cassette deck on which to dub mixtapes (an enviable audio set-up in the late '80s); fat forty-ounce bottles of duty-free Jack Daniel's, which he hoarded for special occasions and honoured guests; and a shiny Zippo to perform party tricks. He would twirl the lighter like a six-shooter and then snap it alight, or douse an index finger in fuel and then extend a blazing digit, like Michelangelo's God, to the unlit cigarette of a startled partygoer.

Wolf also had a creative, introspective side. He had packed high-brow bestsellers in English or English translation—*The Bonfire of the Vanities*, *The Last Temptation of Christ*—that he let me borrow. He was an accomplished draughtsman, too, with an eye for architectural detail. In between parties, he would don reading glasses, sit on the lawn and sketch. His minutely cross-hatched ink drawings of buildings and streetscapes had a Dali-esque flaccidity, like a checkerboard folded and refolded, that contained hidden depths.

In March, the kibbutz planned to celebrate Purim, an unknown holiday to most non-Jewish volunteers. Wolf told us Purim was a major event. "Vee have to do something big!" he urged. The holiday commemorated Mordecai and Esther and the Biblical escape of the Jewish people from annihilation, while the spirit of Purim encouraged excess and irreverence, an overturning of social order and good taste, like

carnivals throughout history. It was the one night, as we would discover, that kibbutzniks cut loose, in an evening of heavy drinking and
dirty dancing. They projected a video loop on a big screen that flickered between abstract psychedelics, old soccer footage and soft-core
pornography. Children guided slurring, semi-conscious parents home,
like soldiers shouldering wounded commanders from the front. The
evening began with a program of "Purim spiels"—satirical sketches
and comic performances—on a stage in the dining hall. As a backdrop,
kibbutzniks erected garish cardboard caricatures of Israeli politicians:
Shimon Peres with a snake's tail, a warty Yitzhak Rabin. They performed Hebrew songs and skits and stand-up comedy. A group of volunteers waved mops and wire brushes and yodelled about the joys of
scrubbing toilets.

Wolf wanted to deliver a show-stopper, and so he enlisted me, two
Brits and an undersized Swedish farmhand named Mattias. Wolf planned
a remake of *Swan Lake* and edited a cassette-tape medley that remixed
Mendelssohn with Little Richard, Tchaikovsky with the soundtrack
from *The Magnificent Seven*, punctuated with gastrointestinal embel-
lishments we recorded in the bar. We toiled for weeks, in secret, on
the choreography and costumes, glue-gunning cotton balls to work-
boots and fashioning pink tutus of synthetic fabric, thick black belts and
white tunics, with feathery wings affixed to our arms. Our baseball caps
transformed into yellow-billed swans' heads. Wolf pressed Mattias into
dancing shirtless in the starring role, clad in a diaper of pink fabric, with
a red ribbon in his hair.

The Purim organizers let us deliver the finale. In our costumes,
we awaited our curtain call in the cool dark of the empty kitchen. The
dining room was packed. Our second thoughts had second thoughts.
Bruce, a well-travelled London hippy, told a cautionary tale about a
bunch of English volunteers on another kibbutz who had offered to
showcase a traditional folk dance for a holiday festival on the theme of

"Peace between Arabs and Jews." Instead they performed the infamous Balloon Dance. The lights went up on the eight Brits, naked except for blown-up orbs held in front of their man bits. Four wore Arab *keffi-yehs*; the others sported Groucho Marx–style masks, with plastic glasses, bushy moustaches and bulbous noses. The music started. The balloons started swinging. Kibbutz families gawked in silence. The Brits only survived demands to expel them from the kibbutz because of the night's theme of forgiveness. For weeks, they faced icy stares in the dining room. Were we about to disgrace ourselves, too?

A liquored-up Wolf paced in the back room like a Broadway impresario on opening night. Mattias shivered in his diaper. "Get warm, Swede!" barked Wolf. Our prospects for success didn't look good. We got our cue.

As the baby swan, Mattias entered stage left, swooned across the stage and collapsed in a feathery heap. The rest of our troupe leapt onto the boards in opposing pairs, cigarettes dangling from our lips. Our arms trailed fabric wings as we jetéd over the writhing baby swan—one part *Nutcracker Suite*, one part *Chicken Dance*. Stage right, Bruce and I gestured and beckoned and tried to rouse the baby swan from his swoon. Stage left, Wolf and Brit #2 did the same. Mattias rose. We called to him. He looked away, looked back again. Who would he choose? Finally, as the music crescendoed, our tag-teams lunged and grabbed the diapered cygnet by the fabric wings, tugging Mattias back and forth, more vigorously, until . . . well, we left the conclusion to the audience's interpretation, but the intimation seemed clear. We had wish-boned the young swan in half, like the baby in King Solomon's parable. We had loved our cygnet to death.

Perhaps our dance was a metaphor for the Middle East, Wolf's parable about the elusive peace between Arabs and Jews. Or maybe he just liked music, costumes, drama, circus pizzazz, Theatre of the Absurd. Whatever the meaning, the kibbutzniks released loud, puzzled applause.

My Israeli friend Yoav declared, "Yours was the best act!" Our oddball performance had drawn us deeper into the kibbutz.

—

Two months into my tenure at Shamir, I was relieved of work duties and sent for a three-day educational seminar. Was this standard procedure for a new volunteer? Or did I need extra reprogramming? I didn't complain about freedom from the kitchen and the optical factory. At the Givat Haviva Institute, halfway between Tel Aviv and Haifa, I roomed in a spartan dorm and attended lectures and workshops with volunteers from the 86 kibbutzes in the Artzi Federation, the most left-wing of the left-leaning kibbutz movement. I filled my journal with notes about Judaism as a religion, the rise of Zionism and how the kibbutz helped to establish the state of Israel. In class, we discussed the recent election and its impact on the political map of Israel and the Occupied Territories. We role-played decisions of an imaginary kibbutz. What should we do about kibbutzniks who wanted to move to Australia to care for a sick parent? How should we discipline a volunteer who had wrecked a tractor?

Givat Haviva shaped my beliefs—and my biases—about Israel, and yet the instructors didn't spoon-feed us propaganda. In one lecture, a teacher in a pink tracksuit complained about the facade of kibbutz democracy. The kibbutz, she told us, had started as groups of 10 or 20 like-minded pioneers who could make decisions around a table. As each commune (or *kvutsa*) grew into a community with a hundred or more members (renamed a *kibbutz*), residents set up committees to preside over social life, work branches, even to make policies about pets. Committees begat onion layers of bureaucracy—and one master committee to rule them all. Every committee was prey to insider influence and favouritism. The bureaucratic scrutiny drove many kibbutzniks to leave. "Kibbutz democracy," the instructor warned us, "is bullshit!"

The happy villages into which we'd been dropped concealed decades of hidden and not-so-hidden grievances.

Twenty years later, I was met at the gates of Givat Haviva by Lydia Aisenberg, a coordinator at the institute's international office. Givat Haviva, founded in 1949, remained a progressive force for peace within Israel, even though the kibbutz movement's national influence had waned. Its Center for a Shared Society conducted tours for international visitors, connected Arab and Jewish kids, teachers and neighbouring towns, digitized old Arabic newspapers, taught the language to Israeli soldiers in the hopes it might ease tensions during their service in the West Bank and ran a "peace gallery" on site. Lydia and I sat down for coffee in the gallery where a group of Jewish and Arab women were curating an amateur photography exhibition. Lydia was a kibbutznik in her sixties, with short dark hair, a hurried gait and a vestigial hint of a Welsh accent. "I came to Israel as a beginning-to-lapse hippy," she admitted. The kibbutz offered a successful model of egalitarian life compared to the foundering communes of the counterculture. "Many of the people who gravitated to the kibbutz at that time were looking to continue what they'd built up in different countries but was turning into drugs, free sex, and all that, with no real commitment to an ideology beyond the personal trip of each and everyone there."

In Israel, she had overseen the volunteers at Kibbutz Mishmar HaEmek, where she still lived, and worked as a freelance journalist when she wasn't running seminars for the dwindling number of volunteer programs in Israel. Lydia was opinionated, even by the high standards of the average Israeli, and led educational tours for foreign visitors along the "Green Line" that divided Israel from the occupied West Bank.

Kibbutzniks, I knew, didn't always welcome foreign volunteers. The older generation often saw backpackers, whose interest lay in socializing not socialism, as an intrusion to be tolerated or a corrupting influence on younger members. We smuggled the temptations of the city through the gates of their villages. We married their sons and daughters and grandchildren and lured them away with the trinkets of consumer culture. We brought with us the spirit of hedonistic mischief. We were the Wolf in their midst.

"Many on the kibbutz blame the volunteers for turning the heads of young people in the kibbutzim," agreed Lydia, "for introducing them to drugs, booze, rock and roll, for creating a situation where the youth of the kibbutz, who had been living in the closest thing to utopia in the world, suddenly wanted everything else. That's bullshit with a capital B! As a volunteer in '67, I was offered hash *from* kibbutz kids. They had brought it back from wherever they had been fighting in the army— later from the Sinai, when they all flocked there."

Kibbutz leaders could never keep out foreign culture, unless they closed off their communities like the Amish. "Television brought the world into young people's homes," said Lydia. "Outside influence came through music. It came through film." It couldn't be stopped. Kibbutz kids shared the urge that drew foreign volunteers to run away from suburban homes. The same restless curiosity that drove the original pioneers from Eastern Europe to Palestine to start a new society. Now the so-called "children of the dream" had grown up and wanted to see the world. They flocked to Europe, Asia, North America. Life was elsewhere. It always would be.

—

I drove across the rolling expanse of Western Galilee and then turned north, descending off the high country of Bible Land, where road signs reminded me of Sunday School lessons—Nazareth, Capernaum, the Jordan River. The highway levelled in the Hula Valley, and I navigated the knuckles of the Finger of Galilee. After 20 years, the landscape still felt familiar. The lush notch of northern Israel, once swampland, fed the tributaries of the Jordan that in turn poured into Lake Kinneret. Twice a year, a great avian migration—500 million birds, on return flights from Africa's Rift Valley to Europe—rehydrated in the protected marshlands. On either side of the highway rose the shoulder-blade ridges that separated the northernmost extension of Israel from Lebanon and the Golan Heights. The traffic thinned. The humidity lifted. I felt home again.

I stopped first at the volunteer ghetto. My old residence lay derelict. Our cabins were now used for storage and covered with Hebrew graffiti. Tall weeds thrust through cracks in the concrete porches and erased the lawns and bonfire pit. Kibbutzniks were renovating our decrepit Volly Bar into an upscale tavern to lure drinkers from town. Nobody lived in the ghetto. Nobody disturbed my reveries as I stood on the broken sidewalk and recalled the names and faces of long-ago friends. The pop and roar of the campfire. Hard laughter and the clink of bottles. How the falling sun over the hills of Lebanon painted the sky with pinks and orange. The cries of jackals and the screeching of rock rabbits at dusk. The grip of youth in our bodies as we rolled out of our cots every morning for a new day in Israel.

The volunteer ghetto was empty. The epic age of the kibbutz had passed. Shamir hadn't accepted volunteers for years. "You lived on a kibbutz?" a friend once quipped. "What an '80s thing to do!" She was right. By the 1990s, young travellers turned their backpacks on Israel and decamped instead to Prague and other post-Communist capitals. They trekked through Southeast Asia and South America. They went "WWOOFing" on organic farms. The kibbutz lost its appeal amid post-9/11 anxiety and the violence of the Second Intifada, buses and cafés obliterated in a flash. Sympathies, especially among young Europeans, shifted from the Jewish state toward Palestinian independence. Life was elsewhere. So what remained?

CHAPTER 3

A Few Grams of Courage

As a volunteer, I read the *Jerusalem Post* every morning but usually flipped past the business pages. If I'd paid attention, I might have read how kibbutzes were struggling with debts even then. One story I did remember hinted at the woes. It was a fairy tale with an ambiguous moral. Once upon a time, there was a kibbutz that fell into financial trouble. Bankers circled like jackals. The future looked grim. Then a bright kibbutznik had an idea. He liked to tinker and asked fellow kibbutzniks to invest their dwindling shekels in his latest invention—an electric tool to remove hair from women's legs. His fellow members were skeptical at first. *This* was their best hope? Still, with the poorhouse looming, they figured: Why not? They had little left to lose, so they bet the farm—literally.

And won. *Big*.

The gadget sold millions around the world. The kibbutz became the richest in the nation. Members bought Mercedes and BMWs, added extensions to apartments, and erected a flashy new sports hall and hotel. And lived happily ever after.

In Tel Aviv, I'd mentioned the parable to a director at the Kibbutz Industries Association, a lobby group for the 350 companies and 40,000 employees managed by Israel's kibbutzes. He laughed and blurted out, "HaGoshrim!" The story was true. The kibbutz was HaGoshrim, close to Shamir. They'd produced a device called the Epilady in 1986 that had made the kibbutzniks rich—for a time. "Do you know the rest of the story?" he asked. I didn't.

Remington, the shaving industry's corporate Goliath, designed and released an epilator of its own. Kibbutzniks didn't want to see their golden goose plucked, basted and cooked by an American conglomerate, so they launched a series of lawsuits. And lost. HaGoshrim spent millions fighting the patent only to become a business-school punchline. Lawyers still cite the case and debate if the judgment was fair. The kibbutz went from bust to boom and back to bust again. It was a tough lesson for kibbutzniks to learn. Capitalism gives and capitalism takes away. Even if you're a kibbutz. I wondered if Shamir had learned that lesson.

—

I didn't recognize the old optical factory at first; it had been swallowed by renovations. A white-sided two-storey addition with tall windows offered an entrance to the corporate offices. A huge warehouse branched off the side. As a volunteer, I hated the optical factory, and I wasn't alone. A shift in the factory was hot, noisy, messy, repetitive, boring. It spoiled the romantic image of kibbutz life—fieldwork under the hot sun, the lowing of cattle, the garden beds of vegetables and decorative flowers, a pocket Eden in a dry land. Few of us came to Israel to operate a row of machines. The optical factory made glass lenses; our job was to polish them. Each shift, we checked in with the factory manager, popped a mix tape into the cassette player, and for the next seven hours, we line-danced between four or five machines like over-sized toaster ovens on metal legs. We grabbed pairs of lens blanks from trays, positioned the raw glass in ceramic housings within the mouth of each machine and locked the lenses against grinding stones. A few minutes later, the door popped open, and we rinsed off the mud and placed the transparent lenses in a new tray. Polish. Rinse. Repeat. All day long.

Nobody knew what the lenses were for. One rumour said the factory was a military supplier crafting laser-sights for guided missiles. Why the air force would subcontract the nation's defences to hungover volunteer labour didn't trouble our conspiracy theories. The truth was more mundane. We were making glasses for grannies—simple bifocals. In fact, the original factory had been built in 1972 for grannies; it supplied jobs for aging kibbutzniks too frail for fieldwork. For years, Shamir's optical factory operated at a loss so that aging founders could feel like they were still contributing. The old optical factory would have never survived on the open market. Its shabby building, cranky machines, lubricant-slick shop floor, sullen managers, cacophony of grinding and shunting and shouting seemed antiquated and inefficient even in 1988.

And yet after I left, the Little Optical Shop That Could turned a village of Romanian socialists into a gated community of high-tech millionaires. By the 1990s, factory managers knew the future wasn't in bifocals but in progressive or "multifocal" lenses with gradations of intensity. Engineers finessed software for a new method of manufacturing lenses. "It's like sitting down at your laptop and thinking you're going to be the next Microsoft Windows," Dagan Avishai, the vice-president of marketing, told me on a tour of the labs. "You have to be courageous. You have to have *chutzpah*."

Shamir did. Its new lens fared well against products by Nikon and Zeiss, and kibbutz leaders attended to the lessons of the Epilady. The optical factory held patents, but managers knew their advantage lay in designing new lenses and capturing new markets. Constant innovation. Get big or die small was the law of the jungle. In March of 2005, a Chicago investment house shepherded Shamir onto the NASDAQ. It wasn't a Facebook-sized billion-dollar IPO—the factory raised $5.5 million—but it felt like a huge step. Dagan and the CEO rang the closing bell at the exchange before posing for pictures in Times Square as *Shamir Optical* scrolled across a digital screen. "Here we are, two nobodies from a little hole in Upper Galilee," he recalled, "on the most famous board in the world!" Kibbutzniks received an annual dividend—often in five figures—and now tracked the company's stock price like a pulse. Investing in high-tech bifocals had made Shamir the envy of Israel. But at what cost?

—

Twice a month, the IDF delivered young soldiers from their bases to a quiet corner of Kibbutz Shamir. These warriors-in-training came to listen to an elderly kibbutznik, folded into her chair, as she told the story of Hannah Senesh, Haviva Reik and the Jewish paratroopers of the Second World War. It was a tragic tale of bravery and loss in which the storyteller had played a role. The dramatic narrative cast the Jews of the Holocaust in a new light, fighting back against the Nazi death machine. The story of the paratroopers was woven into Israel's collective myth, alongside other martyrs to the Jewish nation: the death of one-armed Joseph Trumpeldor at Tel Hai, the rebels of the Warsaw Uprising, the fall of Kibbutz Kfar Etzion in 1948, the Munich Massacre at the 1972 Olympics, the raid at Entebbe. At 91, Surika Braverman considered her pep talks a way to fulfill an annual reserve duty that most Israelis relinquished in their forties. "I'm the oldest soldier in the Israeli army," she told her visitors.

I'd heard that Surika still cast a long shadow over Kibbutz Shamir. Kibbutzniks and ex-members in their fifties and sixties—accomplished artists, academics and business executives—all spoke her name with awe. "She was hard," one told me. "Very ideological." Surika epitomized the generation of pioneers who had left Romania for Palestine— steel-nerved, committed to the cause. The army sent officers to sit at her feet for a reason: the old soldier represented the resolve of the early kibbutz and her nation.

During my original stay, I'd never met Surika. Back then, the founders seemed a blur of stern, wrinkly faces puzzling over trays in the buffet line, muttering questions in Hebrew as I stood with my ladle to serve their lunch. Only later did I wonder what the life of a founder had been like. Could I have been as bold, 19 years old and an immigrant to a nation-in-waiting? Could I have dodged—and even fought—the colonial bureaucracy of the British Mandate, caught between ancient history and modern revival, between tribal solidarity and antagonistic neighbours? In Europe, on the verge of the Holocaust, Surika had left behind her family. In a new land, she united with a handful of friends in the naive faith they could forge a new society on a rough shoulder of swamp and rock.

The lives of Surika and the other founders of Shamir seemed far removed from my own upbringing, coddled as an egg in suburban Ottawa, a government town in a timid nation of farmers and bureaucrats. The pioneers settling Palestine seemed like a race of space aliens who had crossed galaxies to colonize a cold asteroid. As a volunteer, a few hard shifts in the fields—extracting field stones after the cotton harvest, pick-axing irrigation trenches in the orchard mud—quickly revealed my lack of mettle. Drop me in northern Galilee, in 1944, and ask me to build a village? By the first month, my body and my will would have cracked against the rocky foundation from which Shamir took its name. Recruit me to parachute behind Nazi lines? Thanks, but I'll pass.

—

On my return to Shamir, I wanted to meet Israel's oldest living soldier. In a shady corner of the kibbutz, far from the factories and farm
machinery, I sat down like a raw recruit in her sitting room as Surika
Braverman flipped through photo albums and drew memories from a
well nine decades deep. Her voice quavered as she spoke, in Hebrew,
through a translator, but Surika was still as sharp in mind and tongue
as the young partisan who had earned a spot on the paratroop mission.

In Romania, Surika had joined the Hashomer Hatzair or "Young
Guard," a Zionist youth movement like the Boy Scouts reimagined by
Karl Marx and Theodor Herzl. The scouts hiked and camped in the
Carpathian Mountains and bonded over political debates. By their mid-
teens, a core group vowed to start a commune. In 1938, at the age of 18,
Surika travelled to Palestine on a permit as an agricultural student. It
was the height of the kibbutz-building period, with tower-and-stockade
settlements erected overnight in strategic locations on the frontiers of
Palestine. Her group was sent to a "kibbutz among the towns." On
this temporary site, they lived together, trained as farmers and earned
pocket money, while waiting to be assigned a plot of land to settle. Most
were high-school graduates whose agricultural know-how was theory
and little practice—youth-group propaganda about taming the land,
sowing a new Eden, nurturing a socialist paradise in the mountains and
the desert. Pioneering wasn't as easy as the pamphlets promised. The
dreamy young socialists worked for low wages in the citrus groves and
shipyards of Haifa, where labour unrest and political activism earned
the port city its reputation as "Red Haifa."

"In those days, the class war was strong," Surika told me. "The
farmers owned the citrus groves. They were the bourgeois, and we
were the proletariat. There was even a struggle over Hebrew labour,
because the Arabs worked better than we did. We couldn't compete

with their agility and speed."

The kibbutzniks-in-training baked and sold bread to nearby settlements. The men left for work with a slice of halva, a cucumber or tomato and a small tub of pudding. The women devised a dozen recipes to cook eggplant. The group received a supplement from the Jewish National Fund to keep from starving. If a few men got assigned a job, they divided the shifts, so nobody was left idle, and shared the handful of boots they owned. They dreamed of overturning the economic pyramid on which a few rich landowners perched atop millions of penurious labourers. They dreamed that women could break through the "three Ks" (in German) of *küche* (kitchen), *kirche* (church) and *kinder* (children). They demanded the hardest place, the farthest reaches of Palestine, the borders of the future state. They insisted on new ground. They wanted to *earn* their deliverance.

In December of 1944, the young pioneers were told to travel to a rocky patch on the slopes of the Hula Valley, not far from the tributaries of the Jordan River, only a quarter-kilometre from the border with Syria. By then, Surika had joined the Palmach, the elite militia supported by the kibbutz movement. She requested leave to join her own kibbutz's groundbreaking. The pioneers had dreamed of this moment for years. But when they arrived on the site, Surika looked around the desolate hillside and saw little more than rock and swamp and the distant heights of Mt. Hermon. *Only the crazy are capable of such an act*, she thought, but she didn't confess her doubts.

The young pioneers erected a prefabricated wooden hut and staked a claim to the land. They wanted to honour the moment with the *hora*, the Romanian circle dance. Before they could link arms, they had to roll away the boulders embedded in the slopes. They used the stones to fortify the wooden walls of the hut against the valley's funnelling winds. Then they danced. And night fell upon the valley. "It was dark like in Egypt," Surika recalled. "There were no lights, there was no water. There was nothing. Rocks. And snakes. And scorpions." Using flashlights, they signalled via Morse code to a kibbutz on the far side of the valley: *We have ascended. We are on the hill.* A nocturnal flickering returned the welcome. "That night," said Surika, "was the most powerful experience of my life."

She told me to close my eyes. Asked me to picture how the land looked then. Shamir on its first day. "Imagine not one stem of green!" she said. "Not *one* stem! Have you seen how they make lawns now? In our time, there was no such thing." The founders planted seedling after seedling. They watered each plant individually by pail. "If I see in front of my eyes the first day, and then I look at the Garden of Eden that I live in today, I could have no greater satisfaction in what I did with my life in building this place."

Surika believed they were creating a utopia of absolute equality. If her husband received a pillow as a present from a relative outside Shamir, she brought it to the kibbutz secretary to give to someone else. Once, a delegation from Soviet Russia expressed shock that young intellectuals had left Europe to become farmers. "How can you waste so much human resources?" they said. "To take a professor and make him a cowshed worker or a shoemaker!" The kibbutzniks were more socialist than the Soviet guests. "That was the people's greatest dream—to be labourers," recalled Surika. "And to be proud of it. All we learned was called Borochovism." They had faith in the ideals of Ber Borochov, the Marxist Zionist who had co-founded the Labor Zionist movement and described a vision of Palestine in which the traditional capitalist hierarchy would be overturned by a working class revolution that united Arabs and Jews. "When the waste lands are prepared for colonization," he predicted in his last recorded speech, "when modern technique is introduced, and when the other obstacles are removed, there will be sufficient land to accommodate both the Jews and the Arabs. Normal relations between the Jews and Arabs will and must prevail."

He wasn't much of an oracle. The kibbutz movement survived and even thrived. But "normal relations" between Jews and Arabs remain a fantasy. After 1948, the IDF drove the Palestinians of the Hula Valley into exile. Meanwhile, the dream of turning professors into noble shoe-makers and cow herders faded, too. Surika watched with mixed feelings as changes crept and then swept over the kibbutz movement and her home. "I love this place very much," she said. "I'm proud of it—with all the changes. It's impossible for a social movement to live 100 years without changes. But I hope that if they make the changes, it's not in a barbaric way, but rather in a humane way, in a way that considers the person who is weak and who is sick, and supports the families with a large number of children. And that is how Shamir is."

———

During the Second World War, the Palmach drew members, like Surika, from socialist youth movements and kibbutzes, and the British army drafted 250 of these volunteers for a top-secret plan to parachute into occupied Europe. Fewer than half were selected for basic training and they were whittled again to 36 for the mission. Surika made the final cut and joined a group of trainees, in Palestine and later Cairo, who learned English, Morse code, how to operate a jeep and a wireless radio—and, of course, how to jump out of planes.

They performed practice leaps from wooden towers, but on her first real drop, doubt paralyzed her legs. When a British sergeant shouted, "Go!" Surika's friend Haviva Reik smiled and stepped out the aircraft's open door. And yet Surika couldn't step into the void. Her friends offered to jump with her in tandem, but she refused. She crouched on the floor of the plane as the others launched into blue space. British commanders were mystified. They had nicknamed her "the blonde bombshell" for her beauty and unflappable demeanour.

Decades after the war, that lapse of resolve still troubled Surika's conscience. "The fact that I didn't jump was a very big trauma," she told me. "I felt myself worthless." Her commanders still trusted her capacity to succeed behind enemy lines. A British colonel arranged for Surika to be delivered into Yugoslavia and to infiltrate her native Romania by land. She departed from liberated Italy in a small cargo plane with a bomber escort. "Imagine!" she recalled with a deep laugh. "Taking a woman 25 years of age and lifting her up into a small airplane filled with explosives and first-aid supplies that the English sent to the Yugoslav partisans, with two pilots, waiting just for me, and thinking, 'What? With *this* tiny thing I am travelling?'"

Surika landed in Yugoslavia. Before she could reach her home country, a coup turned Romania over to the Russians and the Allies. Surika was recalled to Palestine, her mission aborted. Other volunteers weren't so fortunate. Haviva Reik, her close friend, infiltrated her native Slovakia but never returned. She was captured by the German SS, who shot her and dumped her body in a mass grave. Givat Haviva, the kibbutz education centre where I'd studied, was named after her. Hannah Senesh, another young kibbutznik, was captured by Hungarian police, tortured and killed by a firing squad. Her diary writings, found on her kibbutz, distilled youthful ideals into words that became an inspiration to generations of young Jewish women:

> *My God, My God, I pray that these things never end,*
> *The sand and the sea,*
> *The rustle of the waters,*
> *Lightning of the Heavens,*
> *The prayer of Man.*

Thirty-two Jewish paratroopers left Palestine for Europe. Twelve were captured; seven were executed as spies.

—

The army officials who still sent young soldiers to Shamir to hear Surika's stories forbade her to talk about contemporary politics. Officers didn't want the inspirational message muddied by her opinions about the current state of Israel. So she bit her tongue. If she could, she would tell the young men and women in arms exactly what she told anyone else.

"My whole life, I believed in peace. And I know that there is no solution other than peace. And it will cost dearly. And I say a sentence that very much expresses who I am. I say: 'We have in this country tons of bravery. But we lack a few grams of courage to make peace.' Everyone who fights—Arab or Jew—they all have blood on their hands. Hate is eating us away from all sides. It's true we did great things in this country. But there are many sins still on our heads. Peace must be foremost in our minds, at the head of the queue."

She closed her album of photographs, her scrapbook of mementoes. She shut the vast archive of her own memory and stood stiffly to usher me out of her apartment and back into the afternoon heat. "We talked about everything," she said, a sly smile creasing her cheeks, "and yet we didn't achieve anything." I put away my notepad and thanked the oldest soldier in Israel. I knew I would never see her again. The next news of Surika Braverman would be of her passing and the end of an era.

—

Skeptics like to tell a joke about the kibbutz. In the early years, kibbutzniks happily shared everything—because they had nothing. Today, the few kibbutzes that had redistributed wealth were the ones rich enough to have anything left to split. It's a cynic's view, with a kernel of truth. In the 1980s, Israel experienced a profound economic crisis, with hyperinflation spiking to nearly 500 per cent. Many kibbutzes had borrowed money to expand housing and build factories or gambled in "grey market" investments. By the 1990s, overleveraged kibbutzes were caught in a spiral of compounding debt—and out of options. The banks, the government and even kibbutz federations refused any more bailouts. Younger members were leaving. Managers shut down dining rooms, sold off holdings and let kibbutzniks look for better-paid work in nearby towns. Between 2000 and 2010, three-quarters of kibbutzes abandoned their communal economies. The dream of total equality declared bankruptcy.

But that didn't explain Shamir. It was one of the wealthiest communities in Israel. And its members had still voted for privatization.

As I walked into Shamir's administrative office to meets its *mazkir*—the head honcho—I recognized Itzik Kahana. He greeted me with a hint of familiarity, too. As volunteers, we knew Itzik as the Apple Man. He'd managed the orchards and guided our five-day trips. He had been in his late thirties then, with a full beard and receding crest of afro-prone frizz. As a younger man, he had run away from the kibbutz, married an English girl and returned to Shamir with a broken heart. His time in Britain had flavoured his fluent English with a wry irreverence. On a bus tour through the Golan Heights, he had pointed to a UN base and quipped: "The biggest collection of sports cars in Israel."

Itzik wasn't as prickly as his peers. The cactus fruit called the *sabra* symbolizes the surface brusqueness of the native-born Israeli: spiky on the outside, sweet in the middle—if you get that close. Rumours circulated about Itzik. That he had been a tank commander during the Yom Kippur War. That he had survived the Syrian onslaught on the Golan Heights and performed acts of bravery. During tea breaks in the orchard shed, he snapped open a jackknife and whittled avocado pits into pocket totems, inscribing the woody ovoids with curled limbs and haunted, wide-eyed faces. Over the last 20 years, Itzik had added a few pounds and lost his afro, but his wry half-smile was unmistakeable. His office was strewn with economic reports and agricultural maps and architectural blueprints. He had remarried, a volunteer from Denmark this time. Nearly 60, he was now a father to a set of twin four-year-old blonde daughters. And in charge of one of the richest kibbutzes.

Itzik had lived most of the history of Shamir. His first memories were the sounds of gunfire. Random shots. The odd mortar shell. Almost daily in the early years. In 1958, hundreds of Syrian rockets fell on the kibbutz in a matter of hours. "Some people left because of it," he recalled. "It was too much for them." Over the decades, the economy of Shamir—and the kibbutz movement—evolved from crude plantations and animal husbandry into more lucrative operations. Kibbutzniks experimented. On Shamir, they planted apples, kiwis, avocados, grapefruits. They managed fishponds and beehives. They raised cattle, sheep, even pigs, until kosher laws made it illegal. In the early '70s, Shamir added the optical factory and a fabric factory.

I had worked for Itzik in the orchards, boom years for Shamir's apple business. But the market collapsed when Israeli farmers in the occupied Golan Heights flooded grocery stores with fat, glossy fruit, so the kibbutz replaced its orchards with citrus groves. But these were cosmetic changes. At the turn of the millennium, Itzik and his fellow kibbutzniks embarked on a radical transformation of the community founded by their parents. They did more than industrialize paradise. They *privatized* it.

—

The leaders of Shamir, Itzik told me, wanted to remake the community from a position of strength. They wanted to edit the social contract, one line at a time, with everyone's consent. They didn't want to wake up one morning with the bankers hammering at the door. To be forced into rash decisions and austerity measures. To sell their community for parts, like so many other kibbutzes. Like so many companies. Like so many *countries*.

Kibbutz Amir, down the road, went $250 million into debt when its diaper factory couldn't compete with Pampers and Huggies; it lapsed into bankruptcy and had outside management forced upon it by creditors. On nearby Kibbutz Hulata, members closed the dining hall and sold the school's musical instruments to reduce expenses—like pawning its soul, lamented one member. A laid-off kibbutznik walked into the citrus orchards in which he'd worked, threw a noose over a branch and hanged himself. Privatization opened a Pandora's box.

Shamir didn't want to make the same mistakes. In 1997, in a trial vote, 60 per cent of members wanted change, short of the supermajority needed to rewrite the constitution. A few years later, guided by a privatization consultant named Israel Oz, the vote fell a few ballots shy of the 75 per cent bar. At the end of 2001, a new vote passed. The following fall, Shamir was no longer a village of equals.

Shamir was one of the first kibbutzes to shift its economy from hard socialism to soft capitalism. Its leaders eased members into the new reality. Factory managers were free to hire and fire as they saw fit, but no members were laid off from kibbutz jobs. (One woman was dismissed for gross incompetence.) Older members retired, younger members found better paying work and managers eliminated redundant positions. Nearly 20 women had worked in the laundry; that roster dropped to a pair. The volunteer program vanished, too. Kibbutzniks needed every job that foreign visitors once did. Seasonal work, especially fruit picking, could be done by low-paid Thai labour that didn't need replacing every few weeks.

Shamir's leaders set up an internal welfare system, supplemented by rent and dividends from the factories, to underwrite a minimum wage, retirement benefits, holiday celebrations, groundskeeping, security guards, a library, a pool and a sports hall, laundry service and car rental, health care and education. No family had to pay more than 20 per cent of its income to health costs or school tuition. If members faced extraordinary medical expenses—travel for cancer treatments, say—the kibbutz funded it all. Shamir helped to cover fertility treatments for a couple I knew; when the intervention didn't succeed, the kibbutz underwrote the fees to adopt two children from overseas.

Today, nearly all members are employed. Perhaps 20 people, out of a population of 500, lack a full-time job or a position they like. As Shamir underwent its transformation, managers recommended retraining or alternative jobs, or offered seed money for members to launch a new service or start-up. But there was no more room for "free riders" or "parasites," the work-shy members of the old system. The kibbutz backed low-interest mortgages so members could buy and renovate apartments or build homes. But squeezed between a nature reserve and an archaeological site, the kibbutz was running out of land to develop. On my wanderings around Shamir, I had to admire its suburbanization. The development had become a magnet for middle-class families upgrading to safer neighbourhoods, better schools, newer playgrounds, swimming pools and sports facilities. The American Dream had come to the kibbutz. Revolution could wait.

On other kibbutzes, an entire generation had left, and so the average age pushed 60 or older. On Shamir, 260 residents were 18 or younger. "We never had the number of kids we have now," boasted Itzik. "Never in the history of the kibbutz."

I'd heard privatization meant no more free condoms. "Maybe that has something to do with it."

Itzik laughed. "No, it's the water."

Kibbutzniks had traded in their historical dreams—some might say delusions—of grandeur. They were like everyone else now: hustling to get ahead and carve out a better life for their kids. They could no longer pretend to be visionaries on the vanguard of social and political progress. "We are one of the most hated groups in the country," admitted Itzik. "We are not leading anymore. And we don't have the pretence to lead. The country is already built. We don't have to rebuild it. We have to find new challenges."

What might they be?

He shrugged. Itzik would leave saving the world—or Israel—to a new generation. He had never been tempted by myths.

— CHAPTER 4 —
A Village Under Siege

David Ben-Gurion, the head of the Jewish Agency, faced a dilemma. The State of Israel was four days old and already its rough borders seemed ready to collapse. At four o'clock on May 14, 1948, he had read aloud the Declaration of Independence in the hall of the Tel Aviv Museum. Almost immediately, the battle to defend the new nation opened on multiple fronts. As de facto prime minister and minister of defence of the provisional government, Ben-Gurion had to marshal the Jewish forces. Kibbutz settlements, erected during the last 40 years, stood against armies and irregulars approaching from the surrounding Arab nations—Egypt to the south, Jordan and Iraq to the east, Syria to the north. The tower-and-stockade settlements, ringed with wire, might slow an advancing force for a few days, maybe a week, but could not withstand a siege.

The remote Jewish colonies in the north, including Degania, the first kibbutz, were in a precarious position. On the night of May 15,

Syrian troops with 30 armoured vehicles descended from the heights that overlooked the Sea of Galilee and captured two kibbutzes, Ma'agan and Sha'ar HaGolan. The soldiers continued westward toward the Jordan River, where Kibbutz Degania Alef had been built in 1910 at the river's confluence with Lake Kinneret; Kibbutz Degania Bet, founded a decade after the original Degania, was only a field away. If the Syrians captured the two kibbutzes and the bridge over the river, they could advance into the Jordan Valley to the south or west across Galilee to the Mediterranean coast. Ben-Gurion knew the vital link could not be broken. He gave an order to Moshe Dayan, a young commander who had been born in Degania: "Hold the Jordan Valley."

Before Dayan's soldiers arrived, the Syrians advanced toward the river. Kibbutzniks met them with small-arms fire in an hour-long skirmish that confirmed the superiority of the Syrian forces. Degania's farmer-fighters suffered 60 casualties, including an 18-year-old woman, and retreated behind their fences. The Syrians stopped a few hundred yards from the perimeter to scout a final assault. The kibbutzniks turned the dining room into a casualty station; during a break from the shelling and air raids, a convoy of mothers, children and wounded escaped for Haifa. Under cover of night, Joseph Baratz, one of Degania's founders, slipped away to Tel Aviv.

"You must give us weapons!" Baratz demanded of David Ben-Gurion.

Ben-Gurion was sympathetic, but Jerusalem was nearly cut off from Tel Aviv and kibbutzes in the south were almost overrun, too. "We have nothing," he told the delegation from Degania. "There are no arms anywhere."

Baratz broke into tears. "Don't say this!" he begged. "Do you know what this means?"

Ben-Gurion told him to wait till midnight. A staff officer suggested that Degania's defenders should let the Syrian forces come into the village and then pounce at close quarters. Baratz thought the tactic suicidal. "If we could give you tanks, it would be better," admitted the officer. "But if we can't, this is the only way." Another commander argued for three hours, pounding a fist until Ben-Gurion's glass-topped desk cracked, urging his leader to send new cannons to protect the Jordan Valley instead of Jerusalem.

Baratz returned to his kibbutz through a Syrian artillery barrage and found that at least Moshe Dayan had brought a few reinforcements. At first light, on May 20, the assault began. Syrian planes dove over the rooftops. Tanks, armoured cars and flame-throwers advanced, followed by three columns of infantry. Kibbutzniks returned fire from shallow trenches. One tank nearly reached the fence when a young kibbutznik from Russia, who had fought in Leningrad, hurled a Molotov cocktail. The tank burst into flames and a brushfire raced across the dry fields. At noon, the Syrians were close to breaching the kibbutz defences when Jewish soldiers, sent from Tel Aviv, arrived with two 65-millimetre cannons and opened fire. Tanks in flames, infantry disrupted by the unexpected bombardment, the Syrians retreated. "I am ashamed to say we did not pursue them," Joseph Baratz later recalled. "We could hardly stand on our feet."

———

Outside Israel, the best-known kibbutznik remains Amos Oz, the widely translated novelist and voice of peace who joined Kibbutz Hulda in 1953 at age 14. Oz described life on the kibbutz and the history of Israel's communal movement in many of his stories and novels. He found that fans and visitors to his kibbutz often wanted to know, "Who was the prophet and where is the book?" that defined the movement. They assumed every revolution needed its Bible, its *Communist Manifesto*, a set of tablets authored by a charismatic visionary. "Bearded, fit for posters," added Oz. "Marx, Trotsky, Ho, Che." Oz's reply puzzled many. "There's no prophet, no book," he insisted. "No program. No vision. The kibbutz was created by a band of Tolstoyans out of a novel by Dostoyevsky who landed on the shores of the Kinneret"—on Kibbutz Degania, in other words—"poor, dreaming, with no book, no prophet. If there had been a prophet and a book, the kibbutz movement would have degenerated like the closed, dogmatic communes of the last century, or become corrupt like the socialism of the tyrants."

Among that band of Tolstoyans was Joseph Baratz. Six years after the Battle of Degania, he poured his memories into a book, *A Village by the Jordan: The Story of Degania*, that's one part boys' adventure, one part national history, with dashes of romance and the picaresque. Baratz had been born in 1890 in Bessarabia (in present-day Moldova) after his family had escaped anti-Semitic pogroms in Ukraine. The situation of Jews was hardly better in their new home, and the teenaged Baratz fell under the spell of Zionist philosophy. "It was known that conditions in Palestine were discouragingly hard," he admitted. "Indeed the whole thing still seemed utopian, but with the growing pressure on the Russian Jews it was something even to dream about." He emigrated with fellow *chalutzim* ("pioneers" in Hebrew) from Russia and Poland, and they tramped rough paths and worked for meagre wages near Jaffa and Jerusalem, in the malarial swamps beyond the city limits, on small Jewish colonies in the Galilee ("a savage life," he recalled), with a vision to create "the first Jewish village built by Jewish hands."

"This was not the way we hoped to settle the country—this old way with Jews on top and Arabs working for them," wrote Baratz. "We thought there shouldn't be employers and employed at all. There should be a *good life*. But how was it to be achieved?"

That good life began when he met the sister of a friend, named Miriam, "a pretty, sturdy girl of 18 with a determined chin" and a quick-to-smile disposition, despite the hardships. "There was plenty for her to laugh at in the way we lived," admitted Baratz. His courtship of Miriam gave the early history of Degania the plot of a romance novel: young love flourishing in the troubled fields of a hard land. A nucleus of ten men and two women formed a *kvutza* to live communally and pool their earnings from piecemeal farm labour. Exhausted by long work days, they still danced the *hora*, debated philosophy and took inspiration from other groups, such as the Russian Doukhobors in Canada, experimenting with communal life. The collective learned of a parcel of 750 acres in Galilee cultivated by another group of itinerant Jewish workers and now available to Jewish pioneers. Named Um Jumi after a nearby Arab village, the property sat beside Lake Kinneret and the east bank of the River Jordan.

"Our aspiration was to be independent—to create for and by ourselves," wrote Joseph Bussel, one of the twelve. "We came to realize that it was a Sisyphean task to achieve this if we were working for somebody else, and we began to look back to Galilee."

They moved to Um Jumi and renamed the settlement Degania for the cornflowers that bloomed nearby. Life wasn't easy. The river dried to a trickle in summer and flooded to a mosquito-thick swamp every winter. The pioneers tilled fields, planted gardens, raised cows and erected buildings. When their ranks swelled with new members, they voted to split into a new settlement, called Degania Bet or "B." A true community could only co-exist when intimate enough to debate problems around a table, 20 families maximum. Utopia couldn't scale without losing its soul.

During the 1920s and '30s, the kibbutz by the Jordan celebrated the marriage of and then first-born son of Joseph and Miriam. They mourned losses, too: the death of a member in a Bedouin ambush; the drowning of founder Joseph Bussel during a storm on the Sea of Galilee; the suicides of two young pioneers. "The number who died from malaria and other diseases was far from negligible, as was the number of suicides," observed British-born historian and kibbutznik Henry Near in his definitive chronicle of the movement. "There was a process of selection and self-selection that weeded out all but the toughest, both mentally and physically." By 1948, the pioneers of Degania were ready to defend their kibbutz against any threat.

———

Six decades after the Battle of Degania, a lone Syrian tank rests near the front gate, browned with age. Its snub-nosed turret tilts toward a sun-parched soccer pitch. The rusty artifact seems undersized, less a menacing Panzer than a suburban SUV on treads, because the kibbutz clash looms so large in Israel's founding mythology. I stopped to snap a photo of the famous tank and then parked in the original village square. Degania, I realized, was both a living community and an archive of kibbutz nostalgia. With each generation, new members of Degania grew up in the shadow of giants. They had to make peace with the fact they could never be the first. Never as heroic. Never as vital. Never true pioneers.

No wonder, nearly a hundred years after it began, when the kibbutzim first fell to the forces of privatization this one made the loudest crash of all.

The sprawling grounds I walked across were typical: townhouse residences, a blocky Modernist dining hall, empty playgrounds and basketball courts. Date palms cast shade in the below-sea-level humidity. The only reminders of the kibbutz's storied past were the abandoned tank, a corroded lookout tower and the old courtyard. The original buildings had been restored, along with an antique tractor and a toothy horse-drawn farm implement. I climbed the wooden stairs to the administrative offices and was greeted by Degania's newest leader. Shay Shoshany, 42 years old, had been the director of the kibbutz for the past six years. "I'm very young to be in this position," he admitted. He had the lean physique, sun-tanned face and pushed-back sunglasses of a marathon runner. His office wall and bookshelf held framed aerial photos of the kibbutz over the decades.

Sure, he admitted, Degania had changed. But it remained true to the founders' progressive vision. "I'm still proud," he said, "to be one of the last true socialists in the world."

It was a puzzling claim from the man some critics blamed for hammering the final nail into Israel's socialist utopia.

"Here, in this place, the pioneers arrived from Russia, from Galicia—what I call 'those crazy people'—and created something unique," he said. "Even today, even after all the changes we've made, we can be a model for many communities."

Shay preferred to describe the "changes" as "reforms" and *not* "privatization," with its connotations of corporate takeover. The war for the future of the kibbutz was a battle over language. Every word mattered.

To claim that the movement never had a prophet isn't entirely true. Degania's founders had welcomed a bearded guru into their community in the early years who shaped their views—and those of the entire kibbutz movement. Shay Shoshany pointed to an archival photo on his office wall; I could barely discern the features behind a brushy white thatch that made Karl Marx's famous beard look like a soul patch. This was A.D. Gordon, the spiritual godfather of Degania and the kibbutz movement.

Aaron David Gordon was born in 1856 to Orthodox Jewish parents in Russia. Later he was inspired by the words and actions of Leo Tolstoy, the hirsute Russian author of *War and Peace* who abandoned aristocratic comforts (and later his wife) for the back-to-the-land simplicity of manual labour, non-violence, vegetarianism and an anarchist's rejection of private property and state authority. In 1904, Gordon immigrated to

Palestine, a middle-aged husband and father who stood out from the younger pioneers. He lived and worked at Degania until his death in 1922 but never officially joined; he didn't think any form of society, even a kibbutz, could cure the taint in the human soul. He believed the Jewish people had lost their connection to the land and should abandon their parents' Biblical faith for Tolstoy's "religion of labour." He was a socialist, a pacifist, a Zionist, a vegetarian, a humanist—and a thinker who resisted the -*isms* his followers attached to his ideas.

Gordon also believed the Jewish immigrants could live peaceably with their Arab neighbours. "Our attitude toward them," he wrote, "must be one of humanity." He penned dozens of essays and books and interpreted the mystical Kabbalah to outline two potential paths for humankind. The way of "contraction" led through egotism, self-ishness and lust to humanity's present alienation; the alternative path of "expansion" opened body and soul to mutual aid and creativity, an embrace of the entire living world or, in Gordon's words, "to immerse the private ego in life, in the sea of life, in the world of life." He was a Zionist Thoreau who anticipated the global awakening of environmental consciousness later in the 20th century.

"Here you have this guy writing in the 1910s prefiguring all these ideas about immediate experience with nature and experiential communication," Uri Gordon, an Israeli activist-academic and author of *Anarchy Alive!*, told me. "He saw Palestine—I think mistakenly—as a blank slate. He thought reconnecting to nature and basing the revival of Jewish national life on principles of equality and cooperation—*kibbutz* principles—would promote human liberation in general. It was an opportunity to create a new society, not just flee persecution. It was not just about a creating a country, like every other country, but creating a libertarian socialist commonwealth."

Today, the occasional tourist or historian stops by the A.D. Gordon Museum and Archives on the kibbutz. His progressive ideas seem quaint in the capitalist culture of modern Israel. His name is preserved on street signs and history books, but his ideas have been purged from the operating system of Start-Up Nation. A.D. Gordon might not recognize Degania either. The kibbutz's economy is now driven not by soulful fieldwork but by a multi-million-dollar factory for diamond-tipped saws. Few people listened to the founding philosopher. Not even on the first kibbutz.

—

In 2007, after seven years of debate, more than four-fifths of the members on Degania voted to privatize. Journalists and TV crews descended. "It was amazing," Shay recalled. "There were articles from Brazil, Australia, China, CNN, BBC." The economic changes dashed the world's romantic image of the kibbutz, where Jewish cowboys flirted with Swedish volunteers, a place where socialism had been preserved like an endangered animal in a zoo. The first kibbutz had gone capitalist. "For god's sake, I don't want to stay as an Indian reserve!" Shay told critics. "The world has changed. The Wall fell down in Germany. The former Soviet Union fell. But I want to keep the idea of the kibbutz alive."

Degania had survived for a century thanks to its ideological flexibility, a democratic willingness to adapt its core philosophy to meet new challenges. Shay drew my attention to the kibbutz communal children's house, where every new generation of kibbutzniks was raised by nannies, away from their parents, to become good socialists—except at Degania. Degania's founders let children sleep at home with their parents.

Still, orthodoxy wasn't alien. When Miriam Baratz gave birth to the kibbutz's first child, members called a meeting to decide who should name the child—the parents or the commune? "Today, it looks ridiculous," said Shay. To Degania's credit, members let the Baratzes name their son Gideon.

Shay picked up a cellphone and pointed to the receiver of his desktop landline. "You see these things?" Around 1971, kibbutzniks debated if their rooms should get telephones. "People said, 'Look, if you will put *this* in my house and David will have it in his house, what will be the interaction? The connection? The society and mobility and the feeling between people?'" He shook his head and laughed. Kibbutz members replayed the argument about the perils of personal tea kettles and showers; both might reduce serendipitous encounters with neighbours, clothed or otherwise. They debated whether private radios and TVs would turn members into a lonely crowd of shut-ins. Kibbutzniks seemed downright Amish in fretting about how technology undermines community. In each case, they argued, and the kibbutz evolved—slowly.

The decision to reform Degania was no different.

Around the globe, conservative columnists, right-wing bloggers and Ayn Rand fans delighted in reporting the end of communism on Degania. They saw proof that socialism didn't work, even on a small scale. Free markets trumped cooperative economies. In his 1946 book *Paths in Utopia*, Martin Buber, the Jewish theologian and utopian socialist, described the kibbutz movement as "the experiment that did not fail." Sixty years later, it was about to. The original kibbutz, once an island of pure socialism, had come to its senses. All that remained were the obituaries.

The engineer of Degania's change tried to straddle the fence on the issue. "Today, we are more of a kibbutz than in the past," Shay assured me. "What was the main idea of the kibbutz? That all people are equal. That's the utopic idea. It's a beautiful idea. Unfortunately, my friend, this is not natural. We can *try* to be equal. We can *try* to give the tools for people to live in a community that respects each other, that has a high per cent of solidarity. But that's the best we can do."

—

Not everyone accepted that compromise. Despite the upbeat spin of leaders, the minutes of meetings and voting records of many kibbutzes contain voices of disillusionment. One academic at the University of Haifa cautioned that I would be unlikely to learn the true story of privatization because the leaders tended to be younger, media-savvy English speakers—good at spin—while the members who suffered under the changes were older, marginalized and often only spoke Hebrew. At Degania, however, the dissent was recorded for the world to witness.

Filmmaker Yitzhak Rubin was a gadfly who loved to shove a camera into the darker corners of Israel's institutions. His documentary film *A Broken Israeli Myth* had investigated the scandal of kibbutznik Udi Adiv, an idealistic paratrooper who had helped to capture the Old City of Jerusalem in 1967 but who became radicalized by his country's unwillingness to negotiate for peace with the Palestinians. In the 1970s, Adiv travelled to Syria—illegal for an Israeli citizen—to meet Palestinian leaders. He was arrested when he returned home and tried as a Syrian spy in a case that made national headlines. Bus drivers refused to stop at his kibbutz. Fellow members didn't want to pay for his lawyer. His perceived betrayal shook public faith in the kibbutz as a patriotic institution. "The Udi Adiv case was one of the reasons people started to despise the left wing in Israel," said Rubin. "It was the match that burned the hay."

Rubin lived south of Haifa, in a cooperative village near the seaside, and often drove past Degania. One afternoon, in 2004, he stopped and asked what was new at Israel's first kibbutz. His timing was prescient. Kibbutzniks were debating major changes, a few years shy of Degania's 100th anniversary. As an investigative journalist, Rubin has the persuasive loquacity of a car salesman and a hound dog's persistence at the scent of a scandal. He talked Shay Shoshany into giving his film crew access to the kibbutz. Rubin interviewed the older generation, including members who had witnessed the Syrian attack, and younger kibbutzniks who confessed misgivings about the coming changes. The debate split families and friends. Why change the kibbutz, lamented one resident, when you could live in a private subdivision anywhere else in the country? Why change the one place that was unique? At the assembly before the final ballot, Shoshany asked Rubin to give the members privacy but the director only retreated to an exit of the dining room and kept his camera rolling.

A film begins its true life after the final cut. Rubin had never shied from pissing people off and the documentary's subtitle—*The World's First Kibbutz Fights Its Last Battle*—didn't hide his opinion. "Shay Shoshany and his friends saw *me* as the biggest enemy ever," he said, with a roar of laughter. "Not the Syrians they fought in 1948!" Degania's leader warned colleagues at other kibbutzes to avoid the film. Rubin couldn't have bought better marketing; kibbutzniks inundated him with requests for screenings. At one kibbutz, members stayed up till three in the morning debating whether to relocate retired members to an old-age home in town to save money. "But once we saw how important it is that you can go with your bicycle to see your parents and grandparents every day," a woman explained, "we decided to reject the proposal."

"For the first time," the director told me, "I felt that one of my films did something."

———

A dozen young dreamers came to Palestine to build a new society. A band of farmers held back tanks to save a nation. Degania will remain the symbol of the kibbutz ideal, the eternal home to the movement's creation myth. Its ups and downs will be scrutinized more closely than any other kibbutz. Degania can never escape that collective nostalgia. "They were giants!" said Yitzhak Rubin of the pioneers. On this one point, he and Shay Shoshany agreed. Who could live up to such legends?

In the fall of 2010, Degania marked its centennial with ceremonies and speeches. The event also honoured five members who turned 100 that year. "We, who authored the history of Israel, not with poetic speeches, but with our hands, our sweat, our tears and our blood," pronounced the secretary of the kibbutz movement, "raise our heads in pride, even if there are those in Israeli society who forgot who we are and what we did." As guest of honour, Shimon Peres, the president of Israel and a founder of nearby Kibbutz Alumot, *did* offer a poetic speech before the crowd. He evoked his own memories of kibbutz life: "I miss savouring the experience of a day's work. I miss the simplicity of the long walks, the wrinkled khaki clothing. I miss the flowerbeds, the bushels of bananas, the dates, the green fields of crops and orchards. I miss the dairy barn, the animal pens and the chicken coops. I miss the hikes before dawn and the grazing excursions, where I fixed my eyes to the stars that were born with the new dawn. To this day a vibration courses through my body whenever I hear the name *Degania*. I ask myself why I miss it, just so I can figure out to whom I belong."

For one afternoon, an entire nation celebrated an institution that had helped lay its foundation. And then Israel's citizens returned to their uncertain, fractious future. Did Degania sell its birthright for a quick buck, as Yitzhak Rubin believed? Or did Shay Shoshany save the first kibbutz from becoming an "Indian reserve" for aging socialists? That will be left for the next generation to fathom. Bloggers and columnists, filmmakers like Rubin and outsiders like myself, we can debate the meaning of privatization. In the end, we don't have to live there.

On a return visit to Degania, I was reminded of the tension between past, present and future. I had finished lunch in the privatized dining hall when I paused to inspect a photo, poster-sized and mounted on a wall. The image was a portrait of the founders posing atop the roof of a new building. An old woman stopped and pointed to a figure in the picture. "*Abba*," she said. *Father*. Pride creased her smile. Every meal in this building was a reminder of the history that her family had created.

I asked if her own children lived on Degania. Her smile dimmed a few watts. She shook her head. One lived in Tel Aviv. The other had moved to America. She shrugged. So it goes. On every kibbutz, in every small town, in cities around the world. What could a mother do? She still had her memories. That was what she wanted to tell me. Under the midday sun, the ghosts of the pioneers cast slender shadows across the courtyard of the first kibbutz. They haunted its paths and its halls. They always will.

CHAPTER 5

The Final Solution

One afternoon, I strolled through central Tel Aviv to Rabin Square. Once known as Kings of Israel Square, the public space had been renamed after the assassination of Prime Minister Yitzhak Rabin in 1995. A former kibbutznik and a fierce military leader in the War of 1948, the Six-Day War and the First Intifada, Rabin signed the Oslo Accords with Yasser Arafat and brought his nation within a whisker of peace with the Palestinians—until a right-wing religious Jew, outraged by the agreement, shot Rabin after he gave a speech in the square. Kibbutzniks I would meet over the coming months and years pointed to this shocking act of violence as the beginning of the end for hopes of reconciliation. On car fenders I still saw *Shalom, Chaver* bumper stickers: "Goodbye, friend"—the final words in President Clinton's eulogy to Rabin.

Down a side street, I found the head office of the Kibbutz Movement, the umbrella federation for the 250 or so secular kibbutzes. (Sixteen religious kibbutzes run a separate organization.) The movement lobbied the government, coordinated economic alliances and arranged cultural exchanges. Rival kibbutz federations once wielded great influence in the politics of early Israel. In 1949, kibbutzniks elected 26 members to the nation's first parliament. For years, kibbutzes delivered blocs of votes in exchange for agricultural subsidies, long-term land leases and tax breaks. Then, in 1977, the election of the right-wing Likud Party ended the era of kibbutz power—and of Israel as a quasi-socialist state.

Kibbutzniks were never more than eight per cent of Israel's population; today, they amount to less than two—just another special-interest group clamouring for attention. At the Kibbutz Movement, politics now took a back seat to public relations. I picked up a glossy brochure. The text spoke little about the values of social justice. It read instead like a flyer for a subdivision, with images of happy families, big houses and tree-shrouded crescents, like the ones I'd seen on Shamir. A sales pitch for a parcel of middle-class paradise.

Aviv Leshem was attending to the demands of his BlackBerry but waved me into his small office. Slender, quiet-spoken and fine-featured, the young spokesperson for the Kibbutz Movement had been raised on Kibbutz Sha'ar HaGolan, not far from Degania, but lived in Tel Aviv. He apologized for his distraction: A cache of weapons, buried since the British Mandate of pre-1948 Palestine, had been found on a kibbutz near the city. He was coordinating with police the safe removal of the old munitions and fielding calls from the press. Every year or two, a trove of rusty guns and ammo emerged from a forgotten hideout on a kibbutz. The communities had formed the front lines in pre-state Israel and still marked the borders in contentious corners of the nation near Gaza, Lebanon and Syria. Kibbutzniks had been hardy fighters as well as socialist farmers. After independence, they took pride in sending a disproportionate number of sons into Israel's elite army brigades and air force fighter-pilot programs.

On the cusp of Degania's 100th anniversary, nobody here believed the kibbutz was dead. They'd heard its premature obituaries before. "The kibbutz today is suffering a mortal crisis," wrote American author John Hersey, on assignment for the *New Yorker*, after visiting several communities. That was in 1952. Still, Aviv acknowledged that the 21st-century kibbutz *had* changed—while explaining the role his organization still played. He began with a family story. "The kibbutz is a very complicated way of life," he said, "and whenever there was a discussion or an argument in our family about an issue that had no agreement, my grandfather used to say, 'Let's hear what the leader of the Kibbutz Movement has to say on this issue, what his opinion will be, and then we will decide.'" The leaders of the various kibbutz federations acted like father figures for its far-flung members and, for decades, ambitious kibbutzniks left their homes to work as lobbyists, bureaucrats and politicians in Tel Aviv and Jerusalem. "They were strong," said Aviv of the heads of the different federations. Leaders like Yitzhak Tabenkin and Meir Ya'ari rose to iconic status. "From the start, they used money to build a state within a state." In the kibbutz, they would create the perfect society. With the kibbutz as a fulcrum, they would bend Israel to their will.

Kibbutz federations held seminars for adult members and built regional schools for children. "They were educated on all kinds of values that you need to be a kibbutz member," said Aviv. "How to be a farmer, how to be brave, how to live in a group." Kibbutz schools were held in high regard. The federations published newspapers and literary journals; many Israeli authors, such as novelist Amos Oz, published their first works in kibbutz publications. A kibbutz orchestra, a dance company and a publishing house promoted the arts—and socialist values. Kibbutz-based teams competed in the premier leagues of soccer and basketball. The federations brought farmers' produce to market, raised capital for factories and redistributed profits from successful kibbutzes to impoverished comrades. Kibbutzniks never lived lavishly, but they shared a social safety net that made a Scandinavian welfare state look like Dickensian London.

And then it all fell apart.

"Lots of kibbutzniks in the last 20 years have the feeling that Israel has abandoned them," said Aviv. "They were educated that they were on the front line of Zionism, geographically and also ideologically. That they were on a mission. All of a sudden, something changed." The myth of the frontier settler had gone to their heads, and kibbutzniks alienated other Israelis. "The kibbutzim were a bit snobbish," Aviv admitted. "We treated ourselves as an elite."

In 1977 and subsequent political campaigns, Likud leader Menachem Begin attacked the kibbutz movement as a country club for champagne socialists and dismissed kibbutzniks as "like millionaires lolling around their swimming pools." The campaign smear struck a chord with poorer, conservative Mizrahi Jews, often refugees from Arab nations, who lived in the concrete housing of development towns. Begin's electoral success tilted the axis of power in Israel to the right, away from its 30-year foundation of soft socialism, and began the kibbutz's decline. Many kibbutzniks blamed Begin for sticking a knife in their backs.

The response from the Israeli right: *You had it coming*.

Aviv's phone buzzed with more calls about the buried weapons. He hoped the only guns raised at a kibbutz in the future would be rusty antiques. The shooting at Ramat HaKovesh, a month earlier, had shocked him.

What would make a kibbutznik snap so violently?

"Old and young people feel weak," he said. "They feel that there is no big brother. No one to talk to."

"The Metapelet Complex?"

The *metapelet* was the woman who looked after the communal daycare until, during the 1970s and 1980s, parents demanded that children be allowed to sleep at home; the last kibbutz abandoned the practice in 1991. The *metapelet* symbolized the entire kibbutz project of utopian socialism: the Nanny State as an actual nanny. Critics coined the phrase "Metapelet Complex" to diagnose the psychic dependence many kibbutzniks developed for their collective institutions. Members had exchanged individual self-reliance for the safety of the group—which explained the anxiety kibbutzniks experienced when that all-encompassing embrace vanished. They woke up one morning to find their nanny had left. And they freaked out.

"Exactly," said Aviv.

It was a conclusion to warm a conservative's heart: the extreme social engineering of the kibbutz had engineered a generation of members too helpless to help themselves—and so their socialist utopia collapsed on their heads.

—

From Tel Aviv, I caught a train north to Haifa, the port city that welcomed so many young Jewish immigrants to Palestine between the wars and after the Holocaust. Downtown, I boarded a vertical subway that crawled up the flank of Mt. Carmel and deposited me near the Bahá'í World Centre, home to the *fourth* world religion that claims Israel as holy ground. The centre's tree-spired pathways, ornate gardens and marble-ringed fountains spill down the western face of Mt. Carmel, a pocket Eden—if you ignore the highway that cut through its grounds and foreign volunteers pursuing foliage with leaf-blowers.

The University of Haifa sits further up the mountain. The summit-top campus is centered quite literally on an ivory tower: the Eshkol Building's 30 storeys of Brutalist concrete and gridded fenestration, with the Institution for the Research of the Kibbutz and the Cooperative Idea in its basement. Since 1990, Dr. Shlomo Getz has surveyed the country's kibbutzes. The kibbutz was always an institution in flux, Dr. Getz told me, not a rigid cult or religious order. Today, however, kibbutzniks talked not about incremental tweaks but of *shinui*: the Change. "The change is total change, multi-system change," said Dr. Getz. "There are three or four crises at the same time."

The biggest change was "differential salaries." Kibbutzes had moved from a one-for-all-and-all-for-one economy, in which everyone took home the same monthly stipend, to fluctuating market-based wages linked to individual jobs. In 1996, nearly every kibbutz ran a communal economy of equal wages; by 2012, only 20 per cent still paid members the same amount of money every month, whether they managed the factory or pushed a broom. For decades, the kibbutz movement had been hailed as proof that socialism could work; now kibbutzniks were tripping over each other to go capitalist. Once a kibbutz embraced so-called "privatization"—as Dr. Getz's home had—it never went back.

"The process is not really a rational process," he admitted.

—

At least one person in Israel thought that, because of these changes, the kibbutz was not just in crisis but dead—or perhaps *undead*. A ragged husk emptied of soul.

I traced the coast highway, nearly to the tide-carved grottoes at the border with Lebanon, to find Dr. Yuval Achouch. I veered east and negotiated a steep switchback, past a metalworks factory and through the gates of Kibbutz Hanita. My rear-view mirror framed a panorama of western Galilee: a haze of brown and green and blue, the humpback of Mt. Carmel, the seaside refineries of Haifa, the breaking waves of the Mediterranean. Dr. Achouch earned his doctorate in sociology for an investigation into the psychic turmoil of kibbutz privatization. He lectured at several colleges and researched at the Institution for the Research of the Kibbutz. In a canary-yellow golf shirt and chinos, he had the dark-eyed, bed-headed good looks and curious mind that makes abstract critical theory sexy to impressionable undergrads. Beneath his college-teacher couture and academic jargon lay the idealistic immigrant from France who became a kibbutznik at 24. At 50, he looked fit enough to haul bananas.

"Hanita is an industrial kibbutz," he explained, as we walked the hallways of the factory that also housed his office. The kibbutz ran three separate enterprises: a contact lens producer, a factory for polyester coating and a metalworks firm that had been sold to a Dutch company. Yuval introduced me to the accounting staff on a tea break.

"Your English isn't bad—" said a middle-aged Brit in wire-rimmed glasses, teasing Yuval, "—for a Frog. Most Frogs can't speak English!"

"I was a Frog who worked in the fields," Yuval replied, "with English bastard volunteers!"

Jibing is the essence of kibbutz life. The fine art of communal bull-shitting lubricates the routines of the workday. The search for community is what drew Yuval to Hanita in the first place. Born in Algeria to Jewish parents, he grew up in Marseilles. At university, his political passions were stoked by debates in Habonim Dror, the Zionist youth movement to which Sacha Baron Cohen belonged. (The actor better known as Ali G and Borat later volunteered on a kibbutz near Hanita.) Yuval answered the siren call of *aliya*—the "ascent" to Israel—and joined the kibbutz.

Hanita had a storied history. It was founded on March 21, 1938, on a rocky ridgetop of land bought by David Ben-Gurion against his advisors' wishes. The 1930s were the height of the tower-and-stockade era of rapid kibbutz expansion, as well as Arab unrest against the Jewish colonists. Zionist tacticians laid the boundaries for a Jewish nation one settlement at a time. Site selection was strategic rather than agricultural in logic. It's hard to imagine any farmer choosing to break ground on these stone-pocked slopes. But Hanita might one day defend a vital pass between Lebanon and Palestine.

Fifty trucks carried 500 settlers to break trail and carry provisions. They intended to erect fortifications in a single day but night fell before they could complete the barriers. A hundred stayed on guard. Two pioneers were killed when an Arab gang tested their resistance. Reinforcements arrived the next day to complete a watchtower and a prefabricated dining hall, its double walls stuffed with gravel to stop snipers' bullets. The IKEA approach to speedy kibbutz-building—out of the box and onto the hilltop—capitalized on a loophole in Ottoman Law, still observed by the British Mandate. Any freestanding building with a roof could legally remain intact. Early photos give Hanita a Wild West look, like Boot Hill or Tombstone, which stoked its frontier myth. Even 70 years later, the kibbutz had the rugged, windblown mystique of a mountain outpost.

After Israel's independence, the border with Lebanon was less hostile than those with Syria, Jordan and Egypt. Kibbutzniks from Hanita took shopping jaunts into villages on the far side of the valley. The neighbourliness changed after Black September, in 1970, when Jordan's army forced PLO fighters to flee from their country to camps in southern Lebanon. From there, the PLO launched rockets and armed incursions at Israeli settlements. The border froze shut. Begun in 1982, the bloody Lebanon War ousted the PLO in exchange for the more radical Iranian-backed Hezbollah and the occasional downpour of Katyusha rockets. Today, the frontier remains closely monitored and heavily militarized. Hanita is still a place for pioneers.

And yet the kibbutz had evolved. Yuval wanted to show me the changes. We drove to its high point and parked beside a tank. He led me along a ridge path that offered views both picturesque and symbolic. Looking north, we stood next to an army outpost guarded by a pair of bored IDF

soldiers. The demilitarized valley and the brown hills of Lebanon undu-
lated like cast-off bedsheets. To the south were the bulldozed foundations
for a new subdivision and beyond that a suburban development attached
to a second kibbutz. I'd seen the same Santa Fe–style pocket neighbourhoods on Shamir, the vision of suburban domesticity advertised in the
Kibbutz Movement's brochures. Come for the mountain air and rural
lifestyle! Never mind the rockets and grouchy Marxists.

The subdivision was a last-ditch effort to inject youth and money
into a community lacking both. "One of the problems of Hanita, like
most of kibbutzes, is the average age is close to 70," said Yuval. In the
1980s, the population peaked near 350; now 200 members remained,
only half of whom still worked. The social services developed by the
Kibbutz Movement—a job for life, universal health care and daycare,
free meals and lodging—had once made these communal villages the
envy of the nation. The struggle to fund these benefits turned the aging
kibbutz into a case study for the demographic problems faced by every
Western nation. How do you manage declining birth rates, mounting
debts and long-living elders who stretch health-care funding? A stroll
through Hanita offered a look at the wobbly future of the welfare state.

"The crisis of the kibbutz," Yuval agreed, "is the crisis of Israeli
society."

The dining room symbolized the kibbutz's decline: the room could
hold 400 or 500 diners but was split in two and remained half-empty
for the lunch buffet. An elderly member operated a cash register. Meals
were now pay-as-you-go. Many members chose to eat in their rooms
instead. Even the workers saved time and lunched in the factories.
"When I used to come into the dining room and take my tray, I would
look for a place and think, *I could sit down there or there—I know this
person or that person*," recalled Yuval.

In 2003, Hanita's members voted to pay members differential
wages. If members worked outside the kibbutz, they could keep most

of that salary; in the past, they'd handed it over to the collective pot. No longer would the dishwasher earn the same as the factory manager.

Yuval wasn't an idle observer of the change. He investigated how kibbutzniks reconciled the transformations of their communities and noticed six "identity forms" or plot arcs in their stories. Optimists maintain a faith in the kibbutz's utopian calling. Pessimists despair that change is inevitable. Kibbutzniks with a "collective assessment" accept change but try to manage it for the good of the community. Selfish members scrutinize every decision through the lens of how they might benefit. Kibbutz-born members with a "native" identity complain about being "parasitized"—working for the benefit of "free riders"—and lobby for privatization; they seek to overthrow the dogmas they inherited, swinging from socialism to capitalism. "Their revolt is against the kibbutz in order to make it like the outside," said Yuval. "Just as the revolt of their fathers or grandfathers was to change the outside to make it like the kibbutz." Those with an "inverted" identity, like Yuval himself, were once fervent believers who suffer a U-turn in ideals. "They close themselves off," he explained. "They have no more connection with the kibbutz. It's what we call in Hebrew an 'internal leaving'—in mind and heart— but their body is still in the kibbutz."

This multitude of competing visions, Yuval felt, had emptied the concept of the kibbutz of any real meaning. Communities like Hanita only remain a kibbutz in the loosest sense. *Kibbutz*, as a word, had been stretched to encompass anything, everything, nothing. It had become, as Yuval put it, a "zombie category."

By 2003, the Israeli government agreed, so it formed a committee of kibbutz leaders, scholars, lawyers and bureaucrats to resolve the outdated legal definition of a "kibbutz"—a designation that still had tax advantages and special status for kibbutz schools. The government drafted Dr. Eliezer Ben-Rafael, a sociologist and former kibbutznik from Hanita, to lead the proceedings. A year and a half later, the Ben-Rafael committee split the old category of the kibbutz into two new subclasses: the *kibbutz shitufi* (or "communal" kibbutz), which retained a tradition of sharing and equality of wages; and the *kibbutz mithadesh* ("innovating" or "renewed" kibbutz), which permitted private apartments, co-op shares and differential salaries but maintained a "mutual guarantee" to help less-well-off members with lodging, health care and education. The committee also added a third category—the *irbutz* or "urban kibbutz"—to acknowledge young Israelis who were forming city-based communes and didn't want to be farmers or industrialists, working instead in education, social work and political activism.

Critics felt the new category of "renewed kibbutz" allowed leaders to sanitize the decision to privatize. *That* had turned the kibbutz into a zombie. Proponents of the new definition countered that the changes had injected vitality into these communities. People could work where they want, own their homes, enjoy the fruits of their labour. Children of the kibbutz were choosing to stay or return to raise families. Membership was rising for the first time in years. Israelis drained by the go-go lifestyle and lonely crowds of the city were drawn to the garden landscapes, the rural settings and the sense of community that existed on many kibbutzes. I'd felt that pulse myself on Shamir as families gathered on the lawns outside the dining room after Shabbat dinner.

—

In the parking lot of Hanita's contact-lens factory, Yuval pointed to the spot where two employees had stepped from a car seconds before it was obliterated by a rocket lobbed from Lebanon by Hezbollah. One man escaped with light wounds; the other required surgery to a shrapnel-filled leg. The incident might give second thoughts to someone considering a suburban home in Hanita.

As we entered the building, a woman furrowed her brow and stopped us. She was a non-member who commuted from outside the kibbutz, like more than half of the factory's 100 employees, and didn't recognize Yuval. "What do you want here?" she asked in Hebrew. Yuval said we wanted to tour the factory. "Stay here," she commanded. "You can wait for the manager."

"You see, I'm not at home!" Yuval said. "It's not my factory. It's no more the members' factory. It's just the factory *in* the kibbutz. I have no more contacts with the factories, with the fields where I worked for ten years. The fields are locked. All the members are closing in on themselves. Everybody is at home."

He had studied kibbutzes that had implemented differential salaries. "There was an improvement in the economic situation," he concluded, "but real degradation in social aspects of kibbutz life. No more cultural activities together, no more informal meetings between people. You have a feeling of—how do you say?—alienation. There is no more 'kibbutz' here."

We looked across the hills of western Galilee. "Haven't you ever been tempted to leave Hanita?"

"That," he replied, with another laugh, "is my *dream* now!"

———

The reputation of Israel Oz preceded his arrival, like a shadow stretched at the end of a summer's day. The paunchy, middle-aged economic consultant didn't look threatening. And yet he had become known as the Grim Reaper of his country's communal movement. He was an expert in the dark art of *shinui*, a pioneer of privatization, a down-sizer, a cost-cutter. Oz had "de-communalized" a dozen or more kibbutzes, including Shamir. Leaders called him to do the messy work they couldn't stomach. Older kibbutzniks would spot Oz as he stepped from his car, briefcase in hand, and whisper to each other: "Here he comes, the man with the Final Solution . . ."

Oz laughed as he told the story. We had met at a roadside café, near his home in Carmiel, in Western Galilee, not far from Kibbutz Hanita, so he could explain how he had liberated Marxist anachronisms from their ideological mistakes. Free your market and your assets will follow—that was his refrain. He sat across from me, in a light blue shirt, shoulders hunched, fingers crossed in a tent over a steaming cup of tea. He was in his fifties, with flat-nosed, hangdog features and a confident, bemused delivery.

"You know what those words mean?" he asked. "Final Solution?"

I nodded.

"My parents were Holocaust survivors," he said. A wisp of a smile neither rose nor flattened. "They were in Auschwitz."

He shrugged. In the paranoid plot line of old-school kibbutzniks who resisted their leaders' calls for change, *he* was Hitler and *they* were the helpless Jewish victims. Oz had an unshakeable faith in his own vision. He had accepted the Final Solution label with perverse pride even when, after a meeting on one kibbutz, he returned to his car to find scratches keyed across the door's paint. He knew he was a polarizing figure. And he didn't care.

The man with the Final Solution called the 80-page how-to guide he brought to each kibbutz his Bible, his Torah, his Talmud. He was a fundamentalist in one doctrine: the power of his book. He would leave the binder and return to guide kibbutzniks through the process laid out in its pages: the cutbacks to services, the hierarchical salary system, the management changes. Then he would say, *Take it or leave it*. Follow his Bible to the letter and save your kibbutz. Deviate? Compromise? Then you were on your own. Lost in the wilderness.

Oz watched kibbutzes struggle to change on their own terms. They got mired in petty politics and endless negotiations, side deals and votes.

"Bullshit, bullshit, bullshit!" said Oz. When these kibbutzes reached a decision, the leaders were so burnt-out they left their homes anyway. They needed an outsider to tell them what to do.

Oz wasn't a kibbutznik. Never had been, never wanted to be. During the early 1990s, he had worked as the chief of staff to the Israeli finance minister and helped negotiate the "Kibbutz Agreement"—the long legal haggling between the major banks, the national government and the Kibbutz Movement over how to restructure the loan obligations of deeply indebted kibbutzes. The settlement would be the biggest such deal in Israeli history—billions of shekels. An initial agreement was hammered out in 1989; a second deal took longer to finalize, dragging into the mid-1990s. That macroeconomic perspective gave Oz insight into how to run the microeconomics of a single kibbutz more efficiently. After he left government, two kibbutzes in the north hired him to steward their economic recovery. He steered leaders toward the vote for privatization and the austerity measures that often followed. When he left, he had a stack of notes that he organized into his Bible. When the next kibbutz called for advice, he was ready. On Shamir, I'd seen the Bible of Oz sitting on Itzik Kahana's desk. With every privatization, his reputation grew.

—

One day, Oz had gone to the crowded *shuk* in Jerusalem to buy a block of halva and stop for hummus and pita with friends. An older couple sat at another table. The woman, in her mid-sixties, kept glancing at Oz. He recognized her face from a kibbutz and offered her a slice of halva. "Who are you?" she asked.

"Try to remember who I am," he said.

"Ah!" she replied. "You are Israel Oz!"

There was a long pause. The encounter might become awkward.

The older generation of kibbutzniks, at the noisy general assembly or roaming the sidewalks on their electric scooters, often resisted Oz's changes—sometimes with words, sometimes with car keys.

"This is the man," the woman said to her friends, "who gave me the freedom of my life!"

Oz corrected his translation. "*Herut*," he explained, is even more than 'freedom'—it is 'liberty.'"

Oz didn't care about the clash of ideologies, this -*ism* versus that -*ism*. There was a simple reason why the old kibbutz had to be remade. "Everything else—privatization, differential salaries, this or that kind of tax—all of it's bullshit. *Bullshit!*" he told me. "The idea is to change from a closed society, a dictatorship society, to a society in which the last person in the group has his right and his freedom to take decisions for himself." Just as the harder-working members on different kibbutzes tired of shouldering the burden, so the rest of the country lost interest in subsidizing the privileges of kibbutzniks, with their swimming pools and private schools, their dining halls and gymnasiums.

I asked if Oz had any regrets. What about the emotional turmoil—even suicides—on privatized communities? What about the laid-off orchard worker who hanged himself from a fruit tree on Hulata, a kibbutz that Oz had helped to privatize?

He cut me off. "This man tried to commit suicide twice before," he said. "You know, during the early years, many people committed suicide on the kibbutzim. Nobody spoke about it. Now, with the big struggle around change, those who are against it say, 'It's because of the change!'" Oz scoffed at the hysteria. Privatization didn't drive kibbutzniks to kill themselves. "Always you can find someone crazy."

And what about the legacy of the kibbutz? Its fading prominence in Israel's history?

"It's complicated," Oz admitted. "The kibbutz movement defined the borders of Israel. Kibbutzniks lived over the borders, they fought over them. They defined that we are the owners of the land. But the question of borders and who are the owners of the land is not a question anymore."

My eyebrows arched. *Really?*

Oz smiled. "Israel has decided we are the only country that can live without a permanent border! It changes all the time."

In the first half of the 20th century, the kibbutz achieved its historical mission as the vanguard of Zionism. In the second half, the kibbutz fulfilled a public-relations function for Israel, said Oz. "The kibbutzniks were for many years what we call in Hebrew 'the beautiful Israeli.' They signified, for us and for outsiders, that we are a society with a high level of, let's say, *values*."

For that reason, the changes to the kibbutz have been especially hard to swallow for people on the outside looking in—foreigners and ex-volunteers like me, tourists to Israel or young Israelis who left the kibbutz. We prefer our pocket utopia of idealized memories to stay unchanged. In the figure of the kibbutznik, we still hope to find the "beautiful Israeli"—the Hebrew Marlboro Man, the rural peacenik.

"It's a kind of symbol," agreed Oz. "Like a museum. We have to keep the old kibbutzes like a reserve to show how good we are. How valuable we are. To show that we are different. That the meaning of Israel is a small house, green fields, red roof, blue shirt, working wintertime, summertime, from morning to night . . . *Bullshit!*"

As our conversation wrapped up, Oz spilled a drop of herbal tea onto his blue golf shirt. He dabbed above his breast with a serviette but only spread the red stain. He looked like a man, we joked, with two hearts.

Two hearts, no heart. You could ask at any kibbutz that Oz had visited with his Bible of Privatization and you would get a different answer. The wizard named Oz was either the man who killed the kibbutz or the man who liberated it from harmful delusions. His solution might not be final, but it was a path that many kibbutzniks had followed. Once they did, they never turned back.

CHAPTER 6

Stories from the Ass

My closest Israeli friend had been a kibbutznik named Yoav. He was my age and recently discharged from his three years of mandatory army service, but I can't recall how we met. I didn't speak Hebrew and his English was rudimentary. He seemed introspective and laconic— except when he drank. Friday nights, he would stride through the doors of the volunteer pub, already half-gone. Booze reversed his shyness and improved his English, too, so we bonded over bottles of gassy Goldstar beer. And yet it still felt awkward to meet Yoav the next morning. We might have talked for hours the night before, but in the breakfast lineup or on a garden path, he barely lifted his head to nod hello.

One afternoon, I went to the town of Kiryat Shmona to catch a bus to Safed, the ancient centre of Jewish mysticism. I wasn't seeking Kabbalistic insight; I only needed to renew my visa. At the station, I saw Yoav and asked where he was going.

"To Haifa and then Tel Aviv," he said. "To find a publisher."

"For your book?"

It was a stupid question. Why else? But anyone who had read the manuscript in Yoav's backpack might have shared my disbelief. I couldn't imagine any serious—any *sober*—publisher investing money to print my friend's surreal, often obscene collection of short-short-short stories. His micro-parables read like semi-pornographic excretions from the drug-addled imagination of an oddball loner in a remote hillside village in the Middle East. Which he was. I doubted Yoav had penned an airport-lounge bestseller.

Maybe I was envious. I fancied myself a writer and had come to Israel to chase that dream while I mended my broken heart. Writing felt romantic—part calling, part costume. It gave purpose to my wishy-washy suburban identity. There I was, like Hemingway in Spain, in a foreign country on a knife edge of violence. At the kibbutz, though, I mostly wrote maudlin or angsty confessions to my diary. More often, I'd go drinking with Yoav and his best friend, Gonan. Yoav was quiet, gentle, slender, with fine handsome features. Gonan was loud and brusque, thickly muscled and bushy-haired, with an uncensored bravado that felt quintessentially Israeli. Gonan had served in the Palestinian Territories, kicking in doors in refugee camps, rifle-ready, to roust suspects in the middle of the night. He was crazy in his own way, with the volume cranked high. (He later suffered a nervous breakdown travelling in Germany, discovered religion and left the kibbutz.) Over beers and bong hits, Gonan translated Yoav's stories from Hebrew to English. The strange micro-fictions rarely filled a page and felt fractured and incomplete. Many featured a recurring character named Haim the Hunchback upon whom the universe inflicted a parade of humiliations. The less scatological tales hinted at a hermetic wisdom.

A story titled "Childhood Memory" ran like this: *I don't remember if this happened in third grade or if I saw it on television, but what's it matter?*

*What was, was, won't come again. Many years later, Rabinovich told me
that, according to him, it never happened. Now, I'm not sure.*

Now Yoav was bringing this "book" to a "publisher." I wished him
luck but didn't hold my breath.

A year after I returned home from the kibbutz, I got a package from
Israel. It contained a letter from Yoav, a photo of a wooden shed on
stilts and a slim book—*his* book. The title, translated from Hebrew,
was *Stories from the Ass*. The cover had the cheap gloss of a vanity press
and featured a blurry black-and-white photo of a gap-toothed couple
surrounded by hand-drawn cartoon centipedes. Yoav's older brother
had inked crude illustrations to accompany each story.

I was surprised the package got through customs. Yoav had managed to get a dozen stories translated onto slips of paper. I tried to decipher the hidden meanings of his parables without much luck. Over the
years, I packed Yoav's anthology whenever I moved. *Stories from the Ass*
remained the most enduring memento of my time in Israel. A token of
the place and its people. A reminder that both might be as fucked up as
I remembered.

—

When I returned to Israel, I assumed Yoav had left the kibbutz. He had
likely moved to Tel Aviv or left the country. His idiosyncrasies never
seemed fit for communal life. And I could find no trace of his name on
the Internet. But when I asked, Itzik Kahana, the head of Shamir, said
my old friend wasn't a member of Shamir anymore but he lived in the
hills above the kibbutz and still worked in the gardens. In Israel, even
hermits have cellphones, so I got Yoav's number from his mother, who
remained on Shamir. I wasn't sure if he would remember me, one more
clown in a circus of self-absorbed volunteers. Yoav sounded surprised
to hear my voice—any voice in English—but he hadn't forgotten our

time together. He invited me to visit his cabin, and so I drove north and traced the first few switchbacks that climb the Golan Heights to find him waiting beside a dirt turnoff, in dark shorts and a light blue button-up short-sleeved shirt. A white sunhat shaded his features. He hadn't changed much. He was lean and handsome, with the same tousled mane of dark brown hair framing his face, ruddier and creased from homesteading in the hills.

"David," he said, as we embraced. "How have you been?"

I followed his truck down a dirt track, past a small army outpost, to an old stone house with two rooms on either side of a small kitchen; Yoav had added a covered foyer, an outhouse and a sun-heated shower stall. He hauled water from the kibbutz or from town. A solar panel powered a small stereo and a few lights, and he cooked on a propane stove. We sat across from each other in his bedroom-slash-living-room and listened to Balkan folk music while he boiled a pot of Turkish coffee. Later, he poured us each a shot of hooch distilled from the *qat* plants he cultivated beside his house. I knew *qat* leaves were a mildly addictive alkaloid, popular in Yemen and Somalia. "Don't worry," my friend assured me. "I chew them all the time." Yoav had never been the poster boy for sobriety; over beers, he had once explained his personal theology, which amounted to the belief that there was no Devil—it was just God when He's drunk. For the next few hours, I succumbed to a tingly out-of-body high, feeling as though I were levitating an inch off my chair. Yoav and I swapped life stories and let the *qat* buzz fill the awkward silences.

Yoav had inherited his bohemian streak from his father, Avraham, a visual artist and experimental filmmaker, but had struggled to find an outlet. His shyness never fit with the garrulous, nosy nature of the kibbutz. That reserve left Yoav an outlier to the macho psychodrama of the average Israeli male, too—the brash boy's network forged by mandatory army service. He had never been a good soldier. When I'd met him, he had finished three years in the Information Bureau. A kibbutz friend told me Yoav had his first nervous breakdown at a debriefing session; he had started shouting and needed to be ushered out of the room. I never asked about the incident. Every year, Yoav had to return to uniform for a mandatory month in the reserves. He had watched over a military installation during the First Gulf War. "I was in the war, I can say," Yoav told me and smiled at the absurdity of such *faux*-heroism. On his third stint in the reserves, he was assigned to guard a penitentiary for Palestinian prisoners in the West Bank. He didn't laugh at that assignment.

He wouldn't do it. Couldn't do it. He would sooner go to jail himself.

He asked to see a psychiatrist. He wanted to claim status as a conscientious objector. Other COs who balked at serving in the Occupied Territories or Lebanon had been sentenced to a month or more of detention. Israelis who wanted out of the reserves often devised subtle strategies to lower their physical or psychological rankings. A professor I knew, rational and liberal, had convinced the army he was a raving racist who might kill Arabs on sight to get an exemption. In a small room, an IDF shrink interrogated Yoav about his failure to uphold the values of the army, his nation, his people.

Yoav didn't mind defending his country but he knew he couldn't watch over Palestinian prisoners in the Occupied Territories. He knew he didn't want to be in this room either, with a bug-eyed doctor trying to break his resolve.

"Have you ever smoked hashish?" the psychiatrist asked.

Was this a trick? Of course he had. *For years!* Smoking up was a form of self-medication. A buffering cloud of Lebanese hash settled his perpetual anxiety. In the middle of the kibbutz, Yoav and Gonan had erected a rough-hewn wooden clubhouse where they could smoke up together. The general assembly ordered their public playpen torn down—the first of Yoav's many evictions.

"Sure," he admitted.

"Ah, why didn't you say so before!"

The psychiatrist dropped the drill-sergeant shtick, signed the medical form and declared Yoav unfit for duty. He wouldn't be called up again. He was free but now also cut off from the fraternity of comrades established by men in the IDF. In Israel, you are where you served. And Yoav no longer served.

He didn't care. He worked on Shamir but decided against membership. Instead, he built his first shack in the hills, the glorified treehouse I'd seen in the photograph he'd mailed with his book. He was forced to dismantle it. And so began a game of cat and mouse with the authorities of the nearby army base and the officials responsible for the nature reserve. For the next 20 years, Yoav would build new cabins, better disguised every time. Weeks, months, a year or more later, officials would discover the illegal habitation and insist that Yoav tear it down. In his unique way, he re-enacted the founding of Shamir, 40 years after the fact. He broke ground. He raised walls. He occupied the frontier. He became a pioneer, a settler and a paradox: the solo kibbutznik, living in a commune of one.

—

The role of an artist or a writer in any utopia has always been uncertain. When Plato laid the ground rules for his Republic, in 380 BCE, he banished poets for a reason: Artists can be a pain. Their versions of reality distort the "truths" of philosopher-kings and lead the next generation astray with romantic visions or irreverent depictions of the world. Utopians prefer PR flacks, not artists, to trumpet the revolution. After the fall of the Russian tsar and sudden rush of avant-garde creativity, Bolshevik officials demanded that artists stick to socialist realism and ennobling depictions of hard-working proles—much like the propaganda posters of the early kibbutz. Hitler's Third Reich purged "degenerate art" (and Jewish artists) in favour of neoclassical homages to Aryan supremacy. In mid-century America, political paranoia targeted the entertainment industry as the McCarthy hearings flushed out "Red fascists" and Hollywood commies. In 2015, the newly appointed culture minister in Israel's right-wing government pulled state funding from an Arab theatre in Haifa for producing a play about the life of a Palestinian terrorist and dismissed Israel's left-wing artists as "tight-assed, hypocritical and ungrateful."

The kibbutz movement never adopted a totalitarian attitude toward the arts. Like many rural communities, though, it struggled to justify a role for creative members. A pioneer settlement needed ploughmen not poets. Building a village and a nation should take priority over the private fantasies of a novelist or playwright. Art that celebrated the collective was encouraged. Dancing the *hora*, decorating the walls of the dining hall, staging a harvest festival or a Purim skit to entertain comrades.

The paradox of the artist on the kibbutz was perhaps best expressed by Rachel Bluwstein, aka Rachel the Poetess or simply Rahel. She immigrated to Palestine from Russia in 1909 and fell for the transcendental "religion of labour" of A.D. Gordon while working at a training farm along the Sea of Galilee. She sublimated her love of art, music and literature to "paint with the soil and play with the hoe." In 1919, she settled in Degania, but she had been infected with tuberculosis while tutoring refugees in Russia during the war and could no longer work outdoors or care for the village's children. Rahel was forced to leave, like Eve cast out from Eden, and died in Tel Aviv at the age of 41. Her poetry's mix of nostalgia and regret became the popular soundtrack for Jewish immigrants. A posthumous anthology of verse amplified her reputation as Israel's Sylvia Plath, the tragic godmother of modern Hebrew literature.

After Rahel, the kibbutz featured prominently in Israeli art as part of the national myth. Naomi Shemer, born on Kibbutz Kinneret in 1930, became Israel's best-known and most-loved folk singer, adapting Beatles' hits into Hebrew, setting Rahel's verse to music and writing many songs that evoked kibbutz life before her much-lamented death in 2004. Moshe Shamir, a young member of Mishmar HaEmek, left the kibbutz for a prolific career as a columnist, novelist and provocateur after his stories were criticized by a leader of the kibbutz movement. His debut novel, *He Walked Through the Fields*, was adapted into a play that toured pre-state Israel during the War of Independence; his kibbutznik hero looks like the epitome of the "new Jew"—earthy, strong-willed, passionate, a man of the land, a soldier of destiny committed to his country. The 1967 film version entrenched the stereotype of the macho kibbutznik, striding the fields, sleeves rolled over thick biceps.

Internationally, the best-known kibbutznik-artist remains novelist and Nobel Prize contender Amos Oz. "The pioneers occupied the highest rung in the ladder of prestige," he recalled thinking as a young boy in Jerusalem. "We admired their rugged, pensive silhouettes, poised between tractor and ploughed earth, that were displayed on the posters of the Jewish National Fund." Once he became a kibbutznik, he carved out time to cultivate a creative life between shifts in the fields, although he admitted he was a "disaster as a labourer" and "the joke of the kibbutz." In his twenties, with a growing literary reputation, he asked kibbutz leaders for an extra day off to devote to his writing; the proposal had to be debated and passed by the assembly. Later, as Oz's books sold well and added to the kibbutz revenue, he was granted more time to write and offered the services of two elderly members, too old to work in the fields or factories, to help "increase production." (Oz declined.) When he needed seclusion to finish a book, the kibbutz secretary paid for a hotel room. Most modern artists would envy such community support for their creativity, and Oz used the kibbutz as a setting in short story collections and novels, such as *Elsewhere, Perhaps* in 1966 and *A Perfect Peace* in 1982. The inconsequential characters and banal dramas of a tiny village in Israel could be transformed into a microcosm for the larger world. "In terms of human experience," the novelist later reflected, "as a writer, it's like the best university I ever attended."

Kibbutz Shamir produced artists and writers, too. None has been more influential or controversial than Joshua Sobol.

—

A hush settled over the dining room. Called to attention, the general assembly of 250 kibbutz members leaned forward and strained to hear the words to come. Joshua Sobol stood up. The young man, in his early twenties, had been asked to address the assembly. To tell a story. Or rather, to tell them *about* a story. To explain to this gathering of friends and colleagues and neighbours *why* he had written his story. Most had read this work of the imagination by then. Its pages had been passed around and gossiped over. Its details were scrutinized in every corner of the kibbutz.

Joshua Sobol wasn't originally from the kibbutz. He was born in Tel Aviv, grew up in the Youth Guard movement and was stationed on Kibbutz Shamir during his army service in 1957. When he returned to Shamir at the end of his paratrooper training, he raised fish in the valley's artificial ponds and worked in the kitchen. Later, the kibbutz sent him to teacher's college, where he studied humanities, but called him back before he could graduate so he could lead classes at the regional high school. His imagination remained alight with the promise of literature and philosophy, and in his free time he wrote stories and sketches. One piece, titled "The Deeds of the Fathers," was accepted and published in a well-read literary review. The allegory suggested the future of the kibbutz movement might not be all trumpets and glory.

Members on Shamir read the story and demanded the author explain to the general assembly why he had written a tale that made his home look bad. Sobol stood up, the accused before a jury, and offered his defence. After the meeting, he received a letter from a parent of a high-school student. "If that's what you think of the kibbutz," wrote the angry father, "how dare you educate my son?" He quit his teaching job and returned to work in the fishponds. "The fish were absolutely indifferent to my story," he later told me, in a bookstore-café in Tel Aviv. "They didn't care. They knew about the grim future already, without my story." He would leave Shamir within the year.

Sobol moved to Paris to study French literature and existentialism at the Sorbonne. Avraham Eilat, Yoav's father, joined him in Paris, where the two friends lived as Left Bank bohemians, far from the cotton fields and controversies of Shamir. The kibbutz sent an emissary to persuade Sobol to return to Shamir, and he and his wife moved back. "We somehow missed the kibbutz life," he recalled. A year later, the Sobols left for good. "We saw that we couldn't fit anymore into the patterns of life," he admitted. "So my kibbutz experience was a split experience. A very unusual one. I left not being angry, not hostile. On the contrary, I left with the feeling that it was a very important chapter in my own life. There were many things—many values—which I appreciated."

Sobol wrote plays and grew into an eminent and provocative figure of the Israeli stage with an international reputation. His nearly 60 scripts have been translated, anthologized, performed—and debated—throughout Israel, Europe and North America. In 1988, right-wing protesters disrupted the Haifa debut of his play *The Jerusalem Syndrome*—which blamed the fall of the Second Temple on Jewish zealots—with shouts and firecrackers. More recently, he produced a series of "polydramas," in which audience members (who Sobol describes as "road companions") wandered between the rooms in which the scenes were enacted. There was no single story, no unifying meaning; every person's experience of the play was different.

Sobol left the kibbutz, but the kibbutz never left him. He wrote the screenplay for *The Galilee Eskimos*, a quirky comedy about an indebted kibbutz whose members disappear one night and abandon the elderly founders in the retirement wing—like aging Inuit on arctic ice floes—until they learn to fight back against the creditors who threaten their community. Sobol's first play, *The Night of the Twentieth*, debuted in 1976 at the Haifa Theatre and dramatized a single evening in October 1920, on a hill in the Galilee. Seven young pioneers from Europe debate what action to take the next morning, and their uncertain future, as they prepare to set off at dawn, into the valley, to break ground for a new kibbutz. What kind of society will they create? What can they expect from the Arab farmers they will displace? Instead of the heroic myth of selfless pioneers, Sobol described a self-doubting, argumentative, neurotic band of youngsters, many still teenagers. Sobol modelled his protagonists on historical figures and drew their words from the ecstatic, anguished entries in a collective diary written by early settlers. He wrote his version of kibbutz history with one eye on the colonial past and another on current events, especially the consequences of the Yom Kippur War and the ongoing occupation of Palestinian territory.

"I was looking for the moments in the history of our country which could be considered the starting point of everything," he told me, "where things could go one way or another." Every nation had such fulcrums on which their futures pivot: the French Revolution, the American Civil War. "My feeling was that," he continued, "the history of the country was always a result of decision-making under pressure, without having the time to think out and develop a real strategy for the long term. It was always a matter that you had to decide today, and tomorrow you're going to do it already."

Since the days of the pioneers, Sobol explained, the Jewish nation has been split between the "activists" and the "moralists," between the doers and the thinkers, between the politicians and the generals in control, and the artists and the social critics on the sidelines. "This kind of splitting up—I don't know if it's a curse or a blessing," mused the playwright. "You could call it a 'curse-blessing' or a 'blessed curse' that accompanies the history of Israel to this day. Because again we are split up between people who preach morals and people who act sometimes immorally or amorally. And our history consists of the integration of these two contradictory currents in our structure of society, in our mentality, in our literature, in everything."

The nation's "split consciousness" had always been there, even in the ideals of the early kibbutz. "The soul of the kibbutz movement," suggested Sobol, "is a combination of these two elements in a painful way, in a very tragic way. First of all, the kibbutz marked the frontiers of the future Israeli state. And if we speak today of returning to the Green Line, it is approximately the line which is marked by Dan, Shamir, Kfar Szold . . ." He listed the names of border kibbutzes that have outlined the nation's borders in northern Galilee since 1948. "You can say that the kibbutz physically drew the frontiers of the state of Israel while going through a very deep conflict with the socialist internationalist ideology that said, 'We don't want to be enemies of the Palestinian Arabs. We want to live with them in a certain *modus vivendi* of fraternity.' This was the slogan: 'Zionism, socialism and fraternity between people—between nations.'" He laughed at the contradictions of that dream. "Three things that did not go together somehow! You could be a fervent Zionist, but then what do you do with the fraternity with other people who don't agree with you? The kibbutz lived all these conflicts very deeply. The soul of the kibbutz was a suffering soul."

—

The souls of kibbutzniks suffered, too. Between evictions, my friend Yoav lived with squatters, worked as a shepherd near Jerusalem and backpacked through India for a year. When he returned to the Galilee, he erected another cabin in the nature reserve that protected the streams and creeks cascading off the Golan Heights. He reduced his life to essentials. He evaded the watch of the Nature Authority—for a time. A conservation officer named Niv became Yoav's nemesis, the Wile E. Coyote to his Roadrunner. For a decade, they engaged in a wilderness match of seek and destroy. Yoav built at least 10 cabins and encampments. Sometimes, Niv would find and remove the cabin before Yoav had finished it. Finally, Yoav discovered a secluded site, deep within thorny overgrowth that shaded a stream. He carved a stone-and-mud house into the bank, like a hobbit hole or hippy "earth-ship," warmed by an adobe stove. He draped a plastic sheet as a roof in the wet season and used a net during the summer. The stream ran beneath his floorboards, so he lifted a plank after meals and dipped a mesh bag of dirty dishes. His girlfriend was studying the Talmud and needed a *mikvah*, so Yoav built a ritual bath for her. His Godstruck girlfriend eventually left, but Yoav lived in the earthen cottage for five more years. It was far from the highway and impossible to detect under the canopy of brush, even from the sky. Every year, a hiker or two might stumble across the site; Yoav occasionally brought a trusted friend there. Otherwise the hideaway remained his secret and began to feel permanent.

One morning, Niv and a dozen staff from the Nature Authority swept through the brush and down upon the house. "Wait a minute!" Yoav begged. "Let me at least make some coffee!" They didn't listen. Niv's men dragged out his belongings, tore down the roof, pulled down the walls and tilled the foundations back into earth. What had taken years of solitary construction vanished in an hour. "They destroyed it completely," Yoav said. "After, it was like nothing was there."

The nature official had come to respect Yoav's commitment to living off the grid. "It's a nice place," said Niv, as he surveyed the remains. "I've destroyed a few hundred places. But this time, I feel different."

Niv told Yoav about an old Syrian farmhouse, still standing, 40 years after the Six-Day War. It wasn't far from Shamir. He deputized Yoav as a "cattle guardian" to watch for stray heifers and midnight rustlers. Technically, the new guardian wasn't allowed to live in the farmhouse full-time, but if Yoav happened to maintain round-the-clock duty, nobody would care. And because he wasn't building a *new* structure in the reserve, Niv didn't need to evict him.

Yoav had to bring water, food and stove gas. He grew herbs and vegetables. He worked half-days as a kibbutz landscaper, tending decorative beds and grooming the cemetery. On Shamir, he visited his mother and used her Internet connection to play computer chess. Israel is one of the most densely populated nations; Yoav was a throwback to the age of desert prophets and solitary monks. Most days, he sat in his stone house, read and listened to music and the wind through the tall grass. He got high on *qat* and contemplated the universe and the corners of his mind. He was rarely disturbed in his stone house. Occasionally, soldiers dashed up and down the nearby dirt road, carrying a stretcher and a wounded mannequin or holding their rifles and yelling, "Fire! Fire! Fire!" instead of pulling the triggers.

There is no *nowhere* in Israel, however, that exists out of time, out of context. In 2006, during the Second Lebanon War, Yoav left his house for the day. By his desk, in the wall, he showed me the divots in the stone, the shrapnel's trajectory, the close call. A rocket had landed 75 feet from his bedroom window.

Yoav knew he was living on occupied land. But nobody, not in Israel at least, imagined the Golan Heights would be returned to Syria any time soon. Did he know anything about the former owners of the farmhouse? "They ran away from here when I was born," he said. In 1967. He smiled. "Maybe they realized I would need a place to live."

He knew that his situation could change. He knew that nothing was certain in Israel or the Golan. The army or the Nature Authority could kick him out anytime.

We drove to Tel Fahr, a memorial to a battle from the Six-Day War. Here, after a four-hour clash, IDF soldiers overran the outpost's Syrian defenders and opened a route onto the plateau that allowed the Israelis to sweep across the Golan Heights. A few visitors snapped photos. Near a concrete trench, Yoav set up a gas campstove and brewed another pot of Turkish coffee. The sun flared as it dropped behind the Lebanese border. We could see other kibbutzes in the distance: white boxes framed by a fiery backdrop. I asked Yoav how Shamir had changed in the last 20 years. And Israel, too.

"The kibbutz is like . . ." He paused. "In the beginning, everything belonged to the kibbutz. Nothing for yourself. And now everything is divided. The same thing in the country. They sell all the factories. It's all private now. They took the idea from America. Maybe it's happening all over the world. The rich get richer."

He shrugged. He had returned, as much as was possible in modern Israel, to a state of nature. It was a strange paradise my friend had found in the hills that overlooked the Finger of Galilee. A Zen-like existence, propped up by *qat*, punctuated by games of online chess.

I asked Yoav if he had written any more books. He hadn't. He didn't even own a copy of *Stories from the Ass*. I remembered one of the short tales from that volume, an abrupt parable that had given his collection its title. It went like this: *Haim the Hunchback says that life is not a story. He says that life is a story from the ass. A story is not like a story from the ass. It's a different thing. That's what he says. How come Haim is so clever? It's only because of his hunchback. The hunchback taught him a lot. That life is not a story, for example. Aside from this, it taught him mathematics.*

It felt good to reunite with an old friend after all these years, and to find he still pursued his own uncompromising vision of peace and solitude in a land that made both difficult. Yoav remained an exile-in-waiting in a land of unclear provenance. Yoav was the true utopian, a citizen of "nowhere." He had become a character from his story collection—a figure of myth who lived in the hills, with a hard-learned wisdom borne of a strange wilderness. A prophet. Or a holy fool. I felt a pang of envy for his simple life. I'd always fantasized about such an escape: living alone and writing novels in a lighthouse, or a forestry watchtower, or a derelict train station in Eastern Europe. Instead, I'd become an overscheduled suburban dad who read more spreadsheets than works of literature.

I felt a sadness, too. I sensed it in the long pauses between our words. Perhaps Yoav had always been unsuited to life as a kibbutznik. His private, eccentric nature didn't square with a place where everyone knew your name and your business, where gossip and the pressure to conform drove others from its gates, too. A business philosophy was the new force on the kibbutz. This, too, felt alien to Yoav. His vision was Zionism writ small, a Jewish nation reduced to a microcosm of one. He only needed a room of his own, a day or two of outdoor labour to earn his food and fuel, and a deeper connection than most of his countrymen would ever feel to the ground—the sacred soil—beneath his feet. He had found all that.

CHAPTER 7

Moving the State

When I was a volunteer on Shamir, I often looked out toward the ridges that divided Israel from Lebanon and wondered what dangers lurked beyond the border: *Here be dragons*. Kibbutznik friends described pulling up lawn chairs, cracking open beers and watching as Israeli F-15s and F-16s decimated the Syrian air force in the skies above Lebanon's Bekaa Valley during the air battle of June 1982. One fall morning, as I dug stones from the cotton fields, the warm air began to vibrate, and several of the IAF's Cobras, slim two-person attack helicopters, buzzed low over the treetops as they circled the Hula Valley. "The effect of watching these lithe metal killers on maneuvers was unnerving," I confessed to my journal. "A sobering reminder that all is not as utopic as it may seem in this deceiving country." I'd read a recent news report about three Palestinians, armed with shoulder rockets, assault rifles and grenades, who were shot and captured in the security zone the IDF monitored along the Lebanese border; the trio had planned to attack and kidnap civilians in Kiryat Shmona, the town where we drank and shopped and caught buses into southern Israel. Two months later, the IDF killed another trio of insurgents as they were cutting through a border fence and preparing to fire a rocket at Kibbutz Manara.

Danger could ride the skies, too. A year before I arrived, a Palestinian terrorist had flown a motorized hang glider from Lebanon into the Hula Valley and attacked an IDF base, killing six soldiers and wounding seven others before he was killed. In the aftermath, a volunteer on another kibbutz was wounded when antiterrorist units ordered him to raise his hands in Hebrew—a language he didn't speak. One morning, as we worked in the apple orchards, we heard a loud explosion and saw to the north, through the hilly notch that framed the Bekaa Valley, a tower of smoke slowly rise into the sky. On dawn shifts, our drivers were sometimes stopped at the kibbutz gates and told to wait because the army had detected suspicious activity in the valley. Judi Sinton, the volunteer from New Zealand, had been killed within the fences of Shamir, so such precautions seemed neither abstract nor overzealous.

And then there was Wolf's party. Following our Purim celebrations, the mysterious German volunteer commemorated his 33rd birthday with a boozy all-night bonfire. We salvaged loose wood, piled it high and doused it in gas; Wolf flipped his Zippo and ignited the conflagration. Flames spiralled into the night sky, and blankets of heat bowled over tipsy bystanders. Someone stuck a Pogues tape into a ghetto blaster. A Dutch volunteer strummed an acoustic guitar: "If I should fall from grace with God . . ." Across the valley, the midnight sky exploded with falling light. Flares, as many as 10 at a time, seemed to break free of a distant constellation and drift to earth. Ghostly auras illuminated the border ridgetops. We had seen flares before but never in such multitudes, one after another, like a host of fallen, falling angels. Behind us, beyond the wire of the kibbutz perimeter, from the plateau of the Golan Heights, we could hear a husky *whumpf whumpf*, like an agitated guard dog. We kept singing and dancing and drinking. The next morning, all that reminded us of the night's revels was the deep ashen pit in front of Wolf's cabin. Were the sounds we had heard just a collective hallucination? When we picked up the day's *Jerusalem Post*, we knew it hadn't been. IDF soldiers had killed nine Palestinian insurgents trying to sneak across the border from Lebanon to attack outlying kibbutzes. That explained the shower of flares. That explained the barrage of munitions being hurled over our heads. That explained the sense that we were, for one night at least, dancing on the border of the end times.

Ten years later, the valley would catch fire again.

—

On a rainy night in early February 1997, two army helicopters hovered above a field in the north of Israel. Visibility was near zero, even before the pilots switched off the powerful searchlights to evade detection. The transport choppers, huge Sikorsky CH-53 Sea Stallions, were preparing to cross the border for a night mission into Lebanon. A rush of wind ripped through the storm as the choppers bent toward the northern border.

The helicopters clipped rotors in mid-flight. In a terrible rending of metal, both lost control, spiralled to the earth and exploded on impact. The conflagration lit up the fields of a border kibbutz. The Hula Valley whistled and roared with exploding munitions. Rescue crews couldn't approach the fiery crash site for hours. It didn't matter. None of the 73 soldiers survived.

News of the deaths—the worst air crash in Israel's history—sent the country into mourning. Nearly everyone had a son or a husband in uniform. *How had this happened? At this time?* To the citizens of Tel Aviv and Jerusalem, Israel was no longer a country at war; residents in northern communities knew better. Fifteen years earlier, in 1982, the Israeli army had launched Operation Peace for Galilee—an incursion to oust the Palestine Liberation Organization from its bases in Lebanon. The planned blitzkrieg against Palestinian guerrillas turned into a bloody and protracted conflict in a country already riven by civil war. After two years of fighting, the Israeli army withdrew from Beirut but still occupied a security buffer along Lebanon's southern border, seven kilometres wide. The Lebanon War achieved one goal: Yasser Arafat and the PLO fled to new headquarters in Tunisia. But victory was Pyrrhic. Thousands of casualties. Beirut in ruins. The massacre of more than 1,000 Palestinian civilians by Lebanese Christian militiamen, under the watch of the IDF, in the Sabra and Shatila refugee camps. The drawn-out conflict became known as "Israel's Vietnam" and tarnished the myth of the IDF as an invincible, moral army.

Even without the PLO, sporadic violence in the north continued for years. Rockets from the newly formed Hezbollah Shi'ite militia, supplied by Iran, landed on border towns and kibbutzes. Peace for Galilee was an oxymoron. IDF foot patrols triggered roadside bombs in the security zone, so the army switched to armoured trucks. When Hezbollah detonated bigger bombs under the trucks, the IDF turned to helicopter missions. The heavy-duty Sikorskys reminded enemies that Israel ruled the skies. The choppers were considered indestructible. They weren't.

—

Kibbutz Gadot sits in the southern end of the Hula Valley, not far from the Mahanayim Reserve Air Base, from where the military helicopters had lifted off. Rachel Ben Dor, a kibbutznik on Gadot for two decades, now lived with her family in a nearby town. After hearing news of the 1997 crash, she wondered, *Was my son aboard one of the choppers? What's going on out there in the dark?* Only in the morning did she learn her commando son was safe. Still, the crash deepened her misgivings about the low-grade border conflict in Lebanon, and so she visited two of her old friends at Kibbutz Gadot, Ronit Nachmias and Yaffa Arbel. The kibbutz mothers discussed their frustration at the endless war of attrition. Their boys had grown up on the kibbutz; they knew families who lost sons in the crash. The mothers also understood the importance of the army, their sons' duty and desire to serve. But were their sacrifices being squandered in Lebanon? Why wasn't the country even *talking* about the war? The mothers could no longer stay silent.

They composed a letter of support for four elected members of Israel's Knesset, from different parties, secular and religious, who had been asking Israel to reconsider its military operations in southern Lebanon. That letter led to meetings with sympathetic politicians and a public debate organized at the kibbutz. Around this time, a kibbutz newspaper printed a diatribe directed at mothers of soldiers, especially kibbutz mothers. *Why*, the writer asked, *were they so passive about allowing, even encouraging, their sons to accept combat duty as inevitable and just, under all circumstances?* "Why are you not shouting, why aren't you demonstrating, why don't you chain yourselves to the gates of the prime minister's office?" The article struck a nerve. The women from Gadot agreed with the sentiment but not the generalization. The mothers *were* trying to make a difference. But it was hard to be heard when they lacked experience in the PR of protest movements and lived far from the country's major cities and national media. Rachel Ben Dor called to thank the editorial's author; he asked to interview the group.

The friends invited a fourth mother, from nearby Kibbutz Mahanayim, to join the meeting. Miri Sela was an activist and part of the Women in Black movement, which opposed the Israeli Occupation of the West Bank, the Palestinian territory surrounding West Jerusalem that Israel had captured from Jordan in the Six-Day War of 1967. She understood the highs and lows of protest in Israel—the solidarity, the isolation, the backlash—and felt ready to engage against the war in Lebanon. After the Yom Kippur War of 1973, her husband served as a soldier in the fortifications along the Suez Canal, when Egypt and Israel exchanged artillery shells almost daily. He would return home, through Tel Aviv, bewildered by the indifference to casualty counts in the Sinai. "My God," he would tell her, "don't they know we are fighting a war?" In 1977, when Miri watched the historic visit of President Sadat to Israel on TV, a prelude to the Camp David Accords, she cried and whispered a promise to her new son: "You were born into a time of peace! You can forget about doing army service!" Naive words, it turned out. Eighteen years later, her soldier-son was ordered to Lebanon.

After the meeting, the journalist mused, "Have we here a one-time outburst of motherly emotion, or perhaps a local political adventure, or the budding of a new movement of political protest?" The article appeared on the Eve of Passover, so the author dubbed the middle-aged activists the "Four Mothers," after the Biblical matriarchs of the Jewish people. The label proved a mixed blessing. The movement grew from four into many—and soon included fathers, sons and daughters. The name deflected criticism under the sacred shield of motherhood, a symbol nearly as potent in Israel as the army. But its feminine connotations led many people to dismiss their efforts as the "hysterics" of overprotective womenfolk who couldn't grasp military strategy.

The Four Mothers appeared on a Friday night broadcast on national TV. Their protest filled in as "balance" to a story about a mother who had lost one soldier-son but felt honoured to send her other boy to defend the nation. The organizers then staged a demonstration at a major highway intersection where troop carriers passed en route to the border. Their protest signs flashed across TV sets:

15 Years in Lebanon: Enough! and *Let's leave Lebanon in peace.* The next day, Miri Sela's kibbutz phone didn't stop ringing. Israelis from across the country, mostly women, wanted to help.

The roadside demonstrations weren't universally popular. Young soldiers swore from the back of troop transports. Passing drivers hollered, "You're women, what do you understand?" "Go home and cook!" and "Arafat's whores!" An army commander called them "The Four Rags." A bus driver tried to run down protesters. One of the original mothers dropped out at the request of her soldier-son.

But slowly, their voices reached sympathetic ears: an article in Israel's largest newspaper. A petition with 25,000 signatures. Soldiers flashing thumbs-up. The Four Mothers found allies among retired IDF officers who had served in Lebanon. David Grossman, the acclaimed novelist and activist, became a prominent supporter. Long ignored, even taboo, the issue of Lebanon rose on the national agenda. The Four Mothers avoided aligning with any one political party, even though most support came from the Left. They reached beyond partisan ideology, beyond the borders of Israel. They mailed letters to UN leaders, foreign diplomats, President Clinton, even the head of Hezbollah. The mothers plastered their faces in mud—a symbol of the morass of Lebanon—and marched on the prime minister's office.

Pollsters charted public support for the Mothers' call to leave Lebanon. It started at 10 per cent, marginal at best, but it doubled and doubled again, until it approached half the nation. Ehud Barak, the Labor candidate, sought to unseat Prime Minister Benjamin Netanyahu of the right-wing Likud Party and sensed an opportunity. The kibbutz-born former army chief of staff promised, if he were elected, to remove troops from Lebanon. His languishing campaign caught wind. Barak won the election and kept at least this one promise. In May 2000, three years after the helicopter disaster, Israel closed the door on 18 years of military occupation within Lebanon. The soldier who locked the last border gate called to thank Rachel Ben Dor and the Four Mothers.

—

The legacy of Lebanon and the Four Mothers remains a subject of debate. Peace along the northern border did not magically materialize after that last gate was shut. Rocket attacks continued. In 2006, a Hezbollah ambush captured two IDF soldiers, and Israel launched a new offensive. Hostilities lasted a month, but the Second Lebanon War proved bloody and costly, especially to Lebanese and Israeli civilians. Three months later, the Israeli army withdrew again, and both sides declared victory. David Grossman supported the initial reprisal against Hezbollah, but as the fighting dragged on, he joined a chorus of authors demanding an end to the war. Days before a ceasefire took effect, Grossman's 20-year-old son died in combat. Right-wing critics seized on the tragedy as evidence the withdrawal from Lebanon had been misguided. If Grossman hadn't supported the Four Mothers, they argued, the army would not have needed to return to Lebanon—and his son might still be alive.

On a visit to the Hula Valley, I stopped at the helicopter crash site and wandered the memorial, near the foothills of Mt. Hermon and the headwaters of the Jordan River. A stone pathway led visitors along a channel of clear water that flowed into a round, reflective pool. Polished black rectangles, submerged along the circumference of the pool's edge, were engraved with the names of the dead. Around the pool loomed igneous rock forms, six feet tall, weathered white and mottled orange, a standing stone casting a shadow for every soldier. The effect was haunting.

Miri Sela still lived and worked at Kibbutz Mahanayim. She felt proud of what the Four Mothers had accomplished, no matter the consequences critics laid at their feet. "Some people told us we did something beautiful and excellent," said Miri. "And other people said we were to blame for all of it—for the Second Lebanon War, for leaving Gaza, for everything." She shrugged. "For me, when we got out of Lebanon, it was great happiness. But I had a sad feeling that we didn't start sooner, that we could have saved more soldiers." Miri recalled the words of her daughter, who delivered a blessing at her 50th birthday party: "You taught us that, if you believe in something, you can even move the state."

After achieving their goal, the Four Mothers disbanded. The organization held no ambitions to leverage the celebrity of its leaders into public office or to fight other injustices. Remaining funds were used to create an archive, housed at Ohio State University, of the movement's letters, posters, news clippings and interviews—a case study in how a grassroots social movement can earn the attention of the fickle media. How activists can survive the backlash when they put their names and faces to a divisive issue in a divided country. "Our message was authenticity," said Miri. "People trusted us. We changed the whole mentality that women don't know anything about the army."

The seeds for the Four Mothers were planted on the lawns of Kibbutz Gadot. Many of the meetings and demonstrations occurred in and around the kibbutzes of northern Galilee. But Miri and the other Mothers tried not to frame the protest as a kibbutz project. By 1997, the kibbutz as a movement had little political or social influence in Israel. But the *spirit* of the kibbutz, the philosophy they had grown up with, informed the actions of the Mothers. Before 1948, pioneers had established kibbutzes throughout the North to define and defend the future border between Lebanon and Israel. After 1948, kibbutzniks filled the ranks of elite fighting units and the officer class. Now, that communal ethos defended the North again, this time by demanding the country give peace a chance and leave Lebanon. Miri Sela had joined her kibbutz as a young soldier because of the higher calling at the heart of the movement. Her fellow mothers shared that sense of service to the nation.

"It might sound immodest," she said, "but I think that, as the kibbutz movement, we have a greater political awareness and influence than the average citizen in the country. It's in our basic makeup."

———

Thousands of parents in Israel owed a debt of gratitude to the Four Mothers. And yet, in the years that followed, their protest movement faded from public memory. When people remembered the Four Mothers, it was often as a historical footnote or a trivia question. "If you ask around," said Myriam Dagan Brenner, an activist and educator at the Givat Haviva Institute, "most people today would say about the Four Mothers: 'They weren't significant, they weren't relevant, they didn't have a real impact.'" Myriam knew better. Her son had been an engineer responsible for detonating the bunkers abandoned by the IDF during the withdrawal and one of the last soldiers to exit Lebanon. She had closely followed the debate that led to the pull-out. "Without the Four Mothers, we would still be in Lebanon," she said. "I don't have any doubt about it."

Why Miri Sela and her kibbutz friends succeeded when other peace movements in Israel flounder reveals much about the status of women in Israel—and in the kibbutz movement, too. Women's views about military topics were usually dismissed, despite their mandatory service in the IDF, because they don't see combat. The Four Mothers, however, circumvented gender bias by appealing to a deeper maternal symbolism. "We had a significance to the struggle not as citizens, not as women, but because we were *mothers*," noted Myriam. "It's so Israeli! As mothers you have legitimacy. It's difficult to fight as anything else."

A similar women's movement has never successfully challenged the Occupation of the Palestinian Territories. "It's not a motherhood issue," said Myriam. "It's a civic issue. It's a political issue. It's a democratic issue." Women in Black, a group that began street vigils in 1988 to oppose the Occupation, remains marginal; it inspired a counter-group of right-wing opponents known as Women in Green.

Call it the Lysistrata Theory—the idea that only women can end war when war is all men know. Unlike the Athenian wives of Aristophanes' ancient satire, the Four Mothers brought the Israeli military to heel not by withholding sex from lusty husbands, but by creating a cause to unite the nation—both men and women. If there is any hope for restoring the dream of Israel, it might lie in listening to women like the Four Mothers. War, they made clear, *is* a feminist issue. Peace must be a feminist issue, too.

The kibbutz once offered a great hope for equality between the sexes. Capitalism treated women as domestic servants, according to kibbutz leaders; the socialist commune would end such gendered servitude. And yet the practice of kibbutz equality never lived up to its promise. In principle, every man and woman was equal. The communal dining hall and children's house freed women from the burdens of meal-making and child-rearing. Mothers had more time to work, to socialize, to engage in the political life of the kibbutz and the nation. But when the shovels hit the dirt, some members were more equal than others. The original communes and kibbutzes tended to be lopsided in gender ratios; the founders of Degania included ten men and only two women. Building the first kibbutzes meant turning soil, digging rocks, draining swamps, planting trees, erecting fortifications and laying foundations. Men's work—or that was the assumption. While half of the women on the early kibbutzes worked in agriculture and other areas of production, that number dropped as communities expanded, and women were diverted into the service, education and domestic branches—traditional and undervalued "women's work."

"The kibbutz is a model example of the problems and plusses of the first stage of feminism and sex role equality in that it made an attempt to include women in the productive sector of the workplace, before she had children," observed Betty Friedan, the pioneering American feminist, in an introduction to *Sexual Equality: The Israeli Kibbutz Tests the Theories*, an academic study published in 1983. "The founders of the kibbutz movement could not see beyond the first stage—that equality cannot be achieved in terms of male values alone, and only in terms of redefining the female role."

Myriam Dagan Brenner agreed that gender quality on the kibbutz never matched its utopian aspirations—especially the famous communal childcare facilities. "No woman was asked if she wanted to give up her children," she said. "And no woman who wanted to be with her children was allowed to do it. It was an awful kind of oppression of the women who wanted to be mothers. It took parenthood from both the parents." Communal childcare was meant to shape future generations into ideal kibbutzniks, no longer dependent on the bourgeois family. However, many members who grew up under the watch of the kibbutz nanny rather than their own parents came to resent this austere experiment in collective reprogramming. "The children are sheltered by the finest theories, surrounded by nurses and educators," wrote Avraham Balaban in a damning memoir of his lonely childhood on Kibbutz Hulda, "but the nurses soon discover that a mother's love no more resembles her feeling for her friend's children than blood resembles sweat."

The gender divisions in Israel add a frustrating wrinkle to the Conflict, as the Palestinian-Israeli confrontation is known. (Hebrew speakers also talk about it as *Hamatsav*—"the Situation.") Few women are involved in the peace process. "The Jewish women think they can't be part of it because they aren't involved in army issues," said Myriam. "And the Palestinian women think that the men are right, so there is nothing to argue about." Myriam leads encounter groups with Jewish and Palestinian women at Givat Haviva to overcome that mutual reluctance to engage in political debate. "The kibbutz movement has never been a subversive movement," said Myriam, who emigrated from France with no desire to join a kibbutz, even as she worked at an institute founded by the movement. "Givat Haviva is seen as left wing but it's very mainstream—a very Jewish thing, a very Zionist thing." That was not a bad quality. "You can change things only from the inside, by consensus, by the centre of the map." The Four Mothers were a case study in how small actions within a society—and small groups of activists—can leverage popular support into profound effects, often more than the noisy vanguard that throws light on a problem. "Being against everyone doesn't bring change," said Myriam. "I put my energy into getting small results every day."

In the century before Israel's founding, early Zionist thinkers, diplomats and even helpful outsiders suggested locations other than Palestine as a home for the Jewish Diaspora: Madagascar, Tasmania, Argentina, Alaska, Grand Island in New York State. Theodor Herzl lobbied for British Uganda (now part of modern Kenya) as a sanctuary for the Jewish people. At a conference, Myriam met a diplomat from the region, who told her, "We could have been neighbours!" She smiled at this alternative reality.

"There is a joke in Hebrew that Moses stuttered," she said, "and when he said where should the Jewish people go, it was to 'Canaan.' But what he really said was 'Ca-ca-ca . . .' And he meant 'Canada'!"

"We've got lots of space," I said.

"Yes!" Myriam released one of her piquant laughs. "Maybe the Jewish people were not meant to be here. Maybe we were meant to be somewhere else."

Like Moses crossing the Red Sea, the Four Mothers had led an entire army from the no-man's zone of southern Lebanon to the safety of the Promised Land. The women of Israel and the kibbutz were still waiting for another historic moment, when the men in power, on both sides, learned to listen to their voices and chart a new course toward peace.

CHAPTER 8

The Shouting Fence

On my first Friday night as a volunteer on Kibbutz Shamir, I finished a shift on the dishwashing machine, showered the grease off my skin and walked to the Volly Bar. A single unsheathed lightbulb swung from a wire and illuminated a low-ceilinged bunker. Puddles of beer and fuel from portable heaters shimmered on the bare concrete floor. I claimed a stool at the bar rather than join the busy tables and benches along the walls. The Volly Bar's bar looked like a derelict fruit stand slapped together from bare plywood. Over the raw barrier, the bartender slung bottles of Israeli beer and cans of Tuborg or Budweiser from an old fridge, poured stiff vodka-and-oranges and double shots of anise-tasting *arak* into chipped plastic dessert cups. I sipped a bottle of Goldstar and observed a circle of five volunteers at the next table playing a tongue-twisting drinking game called Fuzzy Duck.

"Fuzzy duck!"

"Does he?"

"Fucky duzz—"

"*Drink!*"

The room was underlit and jangly with testosterone. Large dogs lounged under the tables or nipped at each other. Slurred accents exchanged boozy threats. A short, yappy Australian with five-day stubble and a Star of David around his neck leapt onto a wooden seat, kicked the remaining glass from a broken window and pissed a stream into the night. Two burly New Zealanders grabbed the Aussie like a loose rugby ball and projected him through the frame and onto the cactus below. My barstool neighbour didn't seem fazed. I assumed from his olive skin and close-cropped dark hair, his seen-it-all calm, that he was a kibbutznik. He wore a button-up dress shirt, not the wrinkled T-shirts favoured by volunteers, and aviator glasses concealed his eyes.

"I'm Ali," he said.

"I'm David," I replied. "From Canada." I asked if he lived on Shamir.

"No," he said. "I'm from Majdal Shams."

My face went blank. "Where's that?"

His chin jerked toward the door. If I could look out the entrance of the bar, northward, up the slopes of the Golan Heights, nearly to the summit of Mt. Hermon—there, held in a crook of the mountain's folds, sat the village of Majdal Shams. Ali was neither a Jewish kibbutznik nor a foreign-born volunteer. He was an Arab. But he didn't fit the tidy ethnic or religious identities I'd read about. He didn't consider himself Palestinian and certainly not Arab-Israeli. "I'm Syrian," he said. "I'm Druze."

"What's a Druze?" I asked.

The Druze confound anyone hoping to understand the complex relationship between Arabs and Jews in the Middle East. Most live in villages scattered throughout the southern mountains of Syria and Lebanon, with a few settlements in Jordan, and 100,000 or so in Israel's

North, largely in the Galilee, as well as 20,000 Druze in the Golan Heights. Their religion is nearly a thousand years old, a split from a split from the Ismaili branch of Shia Islam, steeped in Greek philosophy and mystical Gnosticism, with a belief in reincarnation. They claimed to descend from Jethro, the father-in-law of Moses. To evade persecution as heretics, the Druze insulated their faith in mystery. Some consider themselves Muslim; others not. (Ali was enjoying a beer, so I figure he was the latter.) The Druze were the Arabs most fully integrated into Israeli society; they volunteered as soldiers in the Israel Defense Forces, elected their own politicians as members of the Knesset and were full citizens. For years, they had been poster models for Arab-Israeli co-existence. While many of the Druze of the Golan Heights worked on Israeli kibbutzes, they had resisted assimilation. Ali's family came from Syria and still considered themselves Syrian. They had relatives across the border. If I went to visit him in Majdal Shams, he said, I could see this divide. I could see how the Druze of the Golan Heights had been split yet again. I could visit the Shouting Fence.

He described the barrier that divided Syria and Majdal Shams. How his people gathered on either side of the wire and called to friends and family members. How they had done this for twenty years—since the Six-Day War and Israel's capture of the Golan Heights—to bridge the distance across which they could never walk.

I never took Ali up on his invitation to visit Majdal Shams. I got distracted by life on the kibbutz, and Ali moved on to other jobs. On a day trip, I joined other volunteers on a bus tour to the Golan Heights in the winter; we passed through Druze villages and had a snowball fight at the side of the road. We skidded down the hills of the ski resort on our bums and stared across the double-fenced border toward Syria.

The geography of the Golan is a crusty, high-stepped staircase of volcanic rock that leads travellers onto its wide plateau and up the side of the mountain that joins Israel, Lebanon and Syria. Concrete houses were stacked along the outstretched ridge. I had arranged to meet Salman Fakhiraldeen, the PR coordinator and assistant researcher of the Al-Marsad Center, at a roundabout with a statue in the village of Majdal Shams. But as I pitched back in the driver's seat and gunned the car up the steep streets, I realized there were a lot of roundabouts with a lot of statues—mementoes to noble moments in the troubled past of the Druze. Once we finally connected, Salman took me to Al-Marsad Center, a few furniture-less rooms and an enclosed office, where young Irish interns and law students sat in front of old PCs. Their job was to document human rights violations and legal abuses against the Arab population of the Golan Heights.

I told Salman I'd met Druze workers when I lived on a kibbutz.

"Ah, if you were a volunteer in Shamir," he replied, "then you were in heaven!"

I couldn't tell if he was joking.

Salman had a squared-shouldered presence that filled out a lavender-striped business shirt. Black and silver mingled in his hair. His smile was jack-o-lanterned with broken teeth. Throughout the afternoon, he catalogued the injustices his people faced, and yet the inflection of his barrel-toned voice rarely rose beyond a dry note of irony. His fundamental message: *We are strong. We are patient. We can out-wait our occupiers. We will get our message to the world.*

"We have a saying in Arabic," he said, as we sat down to talk. "Sometimes God kills the camel to feed the fox." I nodded as though I knew what he meant.

He showed photos of a neighbour. "He died a year ago." Salman gestured out the balcony toward a nearby rooftop. "That's his house." Like many families in Majdal Shams, they'd been split between Syria and the Golan, so the different members gathered on either side of the Shouting Fence to grieve together at a distance. "We are lucky here in the Golan," said Salman. "If we have a funeral, we get to do it twice."

The Syrian Bride, a 2004 film set in Majdal Shams, tells a Romeo-and-Juliet story of two lovers with similarly border-crossed families—and a bride who must travel from the Golan to Syria. "It was based on a girl from that family," said Salman.

Staff and volunteers at the Al-Marsad Center record violations against the land once owned by the Druze in the depopulated Heights. "In the whole Golan, only five villages remain out of 160," he said. "We also have problems with land mines." Unexploded mines dot the landscape. Mines fill former orchards and grazing fields. Mines surround houses. Mines form a *U* around one entire village. Mines embedded in a slope were sliding toward a family's backyard, not far from where their children played. Mines wounded and killed livestock that wandered past fences or villagers who didn't attend to the warning signs. Mines were the tools to colonize the Golan.

"Mines are used to increase the suffering of people, to limit their space of life. Mines can be used in the future to confiscate the land. They can say, 'Oh they didn't use the land for 40 years, so we can take it.'" Salman paused, looked across the rooftops of his city in the sky. "This spectrum of suffering is what we investigate at Al-Marsad."

—

Salman was born in Majdal Shams—the "Citadel of the Sun" in Aramaic—in 1954. He dates his earliest memories, etched with nostalgia, as BTO: Before The Occupation. He remembers the flavour of the ice cream his father bought for him when they travelled to Damascus. They would visit family friends and tour the ancient city's historic sites such as the Great Mosque of the Ummayads. "But then the war came," he said, "and erased everything." He was 13 in 1967 and recalled the Israeli army entering Majdal Shams. The armoured trucks. The soldiers removing the Syrian flag from the school's pole and setting it ablaze. "I do remember—it's very clear—when they invaded our village, the soldiers tried to give us sweets and we rejected it. I'm trying to remember why I rejected those sweets. Was I afraid they would be poisoned? I don't remember. It's an open question for me."

Israeli colonization of the Golan Heights began immediately after the victory of the Six-Day War of June 5 to 10, 1967. Kibbutz Merom Golan was founded on an abandoned military camp on the Heights in July of that same year. By 1970, a dozen Jewish settlements dotted the plateau. Elsewhere, in the West Bank and Gaza, religious nationalists assumed the vanguard as settlers in the Palestinian Territories and sought to fulfill the Biblical promise of a "Greater Israel" from the Mediterranean Sea to the Jordan River. In the Golan, it was secular left-wing kibbutzniks who claimed the conquered land and began the occupation that would vex future peace negotiations.

Salman was expelled from high school for political activities. In 1973, he noticed Israeli soldiers mustering near Majdal Shams. He suspected the IDF was preparing another surprise assault, like the first strike of the Six-Day War, and so he snuck across the border, via a mountain pass, to alert the Syrians. The Syrian army was already planning its own unprovoked attack on Israel. A week later, war broke out. The Yom Kippur War—or the Ramadan War, to Arab historians—was a wake-up call for Israeli military intelligence; its agents assumed the Syrians wouldn't risk a full-on assault against heavily mined anti-tank defences. They were wrong. On October 6, more than 1,400 Russian-built tanks, supported by air strikes and artillery bombardment, pushed the IDF's 170 tanks back across the Golan Heights. Arab forces threatened to overrun Israeli positions on multiple fronts. Syrian commandos captured the surveillance station atop Mt. Hermon.

Amos Oz, the novelist and kibbutznik, fought on the Golan. For three days, he was convinced Israel would be destroyed. "I don't think I could convey the experience of fighting to people who have not been on the battlefield," he later recalled. "Battle consists first and foremost of a horrible stench. The battlefield stinks to high heaven. It's hard to imagine the stench. . . . This stifling mixture of burning rubber and burning metal and burning human flesh and feces, everything burning. A description of the battlefield that does not contain the stench and the fear is not sufficient. It is where everyone around you has shit their pants." Oz tried to write about the war but destroyed his drafts. "I could write about sex, I could write about the kibbutz, about envy, about sunsets, about howling jackals. Not this."

Exhausted by three days of intense fighting, Syrian commanders mistook the dust clouds from 15 Israeli tanks as a larger force of reinforcements and retreated. The Israeli army reclaimed lost territory and pushed into Syria when reinforcements finally did arrive. By the time of the October 23 ceasefire, smoking ruins of tanks and armoured personal carriers littered the Golan. When Salman Fakhiraldeen returned to Majdal Shams, he was tried, convicted and sentenced by Israeli authorities to five years in prison. Released in 1979, he took up a new role as a political activist. "The first stage of my life was an underground one," he said. "The second, a public one."

In December of 1981, the Israeli government passed a law to annex the Golan Heights. Two months later, four Druze leaders were arrested for protesting the law, and the Golan Druze called a general strike. They closed shops and schools. They refused identity cards issued by the Israeli army, stopped paying taxes and rejected government support. Israeli authorities paid little attention. The 14,000 Druze lived isolated amid the mountains, far from Tel Aviv and Jerusalem, and hadn't caused a fuss before. The strike continued for nearly six months. The IDF closed access to several Druze villages to quiet the rebellion. Nothing worked.

The Druze couldn't reverse Israel's Golan Law. But they commanded the attention of Israel's public and political class. "We were the first successful popular movement against Israel," said Salman. "In the Golan, the Israelis were shocked. They didn't think that people could resist their occupation." No longer could Israelis assume the Druze were happy and loyal citizens of the nation, that mythical hybrid: the Arab-Israeli. Palestinian leaders in the Occupied Territories studied the general strike as a model of non-violent resistance. Five years later, young protesters in the West Bank and Gaza rose up—and so dawned the age of the *intifada*, the "throwing off" that began in the Golan. Israel would never be the same.

—

Salman and I walked the sidewalks of Majdal Shams. "Come look," he said, and we disappeared through a side door, up a set of stairs and into a white-walled, beige-tiled, loft-ceilinged space that echoed with voices. It was an artist-run cultural centre straight out of Soho or Berlin or Greenwich Village. ("What?" a kibbutznik later scoffed when I described the centre. "The Druze have culture?") Curators were finessing a new exhibition. Huge expressionistic oil paintings hung from the walls. Bug-eyed cartoon faces. Scraggly ravens. A gloomy, cramped scene with joyless red kites drooping off their strings. Rough patches of paint dried like halva to the canvas. Postmodern bummer art. A man atop a stepladder adjusted wires from the ceiling and attached them to the wrists and ankles and waists of three life-sized painted plaster sculptures—two barefoot village women and a man—sprawled face down on the tiles.

In a corner of the room, a young woman sat cross-legged, gesturing like a conductor, as she told a story. Four others, in their late teens or early twenties, listened in a semicircle, pens and paper in front of yoga mats. Their teacher nodded encouragement. A lime-green wooden suitcase sat open, filled with cues and props. The contents of a long-handled Turkish coffee pot fuelled the lesson. The teacher, a Palestinian from Haifa, was training the team of young "story collectors" to gather tales from their grandparents before they were forgotten.

Wael Toraby, the director of the centre, explained the goals of the storytelling workshop and the other projects. The artists' collective organized exhibitions, literary readings and music concerts, produced books for adults and children, and removed high art from its pedestal to share with the people of the Golan. Every year, they put on a festival in a different Druze village and left behind a public sculpture as a gift. They hoped to stoke a pride of nationhood, a reminder of where the Arabs of the Golan all came from—especially those, like Wael, who were born under the Occupation. The new generation, he admitted, sees the benefit of Israeli rule: the economic opportunities, the relative freedom next to the violent autocracy across the border. Israel was a democracy; Syria wasn't—and was lurching into a catastrophic civil war.

"Young people are pragmatic in their life," said Wael, who had studied painting in Russia. "They say, 'We are living better.' They don't think, in a few years, that they will feel they are not citizens. And you will never be a citizen in a Jewish country. At least you have the hope of being a citizen in Syria, within some years, because there is no discrimination in Syria." He noticed my skepticism. "We are all equal in poverty, so we have a hope."

The desire to be Syrian, said Wael, did not equal the desire for the repressive status quo of the Assad regime or an Islamic theocracy of ISIS thugs. "How to be in peace with your identity. How to belong to a place, to a history, to a people—and not to a regime. This is the most complicated question we have right now."

—

The story most associated with the Druze of Majdal Shams was the Shouting Fence—a looming presence that held back waves of distraught relatives. A bleak inversion of the Wailing Wall. A towering wire net to catch the sing-songy calls of the Druze.

On an unfinished roof of a building on the edge of town, the rainbow-striped flags of the Druze, tied to rusty ends of rebar, flapped in the breeze. We were finally here. We were looking at the Shouting Fence. The fence was, in fact, two fences, separated by a heavily mined no-man's land—hence, the need for megaphones and shouting.

The first line of wire was about 20 metres below us, a basic barbed barrier, with a dirt road graded parallel on the other side, and ran along the bottom of the small valley where the village ended. The second fence was 100 metres away, higher up the hill on the Syrian side, beyond a swath of orchards filled with mines. The brush was burned away every year to keep trees from growing as cover. The Israeli military in the pillbox behind us scoped the space. Higher still on the far slope, we could discern a few single-storey white buildings. Salman told me it was a Syrian police station. A wide platform, like a helicopter pad, extended around the buildings, on which villagers from the nearest Syrian community, four kilometres away, could gather to be seen and heard in Majdal Shams. Nobody stood there today.

"This is the valley," said Salman. From platforms on the facing hillsides, the two sides shouted to each other *over*, not through, the fences. "The Shouting Fence is a very cynical name, which doesn't reflect the reality of the place."

"Why?"

"People gather here across the valley. They speak to each other, to their lovers, with loudspeakers. They have to see their lovers through glasses. They have to fly something in their hands to be recognized by their relatives." *Shouting* suggests a clamouring mob, half-human, angry, on the march. It didn't capture the poignant semaphore of longing and regret. "In Majdal Shams, we call it the Valley of Tears," Salman said.

Friday afternoon, the Muslim day of rest, was the busiest at the fence. Today, however, the only shouting drifted up from a soccer pitch in town.

The Shouting Fence—or Valley of Tears—didn't see much use anymore. It was an archaic form of communication, like a handwritten letter, reserved for special occasions. Separated families kept in touch through email, cellphones, Skype. Before Syria's civil war, those who could afford the trip coordinated reunions in Jordan. The valley only echoed with shouting when extended families or the entire community needed to gather. To mark a death. To honour a marriage. To commemorate a political anniversary, such as Syria's Independence Day or the Golan General Strike. I didn't know if the fence had become more symbolic or less.

Earlier, I had asked if other people in Majdal Shams shared Salman's strong political opinions. What percentage of the Druze in the Golan really preferred Syria to Israel?

"The question is a minefield, and I want to walk over it," he said. "People have no right to negotiate the sovereignty of the place. It belongs to Syria. This question should be directed to Damascus, not to me. In the Golan, more than 80 per cent consider themselves Syrians, in spite of the fact that the majority have no memories of Syria because they were born after the Occupation."

A small ethnic-religious group, squeezed for the past thousand years in the vice-grip of far greater forces, the Druze have always been canny about expressing allegiances. Most remain as private about their political preferences as their spiritual beliefs. In Syria, Lebanon and Israel, Druze leaders find ways to work with the powers-that-be. Here, in the Golan, in a purgatory of annexation, many people did not claim the Israeli citizenship offered to them—not yet at least—in case they fall under Syrian rule again, as unlikely as that might be. The Druze must be one of the last people in the world not to demand a nation-state of their own. They simply want a patch of land, a promise of freedom, and for the borders that separate their extended families to dissolve. They want to be accepted for who they are. And then left alone.

What they did share with the Palestinians to the south was a sense that demography is destiny. The biggest issue of all in the Golan, according to Salman, was that of the refugees' right of return. Twenty-thousand Druze and 18,000 Israeli Jews live in the Golan—a fine balance. But the 132,000 residents, including Druze, Christian Arabs and Sunni Muslims, displaced after the War of 1967 have grown into half a million strong, most living in Syria, waiting to return home.

"This is the reality," said Salman. "A state that is afraid of demographics is a sick state. It's afraid of the future."

He led me back to my car, parked near a stony-faced, sword-raised symbol of Druze pride that needed no footnote. The statue was an image of his people's past, eyes upraised, looking ever forward. I drove down the swerving mountain roads, off the Heights and past the cordoned fields marked with trilingual warnings of *Danger: Mines!* As I returned to the familiar grounds of the Hula Valley and Kibbutz Shamir, I recalled one of Salman's parables. It was an old Arabic tale. There once was a king. One of his trusted royal advisors had foreseen an ill omen for his ruler, something bad on the horizon. So the king ordered all of his guards, all of his cavalry, the entire army at his command, out to the road that led to the castle. He told them to stand across the path and stop the future from coming.

He might as well have built a fence.

— CHAPTER 9 —

The Architecture of Hope

When I tell people I was once a volunteer in Israel, they often reply: "Oh, you lived on a *kibitz*?"

"No," I correct them, "it's called a kibb-*utz*."

And yet an accidental truth lies in the confusion between the two words. I only appreciated the connection when I returned to Israel, 20 years after first living there. *Kibitz* is a recent coinage, maybe a century old, and comes from Yiddish slang, rooted in a German verb that means, with odd specificity, "to be an annoying observer at a card game." The meaning of *kibitz* has since brightened from unwanted tableside advice to light-hearted banter or chit-chat. *Kibbutz* sounds similar, but the words are etymologically unrelated. The Hebrew word for "gathering"—and not just around a card table—is both a noun and a verb, a location and an action. The Zionist migration of the Jewish Diaspora back to Israel was called *kibbutz galuyot*: "the ingathering of exiles." By the 1930s, in British Palestine, a *kibbutz* distinguished a large communal settlement from the earliest form of Jewish communes, like Degania, whose founders referred to members as a *kvutza* or "group," or from a *moshav*, a cooperative farming "settlement" also used to colonize the future state.

To be a good kibbutznik, you must be a good kibitzer. Citizenship in any democracy requires an engagement with the wider community that begins in conversation with your neighbours. Life in the original Jewish commune was designed around such social interactions. The gossip trade became the kibbutz's most vibrant economy, a force that kept communities alive during their lean years, even if some members, like my friend Yoav, felt smothered by the your-business-is-our-business lack of privacy. Kibitzing suggests a frivolity foreign to the founding generation; the all-night general assemblies were often vocal, contentious, emotionally charged debates about the big *-isms* of the day: anarchism, socialism, Marxism, feminism, Zionism. Still, casual conversation was the glue of true community, then and now.

Kibbutz members recognized this fact as they built their collective homes. Every design decision was informed by a simple question: How might change add to, or subtract from, the daily connections between our members? Will we kibitz more or less? They built common areas—the dining room, the great lawn, the sports hall, the library and coffee house—to nurture camaraderie. They fretted over whether personal tea kettles, showers, telephones and televisions might undermine the gathering of members in social spaces. They also realized that kibitzing happens best at a walking pace, on the way from one place to another, in the aisles of the general store, at the doors of the dining hall or pub, on the way back from the theatre or sports hall. It's a habit of between-ness, of meeting people halfway—not in their homes or workplaces, not in ours either. It happens rarely when we're locked in our boxes: cars, cubicles, high-fenced yards, the castle walls of suburban manors, or when our imaginations are hypnotized by TVs and smartphones. We need to look up and wander across the paths of the people closest to us. Wander *into* their lives and conversations.

The kibbutz taught me to appreciate that sense of human scale and social intimacy. Fresh from Israel, in the summer of 1989, I stayed with my parents for a few months in the suburban home where I'd grown up. One afternoon, I walked around my old neighbourhood. The streets were empty. All the kids were at school. Their parents had commuted into the city. Every day on Shamir, I'd encountered dozens of kibbutz members and volunteers as I crisscrossed the grounds. Today, I was the only person in sight, as though the entire area code had succumbed to the Suburban Rapture. Heading home, I short-cut across a corner of lawn and heard a shout from the shadows of a screen door: "Get off the grass!" That was my one moment of human communion.

I knew we could do better.

—

The first kibbutzes borrowed their architecture from farm schools in Prussia and looked like military forts from the American West. Kibbutzniks arranged the wooden-walled buildings, including a dining hall, a dormitory and sheds for cows and sheep, to form a U-shaped courtyard, with a water tower that doubled as a lookout, and ringed the compound with fortifications. The tower-and-stockade design allowed Jewish colonists to quickly erect and defend small garrisons among often-hostile Arab populations in Palestine. Coincidentally, the early kibbutzes mirrored the layout of the main house in ancient Qumran of the Essenes, the mysterious Roman-era sect who recorded the Dead Sea Scrolls and who lived communally, an ancient test run of the modern kibbutz. The Essenes had rejected property and money—and sex, too, which impeded their longevity.

After Israel's independence, the tower-and-stockade gave way to a less-defensive design that reflected communal goals and the faith that architecture was destiny. Kibbutzniks looked to a visionary Englishman for inspiration. Ebenezer Howard was a shopkeeper's son from London who immigrated to the United States to try his luck at farming in Nebraska and at journalism in Chicago, where he witnessed the struggles of farm life and city strife, and returned to England with a passion for social reform. In London, he was appalled by the slums, disease, poverty and disorder spawned by the massive demographic shift from country to city. Howard wasn't a Romantic like Jean-Jacques Rousseau, urging citizens to return to an idealized state of nature. He wanted to fuse the best of city and country into what he called a Garden City—a network of six "slumless, smokeless cities," each with a population of 32,000, arranged like atoms around a larger nucleus. The concentric design had belts of parkland and the mini-cities were connected to each other, like spokes on a wheel, via roads, railways, canals and subway. Howard's flexible call to balance the country and the city appealed to urban planners across Europe. He wasn't asking citizens to detonate the economic foundations of society (like the Marxists) or co-habitate in sexually permissive "phalansteries" (as Charles Fourier encouraged). He simply declared, *Let's take what we like from the city and from the country and allow our streets to breathe again.*

Richard Kauffman, the German-born architect for the Jewish Agency, imported Howard's ideas when he immigrated to Palestine and then planned more than 100 kibbutzes. "There is a division between the social area and the working zone," explained Michael Chyutin, the author of *Architecture and Utopia: The Israeli Experiment*, when I stopped by his design studio in Tel Aviv. We were examining an aerial photo of a typical kibbutz. "And *there* is the green belt." The two sides of the community looked like the hemispheres of a brain, conjoined by common ground. At the hub were the dining room, the cultural hall and large central lawn for gatherings. Concentric bands spread from this centre to encompass the children's dormitories and schools, and then adult housing. It formed the template for the six decades of kibbutz construction.

The never-realized blueprints for utopian cities of the past tend to be rigid, from Plato's Republic of philosopher-kings to Le Corbusier's antiseptic sci-fi metropolis. "The uniqueness of the kibbutz is that it's growing," said Chyutin. "It's difficult to design a utopia that's growing because utopia is one state. If it's the best one, why grow? You have to make a settlement that, at each point of time, will be utopian—which is almost impossible." Unlike the garrison settlements, the Garden City layout of later kibbutzes accommodated new members and buildings by adding belts, like growth rings on a tree. As the kibbutz population aged, residences were added farther from the central hub. "A city that doesn't grow its walls dies," said Chyutin. "I'm not sure when the kibbutz died, but that was not the reason." What interested him about the kibbutz was its organic capacity for perpetual change; all it required was a vote. "Even if the borders were fixed, they could always innovate inside," he said, "and they never had a limit to the number of residents."

The democratic nature of change anticipated, by several decades, the public consultations that are now standard for any civic project in Europe and North America. Kibbutzniks felt their opinions mattered as their community decided how to grow. Preserving the communal character informed the architectural debates of the kibbutz. Shared facilities needed to be within walking distance for members. The limit, determined by kibbutz architects, was 10 minutes by foot. Farther than that and members might eat in their rooms rather than at the dining hall or skip meetings of the general assembly; the community would split into cliques. That's why kibbutz members had a say in the details of where and when and what to construct within the greater design. Every kibbutz was created, in effect, step by step, building by building, by a committee of collaborators. Even post-privatization, the social character of the kibbutz's built environment endures.

I asked Michael Chyutin if similar utopian ideals influenced his own architectural practice.

"No," he replied. "Utopia is stupid. Life is more complicated." He paused to qualify his judgment. "But utopia serves its aim, especially in Israel. It's the beginning of a new world."

Beginnings often need extreme ideas. The founding of Israel was a bold venture that demanded personal risk and collective sacrifice, with the promise of a new nation at the end of that long road. Kibbutzniks helped to make real the Zionist dream of a reborn Israel. But that task was done. More than 270 kibbutzes had been founded, most before the nation's independence in 1948, from the mountains to the sea; only a handful maintained the original vision of radical equality. Outside Israel, the idea of the kibbutz never found much traction, except as a metaphor amongst Jewish groups in the Diaspora. I'd seen Jewish summer camps, a campus co-op in Seattle, an artists' colony in New York City, a Costa Rican eco-resort, even a hipster bar in Tel Aviv's port district (complete with haystacks and a tractor) that all waved the banner of the kibbutz. None were truly communal; they simply basked in the twilight of pioneer nostalgia. "The kibbutz is a name, a kind of social good," a scholar of the movement once told me. "It's a brand."

Few people want to embrace the pioneers' original ideals of socialist equality—sharing their labour, their land, their profits, even the upbringing of their children. I certainly didn't. Even if the kibbutz vanished tomorrow, however, its contribution to ideas about architecture and planning might be its most enduring legacy. The utopian architecture of the kibbutz anticipated the humane design philosophy of New Urbanism that came into vogue, elsewhere in the Western world, later in the 20th century as a way to reunite the lonely crowds of the modern city. In the end, even kibbutz architects couldn't re-engineer human behaviour, though, like concrete poured into moulds. The New Jew, the *homo kibbutznik*, the eternal altruist—this species could not be created out of nothing by retooling a few pathways and dining halls and nurseries. A Garden City in the wilderness of the Promised Land had inspired pioneers to come to Palestine and Israel; it had influenced generations of volunteers and other visitors. It might even offer a model for how we might live together as neighbours. But it couldn't bend human nature or overcome the great divide that still haunts the land of Israel.

—

Many of us still feel the nagging will-to-utopia, the longing for a deeper sense of community. We search for ideas on how to remodel our cities, our neighbourhoods, our homes. We might not be conscious of exactly how our renovations, big and small, reflect our social values. The last two centuries witnessed a procession of fads and philosophies, as human populations migrated from agricultural villages to urban centres, from downtown cores to suburban "edge cities" and back again. Today, we don't want to choose from competing spheres of habitation—the city, the country, the suburb—but enjoy a synthesis of all three. Kibbutz planners anticipated the power of that golden mean.

Common space, indoors and outdoors, was the signature of kibbutz design. Early planners looked to the ancient Greeks for how to promote democracy. Architects and kibbutz members created indoor and outdoor areas to mirror the function of the *agora*, the meeting- and marketplace in ancient Athens where citizens could mingle and gossip, haggle and debate. The agora formed the cradle of Greek democracy—and our own. The Roman Forum carried on this tradition. In the kibbutz, the open-concept dining hall formed a multipurpose agora: a place to eat, to debate, to vote, to celebrate special occasions and seasonal festivals. "The heart of the community is linked to food," I was told by Dr. Galia Bar-Or, the museum director at Kibbutz Ein Harod, the first big kibbutz, founded in 1921, and Israel's first museum, too. She had co-curated a show called "Kibbutz: Architecture Without Precedents" for Israel's national pavilion at the 2010 Venice Biennale. "In Judaism and many other religions and cultures, you sit around the table, from childhood to old age, and all these ideas are linked to something that is essential and emotional." Breaking bread is a metaphor for community.

Every kibbutz alerts a visitor to its values. You arrive at the gates and often pass between a corridor of trees—cypresses or eucalyptus—until the main road delivers you to the heart of the community. There's no division into private yards or fenced-off areas; everything is part of the public commons. Wander the grounds and you notice miniature junkyards filled with rusted cars, milk boxes, tractor tires, latticework of two-by-fours. These junkyard playgrounds emerged from an educational philosophy that treated children as adults-in-training and let students explore and experiment and even pick up hammers and nails to build their own mini-kibbutzes.

The dynamic of open social spaces is now the mantra of modern urban planners and social theorists. Great cities set aside parkland for public use: New York's Central Park (and now its elevated High Line), San Francisco's Golden Gate Park, the Luxembourg Gardens for ambulatory Parisians, the democratic tradition of Speaker's Corner in London's Hyde Park. Elsewhere in our cities, though, there is often less public space. And our options for social gathering places have been diminished. Is it any wonder we feel disconnected from a sense of shared geography, from the issues that affect our neighbours and our environment? Or that we retreat into the virtual agoras of social media to satisfy the human craving for gossip and argument that lies at the heart of democracy?

American sociologist Ray Oldenburg coined a name for the informal gathering spots, neither our homes nor our workplaces, where citizens cultivate community over a beer or a coffee. Barber shops and bars, coffee shops and hair salons, main streets and general stores, public parks and other commons—a "third place" is any site that levels social status and encourages public association, that (in his words) "serves the need for human communion" and acts as "a centre for informal life." The kibbutz in its prime had a wealth of third places to knit together its social fabric. At Shamir, I could walk to a library and reading room, a volunteer-run pub and a kibbutznik-managed disco, a sports hall for pickup basketball or Tuesday night movies and a general store where the real news got exchanged. In the summer, life revolved around the swimming pool. Year-round, no third space was more important than the dining hall. Today, there are few architectural sights as forlorn as the husk of an abandoned dining hall on a kibbutz. The decline of the dining room tended to be the first step in privatization. Where kibbutzniks once shared three free meals a day, kitchen service was reduced to lunches, perhaps a Shabbat dinner on Friday evenings. To reduce costs and waste, members had to pay for meals, and so they began to eat at home, and the dining room declined as a social hub. Eventually, indebted communities closed kitchens. When kibbutzniks no longer break bread together, many critics wonder, can a community even be considered a kibbutz?

The global turmoil in financial markets pushed households and even nations to the brink of insolvency. It served as a reminder that life is fragile, that institutions are easier to break than to build. A hundred years after the founding of Degania, the kibbutz might have become a tattered blueprint best preserved in a museum or pavilion for visitors to admire under glass, where we can steal a few ideas from its experiment, a nugget of wisdom to heal our own communities.

"I'm not certain the kibbutz will survive, even in the form of the new kibbutz," admitted Dr. Bar-Or. "But the courage to try—to make the future better—that's the main thing. Even if that disappears, it's like a ghost. It will come back."

—

My nostalgia for the kibbutz, I realized, was steeped in the picturesque rural landscapes of northern Israel, in the social architecture of communal life and the bonds of friendship I'd forged on Shamir as a wide-eyed 20-year-old. Now, like a middle-aged former frat boy clinging to golden memories of campus glory, I looked back to Galilee and saw an image of the good life that, however unreal, I wanted to preserve. Why can't we all live this way?

"I believe for some people there will always be an attraction in a way of life that is like an extended family, where people share everything, where people carry the highest degree of mutual responsibility," Amos Oz said, in a 2006 interview. "I hope and believe that the kibbutz will have a revival. Maybe in another time. Maybe in a different country. We live now in a world where people work harder than they should work, in order to make more money than they need, in order to buy things they don't really want, in order to impress people they don't really like. This leads to a certain reaction, and this reaction will bring back some kind of voluntary collective experience."

Even after learning how far the movement had drifted from its founding philosophy, I tried to share its vision of the good life before my memory of the kibbutz faded. I wrote and I lectured about its lessons, its philosophy and its architecture. I gave a TEDx Talk about how we need to improve the "Kibitz Quotient" or KQ—the collective conversational intelligence—of our cities and towns, our neighbourhoods and blocks, by designing sidewalks and streets to promote random encounters between neighbours and strangers. Such intimacy is what I missed most about the kibbutz. I spoke about other takeaways from a century of communal life in Israel and my visits to different kibbutzes. No, we don't need to go back to the land and live like self-denying Marxists on country communes. But there was a middle way between the radical socialism of the original kibbutzniks and the dog-eat-dog capitalism consuming the world. I'd seen it on Shamir as a volunteer. I'd seen it there again, even on the privatized kibbutz, in a community that cared for each other.

Before one of my talks at a university, a woman handed out pamphlets as I readied my PowerPoint slides and notes. After I finished my spiel, she stood up and demanded, "What do you have to say about how kibbutzes were built on the blood of the Palestinian people?" I tried to reply, but the Q&A collapsed into a shouting match between audience members, pro-Israel versus pro-Palestine. Any lessons from the history of the kibbutz were drowned out in the uproar. The gravity of the Israel versus Palestine debate, the need to choose sides, erased all nuance from the discussion.

A year later, I gave another talk at a conference for the study of international communes, at the New Age eco-village of Findhorn in northern Scotland—and there, too, protesters objected to academics coming to discuss the history and sociology of the kibbutz. "Many supporters of a militaristic movement which was central to the ethnic cleansing of Palestinians are among those presenting papers," warned the Scottish Palestine Solidarity Campaign on its website and in pamphlets distributed at Findhorn. "Kibbutzim are based on stolen land whose owners were driven out with great violence, and virtually all kibbutzim operate a stringent racist policy of refusing membership to Palestinian citizens of Israel." The website outed presenters with kibbutz connections.

I realized then that I couldn't divorce the kibbutz from its colonial legacy and the tetchy politics of contemporary Israel. It was still dangerous to read newspapers. And utopia remained a shimmering mirage on a rocky horizon.

PART TWO

Look Back to Galilee

There is this urge in us for the return to earth and normality;
and there is that other urge to continue to hunt for a lost
Paradise which is not in space. This is our predicament. But
it is not a question of race. It is the human predicament carried
to its extreme.

—Arthur Koestler, *Thieves in the Night: Chronicle of an Experiment*

CHAPTER 10

Born This Way

Roger Waters had an image problem. For more than 30 years, the British bassist and singer for prog-rock mega-band Pink Floyd had been a voice of dissent against the indoctrination of mass society. Now critics were questioning his politics. They accused Pink Floyd's conscience of selling out. Why?

Roger Waters was planning a show in Israel.

The year was 2006. The suicide bombings of the Second Intifada had abated but the construction of the concrete-and-wire Separation Barrier, designed to thwart terrorist attacks, continued to draw controversy. Palestinian arts groups and activists sent an open letter to Waters demanding he cancel the Tel Aviv concert; otherwise, they argued, the songwriter behind *The Wall* would be supporting a less metaphorical barrier to justice. International advocates added pressure. In their eyes, Israel was the new South Africa, an "apartheid state" to be dealt with through BDS: *boycott, divest, sanction.*

In the mid-1980s, a similar campaign had urged performers not to play Sun City, the casino resort near Johannesburg. Now a cultural boycott of Israel asked artists to choose sides. Many refused to perform; others ignored the protests. A few musicians signed contracts and advertised shows, then balked under the glare of bad publicity.

Waters struck a compromise. He wouldn't cancel the show if the venue could be relocated. But he would only play on neutral ground.

—

After my return to Israel and Shamir, I understood that the greater dream of the kibbutz movement had failed. Most kibbutzes in Israel resembled well-manicured North American suburbs, even though they were often within striking distance of a rocket from Gaza or Lebanon. The kibbutz was a shadow of its founders' ambitions. Still, I wondered if its original spirit had survived in other iterations. I'd heard rumours of communities in Israel forging new ways of living and thinking that might yet overcome the fear and violence between the Jewish and Palestinian peoples. Some sprang from embers of the kibbutz movement and tried to repair its mistakes; others were the original creations of visionary founders. Many were as audacious as the first days of Degania. And so I returned to Israel once more on a quest to understand these new experiments. My first stop: the community that offered Roger Waters a safe concert space in a land as politically fraught as any on earth.

The Latrun Monastery sits on a promontory framed by a windbreak of conifers just off the highway from Tel Aviv to Jerusalem. The stiff-backed stone temple of the Trappist monks looms over the foothills, a site both picturesque and strategic. From these heights, anyone might survey and defend the natural gap on the road from the Mediterranean coast to the Golden City. A smudge of whitewashed buildings shimmers near the monastery. The village looks like the mirage suggested by its name. A back road leads up the hill to Neve Shalom/Wahat al-Salam—"the Oasis of Peace" in Hebrew and Arabic—a cooperative village of around 250 people that took its layout and its inspiration from the kibbutz. A gift of the neighbouring Trappist monks, the property rests on the Green Line, the border that divided the new state of Israel from the Hashemite Kingdom of Jordan until the Six-Day War of 1967. The Green Line—it sounds so benign, like a buffer of parkland or a subway route. Instead it is an obstacle to peace in the world's biggest real-estate dispute.

I checked into the Oasis's guest house. My room's balcony looked west toward the sea, and through a gauze of humidity and smog, I could spy the blue tint of the Mediterranean. To the south lay the port of Ashdod. In late May 2010, a month before I visited the Oasis, a flotilla of international protesters tried to break Israel's naval blockade of Gaza. Israeli forces stopped the Gaza Flotilla and rerouted the vessels to Ashdod. Naval commandos boarded the *Mavi Marmara* and met resistance; they shot and killed nine activists, whose bodies now lay in Ashdod, too. At the entrance to the village, residents had strung a banner to protest the deaths. Today, the Oasis of Peace felt like a small island of calm amid an angry sea.

On the office door of Abdessalam Najjar, a bumper sticker read, *Don't come in here unless you agree that war is basically stupid.* Roger that. Abdessalam, the director of public relations and one of the community's founders, was slight of build with a tightly cropped goatee. A mischievous laugh, prompted by the Kafkaesque ironies of life as an Arab in Israel, offset his precise manner of speaking. The bloody events of the flotilla, he admitted, had disrupted life at the Oasis of Peace. Jewish and Arab residents had been split: should the deaths aboard the *Mavi Marmara* be described as "killings" or "murders"? Words mattered in this conflict.

"I'm an optimistic person," Abdessalam told me, even amid the grim news of the flotilla debacle. "Otherwise, I would not continue living here. Against all the difficulties going on outside, we still exist because we are optimistic—more or less." He paused to gauge his level of good vibrations. "Sometimes I feel more. Sometimes I feel less." He released another laugh.

The story of the Oasis of Peace begins with Father Bruno Hussar, a Catholic priest with a complex family history. Father Bruno was half-Hungarian, half-French. Both his parents were non-practising Jews. Bruno was born in Cairo in 1911 and spoke English and French at home. When his family returned to Europe, he attended an Italian high school and, after his father's death, immigrated with his mother to Paris. As a young scholar, he studied engineering but felt drawn to the enigmas of the human soul. He began, as he would later recall, to look for God—"not from the Jewish standpoint that I didn't have, but from the standpoint of nothing at all." At age 24, he converted to Catholicism, joined the Dominicans and was ordained. In 1953, he was sent to Israel to establish a centre for Jewish studies. His close reading of the Bible, the horrors of the Holocaust and the evidence of Hebrew history embedded in the landscape of Israel awakened in Father Bruno his dormant heritage and what he called a "Jewish consciousness."

In Jerusalem, Father Bruno founded the House of Isaiah, a sanctuary where Jews and Christians could study religion together. He led a small congregation of Israeli Jews who had converted to Catholicism. On lecture tours in North America, he ended each talk with a vision of a new village where Arabs and Jews might live in peace. People told him he was mad. Bruno didn't own any land. He had no volunteers for such an experiment in co-existence. And he was talking about Israel. "If God wants, it will not be *agada*," he told doubters. *Agada* meant "myth" or "utopia" in Thomas More's original sense of "no place." It was the same Hebrew word with which Theodor Herzl, the father of Zionism, had pitched his state to the globe-scattered Jews. "If you will it, it is no myth," Herzl had promised the Jewish people—the words were etched on his tomb. *Agada* now drove Father Bruno with a teasing vision of a centre for religious harmony, a citadel on a hill.

The Latrun hilltop—with its monastery, Arab villages and Jordanian police headquarters—had been a major battleground in the War of 1948; Arab legionnaires repelled five assaults from Jewish forces and launched counter-attacks against kibbutzes in the plains below. In the Six-Day War of 1967, Israeli forces swept across this high ground en route to capturing the Old City and East Jerusalem and the West Bank. In 1969, the monks of Latrun learned of Bruno's dream and offered 100 acres on a century-long lease. A year later, Bruno registered a non-profit society and scratched out foundations on the site. Progress was slow. For the first four years, Father Bruno slept in a large wooden crate, cloaked in a mosquito net to deter snakes and scorpions. He celebrated the Eucharist on a cushion and used a prayer mat for an altar. He coaxed a few groups of young Arabs and Jews to visit, but they declined to stay when they saw the bare dwellings, uncultivated fields and rocky plateau without road access or electricity. Bruno hauled water by tractor from four kilometres away. There was no "village" to speak of—it was all in Father Bruno's head. The only residents who stayed tended to be glassy-eyed hippies on the global guru circuit. They sampled Bruno's crude nirvana until the next prophet lured their restless souls. Father Bruno's plan for peace had never been to play caretaker to a commune of peripatetic stoners. In the wilderness, he felt the seven-year itch. Maybe it was the sand fleas. Maybe his cassock needed a rinse. Or maybe the Good Lord was testing his faith, as Yahweh had tormented Job. Bruno had poured his earthly energies into founding the village. Now the Jewish-born Catholic knelt in the dust and delivered an ultimatum to his master: *Send me some families or I'm calling it quits.*

The ancient Greeks had two ways of thinking about time: *chronos* and *kairos*. The first referred to chronological time, the passing of everyday life, measured by the rising and falling sun. *Kairos*, by contrast, described moments of crisis or opportunity, when anything is possible, when something new can be created out of the rubble of the old. To the Greeks, *kairos* was the god of the fleeting moment, to be seized by the ankle or forever lost. Christian theologians used the concept of *kairos* to understand significant religious events in which God manifested his divine purpose, like the birth and resurrection of Christ.

Father Bruno was well versed in *kairos*. Not long after he dropped to his knees and demanded a sign, Abdessalam Najjar heard about the Oasis of Peace. Abdessalam had been born to Muslim-Arab parents in Nazareth, the hub of Palestinian life in Israel. In the mid 1970s, he'd studied agriculture at Hebrew University in Jerusalem with Arab and Jewish students who dreamed of building a bilingual high school. Abdessalam and his university friends met Father Bruno, who was impressed by their vision and invited them to build the school in his village. In early 1976, a group of Arabs and Jews travelled from Jerusalem to Latrun. They couldn't find the settlement. Were they in the right place? Finally, they spotted Father Bruno sitting on a stone, under an awning of bamboo, as poised as the Buddha. "Let's go to the village," they said.

Father Bruno smiled. "You are here! *This* is the village!"

There was nothing but scrub and rocks and neglected olive groves and a few spindly trees Father Bruno had planted. Building a bilingual school would be hard enough in a city. They were tempted to leave. And yet there was something charming, even attractive, about the lone priest and his grand vision, so they stayed. That summer, they organized a camp for adult Arabs and Jews. A nucleus of five families from the camp settled the hilltop the following spring. Abdessalam convinced his wife to join him, and together they raised four children in the Oasis of Peace. The community grew from a handful to 55 families. The month I arrived, the village had accepted 30 new families in preparation for a major expansion.

—

From the beginning, the Oasis of Peace's residents wanted to do more than live in harmony as a mixed community. They wanted to effect change, to bend the nation beyond their fence to their hopeful vision. They wanted to educate about the conflict, so they built a bilingual primary school. Today, nearly three-quarters of its 200 students commute to it. Most parents are well-educated liberals like Yoram Honig, an Israeli Jew who filmed his six-year-old daughter's first term. His documentary, *First Lesson in Peace*, captures the extended family's ambivalence about their granddaughter and niece attending a school with Arab peers. "It's a problematic school," complained Yoram's right-wing brother-in-law. "I hope it closes one day."

The film acknowledges the gap between the abstract dream of educating a new generation and the reality of running a classroom. The students, coalescing into Arab and Jewish cliques, needed to be forced to play together. Teachers broke down in tears as they tried to prevent a clash of competing narratives. How can one school accommodate the joys of the Israeli Day of Independence *and* the sorrows of the Palestinian Nakba or "Catastrophe"—the War of 1948 seen through different eyes? The most telling moment came during Purim celebrations, when the children's ethnic divisions disappeared under costumes. A pair of boys waddle toward the camera, dressed as conjoined twins. "We have to get along," one explained. "We were born this way."

The founders of the Oasis brainstormed other ideas to improve Israel. At the Day School for Peace, Jewish and Arab co-facilitators led workshops for teenagers and adults. The program was based on Contact Theory, a practice developed in the 1950s that brought together opposing sides of any conflict, within a safe environment, to overcome prejudices. Contact Theory informed the desegregation of public schools in the United States. Abdessalam's high-school students met pupils of a Jewish colleague. "What do we do with them?" recalled Abdessalam, with a laugh. "Let's talk! Let's dance! Let's play!" If the students went home happy, the teachers declared the day a success. If students stormed out, the teachers wrote it off as a failure. They invited academics to observe, survey and compare the psychological effects to a control group who didn't take part in the bicultural get-togethers. The results were a shock.

"Our activities and results were the total opposites of our aims," said Abdessalam. "The participants gained *more* prejudice and hatred to the other groups."

Contact Theory had eased relations in other countries. Why had it backfired in Israel? The difference, they discovered, was the control groups of Arab and Jews *assumed* the worst about the opposite side. But the actual experiences of the mixed group didn't dispel prejudice. Just the opposite. "*Our* groups were now sure," he said. The encounters turned suspicions into fact—a depressing revelation. The founders had built an Oasis of Peace, only to discover its well of goodwill was poisoned at the source. "Maybe the reality here, between Arabs and Jews, was not the same as between Americans and Chinese, or French and British, or—"

"—English and French Canadians?" I suggested. I had grown up next to the province of Québec, amid the *séparatistes'* fiery (and sometimes violent) campaigns for independence from Canada.

"Yes," said Abdessalam. "We needed to have a different approach."

Subtle power relations intrude the moment students enter a room. "Even when they're sitting down and discussing, you will find half of the circles are Jews and half are Arabs," explained Abdessalam, who had facilitated hundreds of dialogues. "All Jews on one side, all Arabs on the other." After introductions, the issue of language arises. One person, most often a Jewish student, usually asks, "What language should we speak? Arabic or Hebrew?"

"Hebrew, of course," the other Jewish students respond.

"Why Hebrew?" ask the Arab students. "We don't speak Hebrew as well as you."

"But we're in Israel. And we don't speak Arabic."

Finally, a facilitator intervenes: "I don't understand what's going on here."

"We're deciding what language we will speak in!" shout the students.

"But what language are you already speaking?"

The answer: Hebrew.

The language of the dominant group always dominates. Even the students who resist using the dominant language end up using it. Subliminal bias affects visitors, too. The full name for the village is Neve Shalom/Wahat al-Salam. But it's a mouthful. Most visitors shorten it to Neve Shalom; so does Wikipedia. So do I. Even at the Oasis, the language of Arab residents gets buried.

The organizers realized that contact was not enough to overcome conflict. Only when students took action, together, in their communities could they make real change. The organizers have since integrated dialogue about what cooperative work can be done *after* the groups leave the School for Peace. How might Israeli doctors help Palestinian patients negotiate the maze of checkpoints in the Occupied Territories? How can city planners in neighbouring Arab and Jewish towns solve mutual problems, such as sewage treatment and water pollution?

"Geography knows no borders," said Abdessalam. "They have no other choice but to cooperate."

They were born this way.

—

The kibbutz ideal had inspired the design of Father Bruno's original village. Like a traditional kibbutz, the donated land on which the Oasis of Peace sat was owned collectively, in a trust, although that lack of collateral made it difficult for new residents to negotiate mortgages to finance construction. Like a traditional kibbutz, the village was built in the round, with a ring road and communal facilities near the centre. Like a traditional kibbutz, a general assembly of residents made decisions and elected administrators. Like a traditional kibbutz, majority assent was required to accept new members—and occasionally to dismiss misbehaving ones.

Unlike a kibbutz, the rocky acreage surrounding the residential plateau was poorly suited to farming. Most members were more interested in cultivating peace than cotton anyway. Those who didn't work at the school tended to be professionals with jobs in Tel Aviv or Jerusalem: lawyers, doctors, engineers, NGO directors. Unlike a traditional kibbutz (but like a privatized one), the Oasis of Peace doesn't redistribute salaries; it simply required a basic level of taxation, like a condo fee, to fund facilities and programs. Unlike a kibbutz, Palestinians lived here as equals, not as hired help. The population of Israeli citizens was balanced between Jewish residents and Muslim Arabs, with a smaller group of Christian Arabs. I realized that for all its noble rhetoric, the kibbutz movement's failure to attract and accept, let alone integrate, Arab residents was perhaps its greatest failure. The left-wing Artzi Federation, which founded Shamir, had once promoted a vision of Israel as a binational state. And yet it never created a kibbutz for Jews and Palestinians.

A hundred years ago, Degania was founded as a new way for the Jewish people to live in Palestine. That first kibbutz became the template for many other communal and cooperative settlements, like Neve Shalom/Wahat al-Salam. I asked Abdessalam if they had ever considered using the community as a model to build others. Why not *Oases* of Peace?

He shook his head. "Until today, we still think of the community as an artificial reality. We don't think that all Jews and Palestinians should live like this." He smiled at my puzzled look. The intimate scale of the Oasis of Peace didn't suit everyone, he explained. It took hard work to live cooperatively. But he felt the *concept* of living together could be a model. So while they had no plans to build another Oasis, the villagers would work so that other mixed Arab-Jewish communities in Israel and Palestine might dissolve their suspicion and separation. "I will do all my best to help Akko be like Wahat/Neve Shalom," he promised, listing centres of Palestinian culture in Israel and the West Bank. "And *inshallah* Jerusalem. And Nablus. And Hebron."

The Oasis received no government funding, although the ministry of foreign affairs often cited its work in PR campaigns as an example of how Arabs and Jews get along in modern Israel. Visiting diplomats toured the grounds. Roger Waters relocated his gig, along with 50,000 Pink Floyd fans, to a farmer's field beside the Oasis. "I moved the concert to Neve Shalom as a gesture of solidarity with the voices of reason," the rock star told journalists. "Israelis and Palestinians seeking a non-violent path to a just peace between the peoples."

Living as a symbol of co-existence often made Abdessalam and other residents feel uncomfortable, though. It also made them targets. Vandals punctured car tires and scrawled racist graffiti on village vehicles. Abdessalam's levity vanished and he looked directly at me. The Oasis of Peace should be seen as an exception to Israeli society, he told me, not a microcosm. It was evidence that Arabs and Jews *can* live together. It was not an example that they *do*.

———

With a guest house, a school, a gift shop and a café, a spiritual centre and swimming pool, the community and its international reputation attracted a mix of visitors. A tour group of elderly, liberal Jewish couples from San Francisco wanted to unlock the puzzle of contemporary

Israel. A rambunctious class of Jewish teens from the States were chaperoned by dour, rifle-toting Israelis. An expedition of archaeologists, with thick Texas twangs, departed each morning to dig for Biblical antiquities. A clique of Arab kids escaped the heat in the outdoor pool as their mothers, draped in *chadors*, gossiped in the shade. Overhead, the baritone roar of fighter jets from the nearby airbase reminded us that peace only extended so far beyond the Oasis.

Father Bruno had promised his superiors that religion would form the bedrock of co-existence. On the edge of the village, the Pluralistic Spiritual Centre looked toward the valley and the monastery. It was meant to be an ecumenical shared space where residents and visitors could exercise their faiths without fear of judgment: Christianity, Islam, Judaism or whatever New Age fusion felt right. Earlier, I had asked Abdessalam to explain the religious dimensions of the Oasis of Peace. His eyes bugged out. "You want me to explain what is *spirituality?*" He rocked in his chair as he laughed. Every word in the centre's title, he admitted, was problematic and subject to endless interpretation. "Looking for spirituality," he cautioned, "is like looking for the horse that you are riding."

The empty spiritual centre was spare and sterile, with few decorations or icons on its white walls. A middle-aged Swiss volunteer with a dustpan appeared; she admitted the centre didn't get much use. An occasional meeting or a tour group. A holiday function. It was never the fulcrum of community life. Most villagers tended to be professionals, either secular or not outgoing about their faith. The spiritual void disappointed the original benefactors but it hadn't bothered Father Bruno. He saw the good work being done here.

Outside, I walked the dirt paths on the flanks of the foothills. Scattered along the way I found the headstones of past residents, including the grave of Father Bruno, who died in 1996. Admirers had laid pebbles for him, in the Jewish tradition, across the monument's flat top.

On a trip to Jerusalem 20 years earlier, I explored the vast Jewish cemetery on the Mount of Olives. Upwards of 150,000 graves overlook the Old City. As I walked the narrow lanes of the necropolis, I spied a circle of black-clad ultra-Orthodox mourners in rituals of bereavement, nodding and genuflecting. In my young mind, I was a globe-trotting photojournalist, so I crouched between the graves for the best angle, framed and then focused on the platform of the closest headstone and its Hebrew inscriptions. In the blurred depth-of-field, I captured the wall of the Old City, the Al-Aqsa Mosque and the gold-and-turquoise edifice of the Dome of the Rock. It was a perfect composition, I thought, in which my lens held in tension two competing faiths—except for the scattered stones on the grave that distracted from the effect. Didn't anyone tidy the cemetery? With one flick, I swept aside the pebbles and got my photo.

I'm hardly religious, and yet years later my youthful act of ignorance still gnawed at my conscience. That afternoon, I stood next to the memorial for the man who had tried to bring together the feuding peoples of the Holy Land. Father Bruno had looked into the heart of a conflict and seen only hope. A breeze hurried down the slopes of the Latrun hills. I didn't unholster my camera. Instead I picked up a small stone from the dry grass of the Oasis of Peace and set the rock atop the tomb of its founding father.

— CHAPTER 11 —

Buried History

Along the busy highway from Tel Aviv to Jerusalem, on the way to
Neve Shalom/Wahat al-Salam, a road sign flags a turnoff for something called "Canada Park." The sign always sparks in me a Pavlovian
sense of national pride, like the rush I feel when I spot a maple leaf
on a fellow backpacker or find hockey scores in a foreign newspaper.
It's a reminder of home. And in this case a bit of a mystery. Why is
there a Canada Park in the middle of Israel? I already knew about the
Canada Centre, a recreation facility on the border with Lebanon, not
far from Kibbutz Shamir; Jewish-Canadian philanthropists had funded
Israel's largest rink, where the nation's ice-dancing team now trained
and young Arabs and Jews laced up hockey skates to trade their blood
sport for my country's.

A similar act of international philanthropy had developed the
1,700 acres of Canada Park. In 1975, after the Canadian office of the
Jewish National Fund raised $15 million, former prime minister John

Diefenbaker inaugurated the park for the people of Israel, and JNF Canada still contributes to the upkeep of its hiking paths, mountain-biking trails, picnic spots and archaeological sites.

This is the official narrative. But I soon discovered another side to the story of Canada Park.

In 1991, the School for Peace in Neve Shalom/Wahat al-Salam hired a young activist named Eitan Bronstein. His family had immigrated to Israel when he was five and settled on Kibbutz Bahan, where Eitan absorbed the liberal philosophy of the kibbutz movement. During the Lebanon War in 1982, he refused to serve his annual reserve duty in the army; he refused twice more during the First Intifada in the West Bank. Each time meant a sentence in prison, where he met other conscientious objectors. Later, at the School for Peace, he led encounter groups between Jews and Arabs and read the works of Benny Morris, one of Israel's so-called "new historians" who challenged the founding myths of the nation.

"I started to hear something called the Nakba," Eitan told me when I met him in Tel Aviv. "Then I understood that there was something very big that happened in 1948, that Israel expelled many people and destroyed many places. It was a huge thing that came out in the middle of the encounter, that people didn't know how to deal with, to talk about."

Jewish Israelis knew little about the other side of the War of 1948. They heard only a heroic narrative of Jewish victory against steep odds. Palestinians knew more about the Nakba, or "Catastrophe" in Arabic, through personal experience or family history. But detailed history was spotty. Eitan researched the Nakba. During seminars, he would lead groups through Canada Park. The tree-shaded hills offered a respite from the heat of the day and the intensity of the encounter groups. The more he learned about the Nakba, the more he realized Canada Park was not, like the Oasis of Hope, built on neutral ground.

Canada Park fell within the West Bank borders of what used to be Jordan, but visitors rarely realize this fact. As Eitan walked the park he could find no signs to indicate he had left Israel and entered the West Bank. Only pine forests and nature trails. Only the ruins of ancient civilizations. The Jewish National Fund had erected signs to explain the provenance of archaeological artifacts: Romans, Hasmonean Jews, Mamluks, Byzantines, Ottomans. But the texts mentioned nothing about centuries of habitation by Palestinian villagers. Nothing to explain the rubble from abandoned houses or the old cemetery with Arabic script.

Eitan wanted to revive the forgotten story of the Palestinian past in Canada Park—and elsewhere in Israel. He had an idea for this and mentioned it to a friend who wrote for a kibbutz newspaper. "It's a great idea," the journalist said. "Controversial, provocative. Let's do a story on it." Together, they drew up a list of Palestinian villages throughout Israel, abandoned and destroyed after the War of 1948; many had been absorbed as kibbutz property. They proposed a project to commemorate the history, at each site, with official plaques. Reaction to the newspaper article was mixed—one small part supportive, one large part hostile. Eitan had found his calling: to get fellow Israelis to talk about the Nakba, whether they want to or not.

In early 2002, he founded an organization to teach the history of the Nakba. But he wasn't sure what to call it. Names had power. The group considered using "Nakba" in the title but worried the government's registration office would reject that. They considered words associated with memory: *zikaron* (a remembrance), *lizkor* (to remember). "Memory is a loaded concept in Hebrew," explained Eitan, "because this is a memorializing society. First of all, we remember the soldiers who've been killed. Also, the memory of the Holocaust—the Shoah—is strong." Someone suggested *zochrim*, "men who remember." Another person replied with *zochrot*, "women who remember." The gendered name struck the group as a perfect hook.

Hebrew speakers who hear the name often ask, "Is it a women's organization?" It's not. "But we have a feminine way of thinking about language, about memory," Eitan explained. "It's a narrative that's not being heard. But it is also our narrative, our history. In Hebrew, we speak almost all the time in masculine verbs—also in Arabic. So when you use the feminine form, you imply that the language is not the standard language, just as the memory is not the standard memory of 1948."

In one of their first operations, Zochrot activists joined residents from the Oasis of Peace to install signs in Canada Park that described the Arab villages. The park's maintenance superintendent uprooted the guerrilla signage and called Eitan, who had left his phone number on a post. "They're illegal," said the park employee.

Eitan pointed out that many other unauthorized signs, even advertisements, dotted the park.

"Yours are political," countered the superintendent.

Wasn't listing every other civilization that had occupied the site *except* the Palestinians also political?

Eitan pushed his case. Through Zochrot, he filed a legal suit against the Jewish National Fund and the Civil Administration. These authorities finally agreed to the sign postings just days before the High Court was to hear the case. But the approved text made no mention of "occupation" or "expulsion" or "destruction of villages" or "refugees." It indicated that two Palestinian villages were once situated on these lands and the inhabitants now lived in Ramallah and Jordan. Nothing else. It was, Eitan said, like erecting a plaque in Warsaw, Poland, that simply read: "Many Jews once lived here."

Still, the new signs felt like victory, however compromised. Visitors could no longer ignore the history beneath their boots.

—

Eitan has short hair, greying in places, and was wearing a loose-fitting brown sweater that hung off wide shoulders when I met him in Zochrot's small space near Rabin Square in Tel Aviv. He speaks with the quiet, self-composed intensity of a man who savours the friction of uncomfortable truths rubbing against unexamined dogmas. Later that evening, he would host a talk that explored a radical idea: What might Israel look like if Palestinian refugees were allowed to return to their former homes? How could it work logistically, architecturally? The curatorial experiment was titled "Counter-mapping the Right of Return"—a giant "What if?" that nobody else in Israel dared to discuss.

In Israel, the Law of Return works only in one direction. Since 1950, a person of Jewish matrilineal descent can arrive in Israel and claim citizenship. The law has drawn immigrants from around the word: Poland, Russia, England, France, South Africa, North and South America, Ethiopia, Iraq. Palestinians speak a similar language and demand their own right of return. Historians debate the details of 1948, while activists argue whether the war and its aftermath deserve the label of ethnic cleansing, a term popularized in this context by Israeli historian-in-exile Ilan Pappé. During the independence war, advancing Jewish troops expelled many Palestinians; others were encouraged to leave by Arab leaders or fled their homes to live in refugee camps. After the armistice, all were prevented from returning by Jewish forces. Israeli authorities confiscated land and bulldozed villages. They planted trees on ruins. They made parks.

"We at Zochrot think that preventing the right of return, to have a state only for the Jews, is the basis for the Conflict," said Eitan. "And unless we solve it, we will never have real peace or reconciliation."

Zochrot explores practical ideas for the return of Palestinian refugees to their ancestral homeland. The project is utopian in the tradition of the original kibbutz: a creative vision of a better future, an architecture in which Palestinians and Jews could live together again. And it is utilitarian in its design: a detailed blueprint for how it might all work. A plan of action—even if few people in Israel or Palestine believe action will ever be taken.

In one counter-mapping project, Israeli Jews and displaced Palestinians brainstormed how they might one day rebuild the Arab village of Miska; its grown-over ruins sit between two small farming communities and Ramat HaKovesh, the kibbutz where Yossi Schneiberg killed himself. An architect working on a master's thesis drew up plans for resurrecting the village in four stages, as a new town integrated into the surroundings. The blueprint demonstrated that old Miska could return without demolishing everything around it—the fields, the forest, the existing kibbutz—and might add prosperity to the area.

Where did the utopian ideals of the kibbutz fit within Zochrot's deep critique of Israel's past? Like many ex-kibbutzniks, Eitan had an uneasy relationship with his former home. He still visited Kibbutz Bahan and wandered the fields and hills that were the playgrounds of his youth. The now-privatized kibbutz propped up its economy with a flashy garden centre called Utopia Orchid Park—"the biggest and most talked about attraction in Israel!" according to the website, a PR boast unlikely to withstand much fact-checking. Tourists paid to see 10,000 orchids, butterflies, a rainforest of tropical plants (including carnivorous ones), a two-storey-high ficus maze and a musical water-fountain show. Outside the grounds, on a low and barren hilltop, sits the ruins of an old fortress called Kakun and a high stone tower. Eitan had known the site as a leftover from the Crusader era. It was now protected, like Canada Park, as a destination for tourists and hikers. He had visited hundreds of times. He had sat and eaten a *sabra*, a prickly pear, among the ruins and looked over the Plain of Sharon and the West Bank. A decade or so ago, after he had founded Zochrot, he wondered about those ruins. His research revealed that amid the stones of Kakun lay the remnants of Qaqun. An Arab village of several thousand citizens had vanished into dust after 1948.

For years, in his own backyard, he had walked on the remnants of a Palestinian past, a phantom village, and never known it.

Throughout North America, we lived for generations similarly unaware of the vanished heritage of our First Peoples. I grew up in a city whose name—Ottawa—came from the Algonquin word for "trade," and in a nation-state whose postcolonial etymology traces back to the Iroquian word *kanata*, which (like *kibbutz*) means a "village" or "settlement." In my new home on the west coast, I live on the traditional territories of the Coast Salish and Straits Salish peoples, never ceded by treaty to the British or Canadian governments. I might not find stone ruins in my backyard, but if I retrain my eyes, I can discern the west coast equivalent: once-cultivated fields of camas lilies, fragments of old fishing weirs, sediments of shell middens, evidence of centuries of habitation. In recent years, Canadian authorities have made official gestures to redress that colonial amnesia: treaty negotiations, a truth and reconciliation commission, territorial acknowledgements at events, plaques in parks and educational initiatives. But progress is slow. It's slower in modern Israel.

"For me, it was an important experience showing how deep is the ignorance for us Israelis—even me, someone who was interested in the Nakba," admitted Eitan. "Since then, I hear these kinds of stories by Israelis so many times. People were visiting their grandparents somewhere, and there is always one house, or the remains of a house. They grew up and started to ask questions. And they discover things they never knew about."

—

Eitan had earned his living for most of his adult life as an activist and educator who kept faith in a better future—for his country, for his family. He had lived with a Brazilian volunteer from his kibbutz and had two sons, now in their twenties. With his second wife, Eitan had two younger children, who wear Zochrot T-shirts and sing Arabic songs he has taught them. Eitan had abandoned his kibbutz to live in a housing project in south Tel Aviv, yet his ideals still seemed informed by its egalitarian ideals—and its failures.

One afternoon, he had been leading a tour of a former Arab village abandoned in 1948 near Tel Aviv. A Palestinian guide told the story of her family's displacement from a nearby house. Eitan lingered to snap a few pictures. The new owner of the house opened the front door. "Who are you?" the woman demanded. "Why are you taking photos?"

"We know the history of the place," Eitan replied.

"You should go back to your kibbutz!" she scolded Eitan. "You kibbutzniks stole the most from the Palestinians. We at least paid for it."

"You're right," Eitan told her. "The kibbutzim *are* the ones who stole the most."

Many kibbutzes were built upon land or sowed fields expropriated from abandoned Arab villages and Palestinian refugees expelled after the War of 1948. Eitan believes kibbutzniks ought to repair this historical grievance. "In this, I hope they will be pioneers as they were pioneers a hundred years ago in thinking how we can have a new society here," he said. "But I am not optimistic. Unfortunately, kibbutzniks today are the most mainstream Israelis. I don't think you would find even one kibbutz that would make the common decision for how to return the land to the Palestinians."

He knew of a single example: Kibbutz Baram, on the ridgeline along the border with Lebanon. There, in November of 1948, Israeli forces entered the village of Kfar Birem and relocated its population of Christian Arabs, a thousand or more, to the south. The original Arab villagers petitioned to return to their homes but were denied. The army had reclassified the border village as a security buffer against threats from Lebanon. After the war, demobilized soldiers established Kibbutz

Baram on the grounds of the village. The new settlers felt shadows of Arab families moving around their new homes, so the young pioneers relocated the kibbutz, two years later, a few kilometres north of the village.

In 1952, the Palestinian villagers took the case to the Supreme Court and won—and still the IDF refused to let them return. Instead, the next year, the land was expropriated, and the army and air force bombed the remaining buildings as the families watched from a nearby village. The legal plight of Birem's dispossessed dragged on for decades. They would not relinquish the right to their homes, even after the destruction. In 1977, the new Israeli government promised to allow the villagers to return—and then delayed action. In 2000, the pope pleaded for a return to Birem. Throughout the odyssey, Jewish members of Kibbutz Baram acted as allies in the campaign for justice. "They really tried to help them," Eitan said. "This was the only case that I know where a mobilized group from one kibbutz tried to repair what was done to the Palestinians."

The villagers of Kfar Birem—children and grandchildren of the original residents—hold onto memories of home, and memories of memories, and the dream of returning one day. They visit the ruins of the village for baptisms and burials; IDF soldiers have forcibly removed squatters and protest encampments. Hannah Farah Kufer Bir'im, an architect and activist whose parents once lived there, legally changed his surname to include his ancestral village. For the Zochrot showcase, he created a counter-mapping blueprint for rebuilding Kfar Birem. An enlarged photo of the ruins revealed densely packed homes and buildings, arcades and alleys, roofless and overgrown with vegetation. Around these ruins, the architect reimagined a new village, one that embraced the shattered stones of the old one and didn't replace the past.

Eitan had encouraged another team of activist-planners based in Bethlehem to use the tools of urban design to envision the Palestinian

Territories *after* the Occupation. How might the refugee camps be renewed? How could the IDF's concrete bunkers and the settlers' hilltop outposts be reclaimed and recycled into a future Palestinian homeland? The visions that Eitan Bronstein and his colleagues at Zochrot had organized nudged people to think about the future in new ways— to accept rather than fear change. A few months later, a Jewish architect from France, one of the world's leading bridge designers who had family on a kibbutz and had volunteered there, unveiled a bold plan for a Peace Bridge to link Gaza and the West Bank. Four storeys high, 37 kilometres long, the bridge would bisect the south of Israel and include an aqueduct from the Mediterranean to the Dead Sea, two levels of highway and a rail line. Palestinians could travel between the disconnected territories of a future state while the bridge provided solar energy and desalinated water to rural communities in Israel. The long white lanes and wing-like solar panels of the architect's digital mock-up have the clean, austere beauty of a sci-fi utopia—a future that never quite arrives.

"There are millions of books about the right of return," Eitan told me. "There is moral or legal documentation about why there is a right of return. And there are others against it. But what does the return itself look like? Or how would it work? Nobody has an idea."

By teaching the Nakba, the activists at Zochrot imagined an Israel in which Palestinian refugees could rebuild homes and villages. By creating a gallery space and a magazine and a semipublic forum in which wild ideas could be talked about and drawn onto maps, they found new ways to frame the debate about the future of their country, and what it might look like. They even created a smartphone app, called iNakba, that used GPS and digital mapping technology to help users locate and learn about destroyed Palestinian villages. But was anybody paying attention?

Outside the gallery, Zochrot faces more critics than believers. The kibbutz movement had once been the scapegoat targeted by right-wing politicians; now nationalistic parliamentarians in Israel were drafting laws to shut down, or at least shut up, NGOs like Eitan's that raise uncomfortable questions. A proposed bill tried to make it a felony to commemorate the Nakba; the version passed by the Knesset became known informally as the "Nakba Law" and could be used to revoke public money from government-funded organizations that taught the other side of Independence Day—the alternate history that dares not speak its name.

"The aim of the law is to create an atmosphere that threatens anyone who deals with the memory of the Nakba," Eitan said. "The project of this government is to close all the organizations that criticize the nationalistic aspects of this country. I'm afraid there are much more dangerous laws coming."

CHAPTER 12

Buying Cat Food with the King of Achziv

My return flight from Tel Aviv touched down in Toronto, and I shoved my passport under the Plexiglas edge of a customs booth. The young agent flipped the pages, ready to bless my return, until his finger paused.

"What's this?"

His digit incriminated two blue-inked stamps. The crude markings stood out next to the bureaucratic icons from Israel proper; they looked like a daycare art project, carved and inked into wobbly, spud-like ovoids. On the bottom stamp, Hebrew lettering and the words *Medinat Achziv* encircled a half-ruined mansion with a palm tree sprouting between Moorish domes.

"It's from the State of Achziv," I said, as though the location were common knowledge.

"Where's that?"

"It's a micro-nation on the coast of Israel," I explained, and then added, with the slack authority of a Wikipedia citation: "It's in the Lonely Planet." Achziv's Lonely Planet listing appeared in an eccentric guidebook to "homemade nations," which included a country whose monetary system fluctuated with the price of Pillsbury cookie dough, another that had elected a poodle as president and an island nation known as the Conch Republic that seceded from Key West.

"Is it a Jewish state?" the agent asked.

Why did that matter? Was it a trick question?

I suppose it was true: Achziv *was* a Jewish state. One of only two in the world. But it was so much more.

I simply answered, "Yes."

The agent waved me through.

—

A bonfire threw sheets of flame at the stars. Beyond the circle of dancing light, behind a scrubby lip of eroded dune, the tide drummed against the Mediterranean shore. Pair by pair, kibbutz volunteers descended the stone steps of an amphitheatre toward the heat of the fire pit, like the first animals approaching the ark. There, silhouetted against the inferno, awaited our Noah, our Moses, our Abraham. Decades of salt spray and snorkelling had blanched and bristled his once-dark beard, while the sun had bronzed the wrinkled dome of his bare skull. A long, loose, dirty-white *jalabiya*—an Arab tunic—hung to bare ankles; on his leathery feet were scuffed sandals ready to disintegrate.

Eli Avivi looked like a caricature of a pop-eyed desert prophet. His soft voice lacked oratorical rumble, but his words still carried above the snap and hiss of the bonfire, the pounding of the surf, the snickering of the tipsy audience of volunteers from Kibbutz Shamir. Eli had presided over hundreds such rituals of holy mischief with the solemnity of a temple priest.

"In our time under the sky," he began, "two truthful, naked people have come to join together . . ."

To be truthful, we weren't naked. Not yet anyway. Our wedding procession approached in work shorts and T-shirts, flip-flops and canvas boots.

"Behold!" our host commanded. The first couple stepped forward. "The virgin son of god and the virgin daughter of nature!"

In English and Hebrew, he pronounced a pair of Swedish volunteers husband and wife. We raised a toast with bottles of Goldstar beer and *arak*. More couples tied the knot. Finally, I stood with my intended. Mikkel was a new arrival from Denmark, with a thick neck, square head and blonde crewcut. He peppered his rudimentary English with obscenities, chain-smoked with self-serious nonchalance and owned a pair of elephant-faced gag underwear with an anatomically incorrect trunk sheath. I'm not sure how I knew this last fact or whose idea it was to get married. When our busload of kibbutz volunteers disgorged on the Shabbat trip, Eli had asked if he could perform any weddings. Looking back, I now cringe at our frat-boy hijinks, how we thought it would be hilarious to get married—two beery-eyed blonde bros—by an odd old man in a ratty tunic.

It was the spring of 1989. Even then, I doubt we were the first same-sex union Eli had validated. He adapted his spiel to the moment: "Two truthful people join together, the virgin son of god and the virgin son of nature"—he didn't make clear who was whom—"are getting married!" He produced a certificate he'd hand-written in red marker and then burned the paper's white edges with a cigarette lighter to give the document the raggedy-edged *faux*-antique patina of a pirate map or a Dead Sea Scroll. We signed the top corner, and Eli inked his own name, as witness and legal authority.

Technically, the only authorities in Israel allowed to sanctify marriages were Orthodox rabbis, Christian priests or Islamic imams.

Non-religious marriages weren't permitted, let alone same-sex ones. For a civil union or a marriage between faiths, couples travelled to Cyprus or another country. What Eli Avivi had done that night violated the spirit of his land and the letter of its law. He didn't care. The ground on which we stood was no longer part of Israel. He would never bend to the endless thou-shalt-nots enforced by the rabbinate or the government on its citizens. He had declared his independence years ago. If Eli wanted to wed young, drunk foreigners in mass moonlit marriages, that was his business.

He rolled his passport stamp across an ink pad and slammed it down on our certificates. It was official. Just twenty years old, I was now a married man in the Free State of Achziv.

—

Before I returned to Israel, after a 20-year absence, I looked up Achzivland. It now had an email address and a website, so I decided to return and stay at the ramshackle hostel by the sea. Older Israelis recalled Eli Avivi as a relic of the country's hippy youth. Most thought he was dead or in jail. Eli had been a legend in this land, but his fame, hot and bright in the '60 and '70s, had faded. I wanted to find out what had become of Israel's most infamous utopian.

As I drove the coast road north from Haifa, I spotted *Eli Avivi* on a highway sign in Hebrew, Arabic and English. Israel's authorities generally reserve street names for long-dead Jewish philosophers, Zionist politicians and military heroes, not hippy squatters who caused endless bureaucratic headaches. Achzivland looked unchanged from my wedding night. The old mansion and its hodgepodge of additions dominated the grounds. White stone walls and shuttered windows formed the building's wide ground floor, while a semicircle of stone stairs led to a pair of heavy, sun-bleached wooden doors decorated with a constellation of rusty horseshoes; its handle was made from the hefty thighbone of an unknown vertebrate. Inside lay Eli's museum, where he housed 50 years of archaeological digging and an extensive archive of homemade pornography. I'd seen both.

I knocked on the door of a small modern bungalow, waited, knocked again. Through the screen, a bleach-blonde woman inspected me. If Eli was the founder and figurehead of Achziv, then for the past 40 years Rina Avivi was the firm administrator who made sure the nation ran on time—more or less. She was a large woman, thick-set and unsmiling, with a deep voice and lightning-white bangs hanging over thick, dark eyebrows. Her bare arms were mottled by the sun and wrapped in silver bracelets that jangled as she swung open the screen door. "One moment," she said, took my money and disappeared.

I waited in the foyer. Through an open door I could see a small bedroom with a leopard-print sheet thrown over the mattress. One wall was a shrine to Rina's early years in Israel. Eli had framed and hung a dozen photographic portraits, in colour and black-and-white, some candid, some posed. In the earliest images, she looked into his camera lens with the wide, distant eyes of a prepubescent starlet. In the living room, I spotted a stuffed mongoose perched on a shelf with bared fangs. Eli lounged on a sofa-futon in his sandals and *jalabiya*, watching *The Karate Kid* on a plasma TV the length of a surfboard. He looked up, nodded and returned his attention to the high kicks of Ralph Macchio.

I dropped off my bags in my room and strolled to the sea. The water at dusk was long past wine-dark. At the old fire pit with its amphitheatre of stone seats, I wondered how many weddings had Eli conducted here, how many vows were made, and broken, in the licentious revels that followed. (I'd married a Mikkel in the evening and woken up with a Mandy in the morning.) The stone rings sat empty. In the lagoon, a lone swimmer from the neighbouring park splashed in the sea. I was Achzivland's only guest.

Eli appeared. The *Karate Kid* was done and he'd noticed my car. "Are you hungry?" he asked. "Do you want to go into town?" I'd already eaten. "Nahariya has lovely girls," he pressed. He was angling for a night out and I was the only chauffeur. I helped Eli into the passenger seat. His health had deteriorated in the last few years, he told me. His body was frail, his eyes glassy, and he spoke in a hesitant rasp. In town, we stopped at a sidewalk café owned by a Moroccan-born friend. Eight middle-aged men idled on the patio, smoking and arguing about a reality show on a small TV. They looked up, greeted Eli and returned to the debate. I talked briefly with the café owner. "His daughter is very beautiful," Eli whispered, after we'd received our espressos. "What happened to the boy you married?"

"I never heard from him again," I said.

The kibbutz had once brought regular tour groups to visit Eli's compound. "Always, they were very nice from Shamir," he recalled. "They came often but not in the last years."

I told him the kibbutz had privatized and no longer took volunteers. The 2006 conflict with Hezbollah in southern Lebanon hadn't helped Achziv's economy either. Katyusha rockets landed as far as Haifa; eight railway employees were killed at the city's train depot, as were several Arab residents. Eli told me 150 buildings had been damaged in Nahariya. All the missiles passed over Achziv, but visits still plummeted. A Club Med resort along the beachfront closed.

Eli encouraged me to stay longer. We could visit a nearby kibbutz, he said, and sample its organic yogurt. We could tour nearby Druze villages. I could join the revelries tomorrow evening. "Friday is full of people," he promised. "They make fire. Full house!" Where did they come from? "Everywhere. Tourists. Young people. *Girls!*" Summer weekends offered a faint echo of Achziv's glory years.

As we idled in the warm night air, Eli retold the creation myth of the nation he had founded. He had been born to stern, religious parents in Iraq who moved to Tel Aviv in 1931. He longed to escape their house. As a teenager, he vandalized railway lines to protest British colonial rule and joined the underground Jewish navy. He smuggled illegal immigrants from Europe and, after the declaration of independence, took part in guerrilla action, including a midnight mission behind enemy lines in the spring of 1948. "We were 35 people from the commandos," he said. "We left from Haifa to Lebanon and destroyed a village. Somebody died there, some people were wounded from the big fighting." His voice trailed off.

After the war, Eli renewed his romance with the sea, the longest of his many affairs. He left Israel to work aboard a deep-sea fishing boat that plied cold waters far from his Mediterranean home. "The North Sea?" I asked. "No, further north," said Eli. Greenland, Iceland, beyond. "The North Pole almost."

When he returned, five years later, Israel was a fledgling nation, a new society being built from the ground up. The only independence that interested Eli, however, was his own. One evening, walking along a remote stretch of Mediterranean foreshore, far from any city or major settlement, he noticed a rocky promontory and the remnants of an Arab village, abandoned during the war, which overlooked a saltwater lagoon. An ancient palm tree leaned like a forgotten flagpole. As night fell, he explored the ruins. He felt as though he had met his true love: *Ach ziv*. The name of the old village, in Arabic, proved to be prophetic. It meant "The Trickster."

By day, Eli explored the coast in swim trunks, catching meals from the lagoon with a snorkel and spear. After sunset, in the glow of a candle, he inspected artifacts he had extracted from the sea and sand. The tiny settlement and seaport had passed from one empire to the next, as far back as the 11th century BCE: the Canaanites and the Jews, the Assyrians and the Phoenicians, the Arabs and the Crusaders, the Ottomans and the British, and now back to the Jewish people again.

Each civilization had left behind shiny baubles and sacred vessels, rusty armaments and maritime gewgaws, hidden in the sediment. Eli preserved these stories piece by piece.

He indulged a Robinson Crusoe fantasy of absolute independence—except he wasn't, as the government kept reminding him, alone on a desert island. The outcrop of land, so close to the Lebanese border, held strategic value. In 1946, Jewish resistance fighters in a guerrilla campaign against the British Mandate had tried to blow up a railway bridge over a nearby creek; 14 died during the operation. The Israeli government now wanted to evict Eli; officials had plans for a park around the archaeological site that included the old Arab village. Eli wouldn't move. And so began a running battle of threats and counter-threats, lawsuits and government injunctions, passive resistance and active outrage—and worse. When officials began to erect a fence next to Eli's house, he climbed atop the roof, in a bathing suit, and fired a salvo overhead with an old tommy gun. Then he lowered the barrel at the workers. "If you don't move," he told them. "I will kill you." They stared at the machine-gun-wielding hippy in a Speedo and decided the fence could wait.

After years of harassment, Eli was fed up with the government. "I'll make my own government," he decided. "I'll drive them crazy!" He launched his own Two-State Solution and seceded from Israel. (Like Palestine, he is still awaiting full UN recognition.) He declared himself ruler and sole authority of Achzivland, also known as "Aviviland." He performed marriages and stamped passports and set the rules for his new nation. (Rule #1: There are no rules.) He maintained a hermetic solitude during the winter. Come spring and summer, his beachside republic—his Temporary Autonomous Zone—became a magnet for Israel's growing counter-culture in the 1960s. Achzivland hosted protests and "be-ins" and rowdy folk and rock concerts. Young Israelis grew their hair long, shucked the stern morality of the secular kibbutz and the religious *yeshiva*, and embraced a Hebrew Summer of Love. "Every year we come back here," wrote Yehuda Amichai, Israel's leading poet, in a lyric titled "Return to Achziv." "This, too, is the beginning of a new religion." Achzivland drew others with rumours of a strange man who lived in a cave—Eli was described as "a kind of pharoah"— and only emerged to lord over a hallucinogenic host of merry pranksters. When officials tried to oust Eli again to create a national park, his hippy acolytes and artist friends protested. He photographed the government's attempts to evict him. Bulldozers ploughed into the foundations and knocked Eli off a stone wall, camera in hand. His case rose to the heights of power and troubled the agenda of Prime Minister Golda Meir. Eli also took pictures of famous visitors, like Sophia Loren, who cooked spaghetti for him, and various happenings, like the "Night in Achziv" rock festival in 1972, Israel's own Woodstock moment of musical madness.

With his camera, Eli captured intimate moments, too. He convinced hundreds of young female visitors to pose naked, atop the shoreline rocks or amid the village ruins, as the morning sun rose over Achziv. Then he rushed into Nahariya to develop the film. From behind his viewfinder, Eli built, shot by shot, one of the largest collections of beach-blanket pornography in all of Israel, if not the Middle East. By his own accounting, the collection of lithe young nudes numbered more than a million negatives and prints. I remember, on my first visit, stumbling upon a photo album of young women, in various states of undress and sandy repose, strewn amongst the artifacts in his museum. It was like finding a copy of *Playboy* in your father's underwear drawer, the same unsettling jolt a young man feels when he discovers that lust never sleeps, even in the wrinkled flesh of his elders. Two decades later, Eli locked his pictures away in a stone vault filled with plastic milk cartons stacked 10 feet high, where he indexed the folders and envelopes of photographs with a curatorial eye for erotic detail: *A Blonde from Sweden.*

A Sort of Auburn. Two German Girls. A nearby kibbutz had offered to archive his vast collection of artisanal smut.

Eli's reputation as the Hugh Hefner of the Jewish state was six decades old. He never shied away from his own libertine proclivities, his lust for a life less ordinary, even after 40 years of a very open marriage. As a nation, Achziv's philosophy had always been more amorous than political. It was a free-love zone, a celebration of the hedonistic urge, founded amid a national culture that was puritanical from its inception. Kibbutz pioneers shared everything except their sexuality. They sublimated the erotic urge for the greater good of the collective—mostly.

Achzivland was the anti-kibbutz, the reverse negative of the communal ideal. Instead of working for the common good, Achziv boasted a utopia of individualism, a hippy paradise of infinite freedom, a garden of earthly desires that rose from the beach like a mirage.

—

No real estate is neutral in Israel. That was the biggest lesson I'd learned on my travels. The first kibbutzniks hoped to build a socialist utopia in Palestine where Jewish colonists might ally with Arab workers for the greater good. That dream collapsed under the weight of its own contradictions: one land, two peoples, too much history. Even here, in splendid isolation, Eli Avivi and the independent state of Achzivland were entwined in the larger conflict. Eli had pitched his battle against bureaucracy as a David-beats-Goliath tale, one man versus the state. But his situation was more complex than he admitted.

Achziv had been populated before Eli found it empty. On his commando mission to Lebanon, in May 1948, the boat passed Al-Zeeb, a fishing and farming village of 2,000, and the Arab villagers hurled rocks and curses at the Jewish partisans. By the time the mission returned, the village was empty of residents. Jewish fighters of the Carmeli Brigade had fired mortars at and then captured Al-Zeeb. Most villagers fled to Lebanon; the few who remained were relocated to Mazra'a, a village to the south. The Jewish commander ordered Al-Zeeb destroyed; only a handful of buildings were left standing, including the mukhtar's two-storey house to which Eli had claimed squatter's rights. In 1971, Palestinian militants from Lebanon landed on the beach to kidnap the ruler of Achziv. Tipped off about the assault, Eli or Rina—their stories vary—grabbed a pistol and disarmed an insurgent, as the army swarmed Achzivland to capture the others. The next day, a tabloid newspaper ran the headline: "Terrorists wanted to kidnap Israel's number one nude photographer!"

Eli's opinions about his nation's former occupants remained elusive. In the past, he told visitors he was a caretaker for the property who awaited the return of the original Arab owners. More recently, he seemed to consider Achziv his private fiefdom. Others could debate its status after he died.

Achzivland was a metaphor for Israel itself—a splinter of the country that symbolized its triumphs and troubles. Eli had imagined a new world out of nothing. But this nothing had a history, another people in exile, a counter-narrative with a plot line a thousand years long. "It's an illegal settlement what Eli has done," one of his supporters admitted to an interviewer. "A charming one, mind you." How different was Achziv from a kibbutz in the Golan Heights or a settler outpost on Arab lands in the West Bank? Was Eli a freedom fighter against bureaucratic conformity and capitalist greed? Or was he another cog in the colonial machine that had dispossessed so many Palestinians? I'd laughed at his irreverent antics, his audacious act of self-determination, but his utopia-building had a dark side. That tension confounded the history of the kibbutz, too.

—

"Fifty-eight years, it's a long time . . ." Our coffee was cold. Eli was feeling reflective.

I asked if Achziv was his utopia.

"I love it here. If I did my life over again, I would do the same." He considered the texture of his autobiography, the smooth and the rough. "Even with all my problems here. With the government. With the permissions. They try all the time to destroy everything here."

His tenure in paradise had been secured only through decades of struggling. How had he fought the law and won?

"I was strong," he said, "and I didn't care."

I mentioned the road sign with his name. It had appeared one day, he told me, without any notice. Did that mean the authorities accepted Achzivland?

"Some people," said Eli. But others were biding their time until he grew ill or died. "The Israeli government doesn't like individualists. They want everybody to look the same. They want your number, so they can find out about you."

We stopped at a grocery store, and Eli shuffled between the neon-lit aisles, searching out cat food for the feline menagerie that roamed his compound. Kibble in the trunk, we drove along an unlit side road that paralleled the beach, with only flickering cottage lights to remind us this wasn't the barren shoreline Eli had walked a half-century ago.

The next morning, I joined Rina and Eli on the patio for tea and strudel. She had arrived in 1967 and stayed. After their wedding, Eli had tossed his wife into the sea and carried her back to the sheikh's bedroom. They were two months shy of their 43rd anniversary, so I asked for the secret of such a long marriage.

"Because he don't love me," said Rina, "and I don't love him."

Eli nodded. "I have to find a nice girl, 16 years old," he said, "like she was in the beginning." They both laughed.

I asked again what would happen to Achziv when he was gone. Eli shrugged. "Do you have children?" I pressed.

"No, I didn't want children. Not me, not my wife."

Even if he acquired the legal title to the property, Eli had no second generation upon whom to bequeath Achziv. All that remained were his memories, his museum of artifacts, his trove of erotica, his unshakeable sense of independence. "My country is doing the best in the world," he said. How can you have an economic crisis when your nation barely has an economy? Eli and Rina eked out a living from camping fees, hostel guests and wedding parties. Life, liberty, the pursuit of happiness— these weren't empty slogans in Achziv. "Everything is better here than any other country."

I said goodbye to the royal couple and glanced in the rear-view mirror as they soaked in the warmth of a new day and listened to the Mediterranean tide lap against the sands of their kingdom by the sea.

— CHAPTER 13 —

Living in Glass Houses

I had crisscrossed Israel several times, and yet the community of Nes
Ammim always evaded my radar. Only later on the Internet did I stumble across a mention of the paradoxical place: a Christian kibbutz built
in the heart of Arab Galilee as common ground with the Jewish people.
A village started in the shadow of the Holocaust with only a dream and
an old school bus. None of my Israeli friends had heard of the place. I
wondered if Nes Ammim was a hoax.

The Christian kibbutz, it turned out, was no mirage. It was a living place, with a history stranger than fiction and a future as uncharted
as any utopia. Tucked off the coastal highway, near the Arab town of
Mazra'a, the gates of Nes Ammim led into the familiar circular plan of
a traditional kibbutz, centred on a large dining hall—and an old school
bus. The bus wasn't the classic yellow model of childhood mythology.
It was a shorter, older camper van from the 1950s that hadn't budged
in decades, with an extension bolted to its flank to house a museum.

On the walls of the addition, black-and-white photographs and signed documents chronicled the origins of Nes Ammim. The bus itself held a long wooden table with eight china place settings and two serving bowls, as though members might return from chores at any minute to say grace.

Even in its sedentary condition, the bus implied the same question printed on a mounted photograph of the founders: "Why have you come?"

Nes Ammim, like Israel itself, emerged from the collective guilt of the Holocaust. European Christians felt haunted by the wilful ignorance and willing collaboration of many of their faith in the extermination of six million Jews. Throughout Europe, the Nazis had reduced once-thriving Jewish enclaves to shadows. How had the loving philosophy of Christ allowed such atrocity? How could they repair relations with the Jewish people in the new state of Israel?

Dr. Johan Pilon, a Dutch physician, moved to Israel in 1950 to work at a hospital in Tiberias, where he dreamed of restoring the bridge between Christians and Jews. A Christian community in Israel could provide a sanctuary of healing for the two religions. But he needed money. And land. And permits. And people who shared his vision. Dr. Pilon found fellow utopians in Hans Bernath, a Swiss doctor, and Shlomo Bezeq, a Dutch Jew sent to Palestine by his parents before the Second World War. The three men imagined their new village as a home for "Messianic Jews" who had converted to Christianity. Later, they envisioned a communal settlement, modelled on the kibbutz, for Christians visiting from Europe. Bezeq lived on a kibbutz that let him work as an advisor for the new community. Over the next decade, the three men drummed up support. After Dr. Bernath treated a gravely ill Druze elder, the sheikh granted him any favour. The Swiss doctor made his one wish: real estate. From the Druze sheikh, the founders bought 250 acres in 1960. Then they got the blessing to build from

Israel's Prime Minister David Ben-Gurion, as well as future prime ministers Levi Eshkol and Golda Meir.

News of the plan, however, was greeted with skepticism. The chief rabbi of Western Galilee protested; Nes Ammim, he warned, was a cover for Christian missionaries to slip into the country and convert Jews, an act forbidden by Israeli law. Thousands of protesters marched in Nahariya. Their message to the Christian kibbutzniks: *You're not welcome here.*

The founders persisted. In 1963, they signed a memo with the Israeli parliament to establish the new village, including a vow never to proselytize. By respecting each other's faiths, Christians and Jews might bridge the "depth of the abyss between the two groups," read the memo, and recognize "the extent of Christianity's moral failure." The first Swiss families drove from the heights of Nazareth in the donated bus with dodgy brakes and coasted downhill until they reached the plot of land. They parked on a low hill overlooking the untilled fields. The Swiss bus served as one family's bedroom, bathroom, kitchen and dining hall. The pioneers were joined by others, many from the Netherlands, who added cabins and new buildings. The bus acted as the hub for a community they christened *Nes Ammim*—"Banner of the Nations" in Biblical Hebrew.

Neighbours saw the outreach efforts of the Christian leaders and volunteers and came to accept Nes Ammim. The once-skeptical rabbi gave lessons in Judaism at the kibbutz. In 1971, Germans were allowed to volunteer for the first time, to work and to listen to stories from the Holocaust survivors on nearby kibbutzes. Dr. Pilon died in 1975 and his wife carried on his legacy for the next 30 years. And yet Nes Ammim remained a transient community. Few volunteers or hired pastors stayed more than a couple of years. Yet every volunteer passed on the guiding spirit of Nes Ammim to those who came next.

As the 21st century dawned, the bottom fell out of Nes Ammim's economy—an echo of the larger kibbutz movement's financial turmoil.

The Dutch founders had developed a thriving greenhouse operation that sold roses throughout Israel. Foreign dignitaries received bouquets from Nes Ammim—until cheaply harvested flowers imported from Africa undercut the market. After much debate, residents shut down the money-losing "glass houses." Residents leased their avocado and olive orchards to neighbouring kibbutzniks and Arab farmers. They rented empty houses and apartments to Israeli families. The violence of the Second Intifada and Second Lebanon War, from 2000 to 2006, slowed the arrival of European volunteers and visitors to the guest house. Nes Ammim's population shrank. Its mission drifted. The kibbutz faded from relevance.

By the time I found its gates, in the winter of 2012, Nes Ammim was suffering an identity crisis, like almost every kibbutz in Israel. Frans van der Sar had been charged with remaking the community. The greying Dutch director had a stooped, hangdog demeanour and spoke in the monotone of a man who had shouldered other people's worries for too long. The stress of change weighed on his health, and yet he remained committed to the vision of Nes Ammim he had discovered as a young theology student from Amsterdam when he had first visited in 1977. He had returned to Israel many times since that formative encounter. In 2009, he moved with his wife to assume the position as pastor and director—and to midwife the community into its next stage of evolution. It hadn't been easy.

"The challenge of the place is that you work with the people who come to utopia, so it's a special kind of people," he explained. We had strolled the quiet grounds in the dusk of a summer evening and were now examining the archives in the school bus. "But then they have to live together, with all their own ideas of utopia, with the different religious Christian perspectives. That has been a struggle." Who's in charge? Who's the successor? Personal politics was the bane of every intentional community. He shrugged. The founders wanted to create a

Christian kibbutz—and so they had, with the original kibbutz's flaws and frustrations, the lack of expertise, the constant improvisation. "We made the same mistakes."

And yet for the many Europeans after the war, Nes Ammim was also a place to confront the dark legacy of anti-Semitism. "A feeling exploded in the '70s but started before that: 'My God, what have we done?' It was utopian—a place of reconciliation, of rethinking. And it has served that purpose."

—

It didn't surprise me to discover Nes Ammim in the Galilee. The north of the country has the highest density of utopian ventures in Israel—perhaps the world. On his one visit to Palestine, in 1898, Theodor Herzl looked over the rolling hills above Tiberias and declared, "At least it's like Europe." Galilee became home to the dozen pioneers of Degania and the heartland of the kibbutz movement. It still contains the most diversely mixed populations of Arabs and Jews.

In the Galilee, I discovered a dozen or more unique communities: Amirim was a valley-shrouded village of vegetarians founded in 1958. In Klil, eco-settlers and peace activists had created an off-the-grid enclave on land purchased from the Druze. On Kibbutz Hannaton, conservative or Masorti Jews, many new immigrants from English-speaking countries, were trying to bridge Israel's Orthodox and secular divide. Kishorit had resurrected a defunct kibbutz into a "home for life" for adults with special needs, both Jews and Arabs, so they could do meaningful labour in a woodworking factory, kennel, TV studio and democratic school. Kibbutz Harduf also ran a care facility for the disabled, based on the spiritual principles of anthroposophy underlying the Waldorf educational system. In Haifa, the ornate and garden-ringed World Centre of the Bahá'í faith was home to the *other* major religion in Israel. On the southern slopes of Mt. Carmel, Dadaist Marcel Junco and fellow creative eccentrics had coalesced into the artists' colony of Ein Hod. In 2009, Kibbutz Ein HaShofet, near Haifa, accepted as a member a Bedouin man who worked in the gardens—the first Arab kibbutznik in the history of the movement. At Kibbutz Ga'aton, a Holocaust survivor turned choreographer started the renowned Kibbutz Contemporary Dance Company, and the privatized dining hall was transformed into rehearsal space for the Galilee Dance Village. And then, of course, there was Achzivland, Eli Avivi's revolutionary republic of love. You couldn't throw a stone in the Galilee without hitting someone's take on utopia.

Davi and Asueli Windholz, Jewish activists and artists in their fifties, were drawn to Nes Ammim because of the reputation of the Galilee. Both sets of their parents had fled from Nazi Germany to South America in the early 1930s, and they had met as high-school students in São Paolo. After immigrating to Jerusalem, Davi worked in NGOs to promote co-existence between religious and non-religious Jews, between Mizrahi and Ashkenazi Jews, between Jews and Arabs, between the white middle-class and the Yemeni and Ethiopian underclass. Asueli was a dancer and a teacher. Over the years, the Golden City felt increasingly oppressive: overzealous, intolerant, with a deepening fundamentalism. Their friends kept moving away—to the suburbs, to Tel Aviv, abroad, elsewhere. They decided to move, too.

"Our dream was to come to the Galilee," said Davi, a plump and garrulous middle-aged hippy with wispy dark locks and an effervescent demeanour. In the Jewish tradition, he explained, the Land of Israel consists of four elemental geographies: Jerusalem is the fire, Hebron is the earth, Tiberias is the water. "And Galilee is the soul," he said. "So we came to the soul."

Davi had watched the kibbutz movement transform and adapt to the new capitalist society of Israel over the past decade. "But there are principles that stay in the Israeli culture," he said. "And one is utopia." An adult son was starting an eco-village; his other son, after a degree in marine biology, was studying alternative medicine and the Kabbalah, and hoping to create a spiritual community less orthodox than traditional Judaism.

A new generation was experimenting with alternative forms of community. Near Nazareth, I'd visited Kibbutz Mishol, a network of urban communes, one of many across the country. Young pioneers from Zionist youth groups in Israel, Britain and North America lived communally—pooling their income like the original kibbutzniks—and worked as teachers, social workers and activists in underprivileged neighbourhoods. The Galilee remained one of the most fertile laboratories for alternative living.

Davi wasn't especially religious, but he understood the Messianic impulse that fuelled the faith of his Orthodox countrymen. He thought the Messiah existed in every one of us, that we all ought to work to bring heaven to earth, not wait for a supernatural deliveryman to knock on our door. "Part of the Jewish people is to believe it is possible to transform our utopian idea into a practical idea," he said. He pointed to the street protests, tent encampments and social-justice marches that had swept across Israel in the summer of 2011—a prelude to the Occupy Wall Street movement. Half a million people took to the boulevards of Tel Aviv and other cities to demand economic equality. "I am an optimist!"

For decades, progressives talked about resolving the Arab-Israeli crisis with a Two-State Solution—a Palestinian nation adjacent to Israel, roughly bounded by the Jordan River and the Green Line border that existed between 1949 and the Six-Day War of 1967. The other option is a One-State Solution: the absorption of the West Bank and Gaza into Israel, with full citizenship for the Palestinian people (an idea most Israelis reject, because it might mean an Arab majority) or continued occupation by the Israeli military (an idea Palestinians spurn for obvious reasons). Neither solution seems imminent.

Davi had published an article that proposed overcoming the political impasse with a *Three*-State Solution: Israel, Palestine and an independent Galilee. "If you want to fight one with the other—Israel and Palestine—it's open to you," he explained. "But from Haifa to the North, we want an independent Galilee. We want to live together, 50 per cent Jewish, 50 per cent Arabic. And we will live fine." He was only half-joking. Galilee was different. Galilee held out hope. Galilee hadn't been sundered completely by ethnic suspicions, high-wired fences, religious hatreds and sectarian feuds.

Frans agreed. He explained the name itself implied tolerance: "Galilee" came from the Hebrew *galilee goyim*—the "land of the heathens" or, in a more generous translation from the *Book of Isaiah*, "Galilee of the nations."

"There is an idea of pluralism that's still here," said the director of Nes Ammim, "and that the people have been proud of."

———

Over the last two decades, the attitudes of many Europeans about Israel have shifted. The image of the Jewish Israeli that springs to mind is no longer the Holocaust survivor or the hardy kibbutznik. The plight of the Palestinian people intrudes on that old narrative. The stereotype of the Israeli is often an IDF soldier manning a checkpoint or suppressing a protest. "The story of Palestinians rose more to the surface," said Frans. "The children of some of the parents who lived here have become very radical on the Palestinian side. You see that kind of generational shift. When people now come to Israel, to Nes Ammim, they want to hear both stories."

The volunteer program was once again thriving, with an eccentric mix of young Europeans—Swiss, Dutch and Germans—and older Christian couples from the Continent. The volunteers' experiences were enriched by work opportunities and educational programs. They taught English to and played soccer with children in the Arab village of Mazra'a. They helped on Kibbutz Lohamei HaGeta'ot—the Ghetto Fighters Kibbutz, founded by survivors from the Warsaw Uprising— with German translations of archival materials and displays for the Holocaust museum. They learned Arabic and visited the West Bank. Their time in the Galilee connected the two worlds of Palestinians and Jews in Israel in a way my own kibbutz experiences never did. They were never asked to choose a side.

—

And so an idea arose on Nes Ammim that the village could renew its mission in Israel by organizing dialogue sessions between Arabs and Jews. Like the Oasis of Peace, the kibbutz could serve as neutral ground. "It's a good meeting place because it's easier here for people to feel equal," said Frans. "You're not in a Jewish environment, you're not in an Arabic environment." Nes Ammim had once opened a safe space for dialogue between European Christians and Israeli Jews; now it could do the same for the two peoples struggling to live together in the Galilee.

These encounter groups sparked a bolder idea. Why not create a community of co-existence where Palestinians and Jews could *live* together rather than just talk? Nes Ammim's leaders were already planning to build a 90-unit subdivision. A new piece of national legislation allowed small rural communities in Israel's north and south to decide who was permitted to live within their boundaries—and who wasn't. The law had been controversial, especially in the Galilee. Critics argued it sanctioned discrimination against Arabs and other minorities. It was the same bureaucratic tool older kibbutzes had used to keep Mizrahi immigrants (or "Arab Jews") from joining as members. It was the same covert racism that the first commuter suburb in Levittown, New York, had deployed to ensure neighbours remained as white as their picket fences.

The members of Nes Ammim would bend the law to higher purposes. They would self-select for a *mixed* community rather than an ethnically "pure" one. They would identify and recruit people who wanted to live together, Muslim and Christian and Jew—and Druze and Bahá'í, and whoever else wanted to join.

After years as a home in Israel for European Christians, not everyone was thrilled that Nes Ammim was handing over its keys to Arab and Jewish residents. Arab families were keener than Jewish ones to sign up for an apartment on the pastoral grounds of the kibbutz, with its fresh air and swimming pool. Co-existence might not be good for the bottom line. The developer of the original subdivision was upset: forced desegregation complicated marketing the suburban dream for maximum profits. "It's ideology meeting reality!" admitted Davi. A very kibbutz dilemma.

Other skeptics worried that Nes Ammim would become a watered-down version of Neve Shalom/Wahat al-Salam. The Oasis of Peace had tried to create harmony between Arabs and Jews, Davi argued, by ignoring cultural and religious differences, by seeing residents as post-racial "universal beings." He thought the idea that religion and ethnicity can be shucked for a secular identity was naive. "It's not like, 'If we want to live together, forget all our ideologies.' No! We *are* different. And this is the principal factor to accept in this region." Only by accepting difference can true acceptance emerge. "We have a heterogeneous community and respect about difference—*this* is the principle."

Frans nodded. "At Nes Ammim, we leave it more open," he added. "We try not to transcend our religion—to transcend it to a common political agenda, like Neve Shalom tries to. They struggle with it and fight about it. That we won't do in Nes Ammim. But it *is* about co-existence. Living together as Jews, Christians and Muslims with different religions, different cultures. To just show that you can live together, that you can find practical solutions for the things of ordinary life and live together in a group way. I am always surprised by the response. There are people who work for such a utopia—it is something that appeals to people. It would be a challenge. It will not be easy. But this could be a good place for it. To *try* it."

Other skeptics wondered why Nes Ammim was drifting from its original mandate to connect Europeans and Israeli Jews—and address the threat of anti-Semitism. "Nes Ammim is a unique place that has no one to talk to, so they have to invent every solution again and again—on their own," observed Tanya Ronen, whose parents had worked with the founders of Nes Ammim. One afternoon, I'd visited Tanya, a wry and opinionated middle-aged Israeli, in the Holocaust Museum at the Ghetto Fighters Kibbutz where she worked, minutes from Nes Ammim. She offered a critical perspective on the transformation of Israel's Christian kibbutz. "Times have changed so much. Ideologies do not appeal to people anymore. You have to find another way to attract them. The Christian world is very tired of the whole Jewish-Christian dialogue, which paints the Christians in a very bad light. They found a very nice escape: 'The Jewish people are not saints. Once they are in power, they are not behaving in a way that was dreamt!'" The new focus on the occupation of the Palestinian Territories, Tanya told me, allows Europeans to wash their hands of the past and say, "We can put our guilt aside because they are as guilty as we are. Let's forget about our crimes and focus on theirs now!" Or in *Fawlty Towers* terms: Don't mention the war.

For Nes Ammim's European leaders and volunteers to revoke the original vision would be a great loss, especially with the rise in anti-Semitic rhetoric and violence against Jews in Europe and beyond. "It has an amazing role to play, but I don't know how to sell it. Israel and the Middle East are not Europe—and never will be," she said. "Now is the real change when Nes Ammim really, *really* need their founders— and they don't have them—to keep the balance in a dialogue with the Arab world on the one hand and a dialogue that is still very necessary with the Jews. Because anti-Semitism and racism have not vanished." I'd heard the same refrain across Israel, even from my most left wing of kibbutz friends: "Why does the world hate us?" Nes Ammim had once answered that call with "We don't."

—

Visits to the guest house at Nes Ammim had picked up in the relative peace of the past few years. No major bus bombings. Few rockets launched from Lebanon. The Galilee was a quiet corner of Israel and a comfortable starting point for pilgrims and other tourists looking to explore the Biblical sites of the North, the stomping grounds of the teenaged Jesus. Nes Ammim was far from the corridors of power in Tel Aviv and Jerusalem, distant from the strife in Gaza or the occupied West Bank. The community of former florists hadn't made headlines in decades.

As sleepy as it seemed, a community like Nes Ammim will always attract a whiff of controversy. How can you bring together the three religions and not expect friction? The tension between harmonious aspirations and contentious reality was embodied in the sculpture in the foyer of the kibbutz's "church." Like the Spiritual Centre at the Oasis of Peace, the building had been stripped of religious symbolism. No crosses, no Torah ark, no Koranic calligraphy. A few chairs faced a bare altar. The entrance foyer had a *koi* pond and rock garden. Emerging out of the green water, a stone disc displayed a diorama of miniature sculptures. Three sets of terracotta figurines, four inches tall, faced the three doors of a central tripod in V-shaped wedges. Some lay prostrate in prayer; others knelt; a minyan of 10 stood with holy books in hand.

The symmetry of the statuettes tried to suggest harmony between the faiths. In Israel, however, religion is often a zero-sum equation of holy, holier, holiest. Some visitors inspected the diorama and asked, *Why is one of the doors not open? Is there a message hidden in the hierarchy of poses—standing, kneeling, prone? Where are the Druze? The Bahá'í? Aren't there more than three religions in the Galilee?*

Over the years, figurines had been knocked over and broken, by accident or design. Thin cracks at their throats reveal where decapitated worshippers needed their heads glued back on. Members of the kibbutz had erected a low wire barrier around the installation to keep back the curious. Here, in the Galilee, in Nes Ammim—in a place trying to bridge the divides of faith—a fence now guarded this tiny representation of collective equality before the Almighty, this microcosm of the community's higher ideals. *Come worship with us*, it whispered. *But don't get too close.*

— CHAPTER 14 —

A Dry Season in the Garden of Eden

It wasn't every morning that a pretty young hippy in a peasant dress asked me to hold a palmful of poop.

Neta Sukenik and I were standing in the well-named "Kaki Classroom," a shady corner of a lush oasis amid the vast desolation of the Arava Desert. On one side, she pointed to stalls of composting toilets. Next, we inspected the output end of the equation: tall plastic bins filled with months of human excrement, mixed with straw, filtered, drained and stirred each week by the kibbutz's most unlucky volunteer. Hungry micro-organisms catalyzed the process. Neta popped the lid on a tub that had aged, like a cask of Highland scotch, and extracted a fistful of brown matter.

I recoiled, but she insisted I take a handful. I'd never met anyone as excited by the promise of fermenting shit. Not even a bouquet of loam, however, suggested its outhouse origins, as I let the fine, dry mulch sift through my fingers. "This is all real," Neta said. "I'm not making it up!"

Composting toilets didn't need a drop of H_2O, a rare resource here in the Arava Desert, where the average annual precipitation of four centimetres tended to evaporate as fast as it fell. "Every time we flush a normal toilet," she said, "we use nine litres of water. That's *drinking* water, which we pollute and send to the ocean. It's not sustainable."

Like many immigrants, the first generation of kibbutzniks described themselves as "compost for the future." They hoped their sacrifices would bloom into better lives for their children and grandchildren. On Kibbutz Lotan, members took a less metaphorical attitude to composting. But they still saw their efforts as fertilizing the future. They hoped to rejuvenate the withered branches of the nation's communal movement with the green shoots of environmental action. They hybridized the secular vision of the traditional kibbutz with spiritual traditions for a skeptical age. They linked the kibbutz, one compost crapper at a time, with the most important trend in utopia-building since the dawn of Degania: an international movement of eco-villages, thousands strong, springing up around the world like mushrooms after a rain shower. If the shit did hit the fan, in our era of peak oil and climate change, these sustainable communities could live off the grid like arks. An Israeli eco-village in the desert hoped to teach us all how to live more lightly on our planet.

—

In the late 1980s, I had passed through the Arava Valley on my way to the beach resort of Eilat. Our volunteer group had trudged through the desert, heads bent under the autumn sun like a column of foreign legionnaires, to visit the site of King Solomon's mines. Nothing moved fast in the Arava. Every organism conserved its energy or became carrion. It was hard to imagine anyone settling this exposed fissure that linked Africa's Rift Valley and the Dead Sea; the Arava Valley seemed an unlikely spot to reseed the Garden of Eden. Only when I returned to Israel did I hear rumours of a "green" kibbutz movement and "eco-Zionism." "There's something interesting in the south of the country," Yuval Achouch, the sociologist from Kibbutz Hanita, told me. "It's less ideological. They are in the desert, and they have all kinds of New Age ideology and anarchism. It's more like the experience of the '60s and '70s than the kibbutz."

Kibbutz Lotan was one of these experiments. Just off the southern highway that led to the Gulf of Aqaba, Lotan's Center for Creative Ecology drew students and volunteers from Israel and abroad to live in geodesic domes and learn in the Eco-Kef Park—part playground, part garden, part mad scientist's lab. Mike Kaplin, one of the centre's founders, looked less like the granola-crunching, pony-tailed caricature of a commune dweller and more like a middle-aged refugee from a British biker gang. He had a bouncer's bullet-shaped bristly head, the thick-framed spectacles of a shop teacher and a black handlebar moustache with a chin strip that deserved a spot in the Motörhead Facial Hair Hall of Fame. He was wrapping up a demonstration for his permaculture students on how to jerry-rig a geodesic dome out of tree branches and PVC pipes.

Mike had grown up in a development town in England, where his parents had become fixated on back-to-the-land philosophies during the oil crisis of the 1970s. He learned to milk goats and midwife baby ducks in his bedroom. His parents took the goats to the local football field to graze because there wasn't room in the back garden. On vacations, the family visited the Centre for Appropriate Technology in Wales. "My parents were different than everyone else," he recalled, "and I hated it."

After graduating with a degree in furniture building, Mike bought a one-way ticket to Israel and landed at Lotan, which had been founded in 1983 by progressive Israelis and American Jews from the Reform Judaism movement. "It was like a summer camp all the time. We were young, working hard, getting up early, picking melons, sorting in the packing house until eight or nine. There was that feeling of togetherness. And that understanding that everything we do we do for ourselves. We're the bosses."

Whenever Mike's mother visited the kibbutz, she would set up a compost pile in the garden and six different recycling bins in the dining room. In Israel, at the time, it was an alien concept. After Mike's mom left, kibbutzniks returned to old habits. Over the years, however, her influence filtered into their collective conscience. A few members cultivated an organic garden. Another started an eco-volunteer program. Outside experts offered lessons in alternative technology and mud-building. Mike enrolled in a permaculture course to learn how to work with natural cycles; his parents' choices began to make sense, and he realized how much he'd learned as a boy. The organic garden evolved into a teaching garden. Bird-watching tours sparked a plan to divert wastewater and develop a nature reserve. "That project was bigger than ourselves," said Mike. "It wasn't selfish." One-off visits by overseas youth groups grew into larger educational ambitions, and the Center for Creative Ecology emerged to consolidate these efforts.

The greening of Lotan during the mid-'90s mirrored shifts in the global zeitgeist. In 1995, 400 self-described "eco-villagers" from 40 countries gathered at Findhorn, a New Age "planetary village" in the north of Scotland, to establish the Global Eco-village Network. "We have more in common with those communities around the world than we do with kibbutzes here in Israel," Mark Naveh, the director of Lotan admitted to me. Environmental awareness fused with Reform Judaism into what members called eco-Zionism. The Hebrew word *avoda*—"to work"—has a double meaning: to do physical work, like tilling the soil, and the spiritual act of worship, to "work" with God. "Everything we do is because we're an active part of creation," explained Alex Cicelsky, a co-founder of Lotan from upstate New York. "It's all in that word."

Lotan recently completed an EcoCampus of mud-covered, straw-bale igloos. International students in the Green Apprentice program, kibbutz volunteers and other non-members stayed in the semicircle of energy-efficient adobe domes that usually did not require air-conditioning—even in the 45°C summer heat. Lotan's builders navigated years of red tape to demonstrate the fire resistance of the mud-and-straw walls before civil authorities approved the dormitories. A larger geodesic dome, draped in dark fabric, shaded an open-air classroom and siesta area. Residents cooked rice and vegetables and baked bread in the mirrored black box of a solar oven. Another reflector stove looked like the Doomsday weapon from an old James Bond film; its rotating silver dish focused a beam of intense energy at a metal pot dangling from a chain. Descending a set of stairs near the dining room, I interrupted international students gathered in a bomb shelter for a seminar about peace and justice in the Middle East.

The Eco-Kef Park had the scrapyard look of a post-apocalyptic film set. A psychedelically painted VW Bug lay half-buried in the sand of the playground. An improvised greywater system filtered old tap water through settling tanks and the roots of hydroponic plants to be reused for irrigation and to flood a man-made lake intended as a rest stop for migrating birds. Talmudic eco-quotes were embedded into signs and pathways. Bushy herbs and fat cabbage heads sprouted from an expansive organic garden. Almost everything built—the domes, the playground, the garden beds—was the work of dozens of hands, visiting students as well as kibbutzniks. It was all part of the creative part of the ecology—and an ethic of self-reliance lost elsewhere in Israel. "It's a bit sad," Mike said. "Modern kibbutzniks don't work in the fields anymore. They used to tinker with things and get their hands dirty." He glanced at the scattered tools, the half-finished geodesic dome, the open-air campus and gardens, the flourishing date plantation and bird preserve beyond the boundaries of the kibbutz. "I want people to learn things and take them home, not for us to be a museum. Not for us to be these weirdos," he said. "I don't think we're creative *enough*. We've got a lot more work to do."

Modern straw-bale homes are often designed with a "truth window." A small decoratively framed opening in a mud wall reveals the densely packed natural innards. Truth windows remind skeptics the Three Little Pigs were wrong—straw *can* be better than brick. On Lotan, I noticed a truth window framed by the plastic frame and dials of an old TV set, its "screen" broadcasting a perpetual fuzz of straw. Another truth window in the eco-park revealed the old truck tires and garbage that had been slathered in mud and transformed into outdoor furniture. Lotan lived with a truth window embedded in the entire kibbutz. The thousands of visitors who passed through its gates every year were encouraged to study what they saw, steal ideas, pass judgment, take part, get muddy. Stare hard enough and we might see our way to a greener future.

—

Inside the gates of Kibbutz Ketura, across the highway from Lotan, a raggedy camel was tied to a post. It might not be the best mascot for the Middle East's leading centre of ecological education. Nature on a leash. The desert tamed. The symbolism seemed a bit . . . well, *off*. Still, I stopped to take a selfie with the grumpy beast—which turned out to be a pet as well as a local landmark. "Take a right at the camel" was a common set of directions. Outside the offices of the Arava Institute for Environmental Studies I found a more appropriate emblem for what Kibbutz Ketura hoped to become known: banks of solar panels being tested for durability and efficiency under the blazing sun of the desert.

The big question critics often ask eco-villages like Kibbutz Lotan: *Can it scale?* Intentional communities of 20, 50, even a couple hundred might adapt their patterns of production and consumption to minimize their ecological footprints on our planet. But then what? Not everyone wants to live in a straw-and-adobe dome, cook with a giant mirror and ferment their own poop. An archipelago of eco-villages around the world seemed like meagre protection against the far greater issue of climate change. We need solutions that work for cities, too.

If Kibbutz Lotan was a hands-on playground for local permaculture, Ketura harboured ambitions for *global* change. Founded in 1974 by American Reform Jews, the kibbutz had become a nexus for innovation in solar energy in Israel. Yossi Abramowitz, a volunteer from Boston in the late '70s, immigrated to Ketura in 2006. As co-founder of Arava Power, he was building the biggest solar power field in the region, backed by Siemens, the German electrical engineering conglomerate, with the goal of providing 10 per cent of Israel's power needs. At the launch of the first installation, he invited a Belizean-born hip-hop star named Shyne, who had rediscovered his Hebrew roots doing time in a U.S. jail, to perform. "No oils, barrels. Powered by the sun," Shyne rapped. "Solar energy—the revolution has begun!"

Founded in 1996, the Arava Institute is now an education and research centre that offers university transfer credits, summer courses and a master's degree in desert studies for Israeli Jews, Arabs from Jordan and the Palestinian Territories, and international students. The core philosophy: Environmental problems don't respect political borders, so future leaders must understand issues on every side of these arbitrary lines. On Lotan, the eco-park had the improvised air of an artists' colony. At the Arava Institute, the campus felt more orderly and academic. Students crunched statistics on a computer, pored over textbooks and journal articles, crammed for exams and end-of-term presentations. The former turkey run that housed the institute's main offices had been rewired into a high-tech hub.

—

With a scrubby beard and intense eyes, David Lehrer, Arava's director, embodied the intellectual drive of the institute—a touch impatient, like many frustrated environmental scientists whose warnings keep falling on deaf ears. As he spoke about his students, David allowed a thin smile to break free. He had arrived from North Carolina in 1978; back then, Ketura felt beyond the edge of civilization—and an exciting experiment in building a new society. Students new to the institute often experienced a similar honeymoon period in which the congeniality of the classroom and the novelty of kibbutz life made everyone instant friends. Tensions later bubbled up as family histories, national prejudices and personal opinions prickled consciences. How should a Jewish student react when bunking with a Palestinian activist who may have lobbed rocks at IDF patrols? Or how will an Arab student feel rooming with a former (and future) soldier who might aim rubber bullets (or worse) at family members in the West Bank? To address bottled-up emotions, the teachers designed a course in "peace-building and environmental leadership." The seminar offered an outlet for students to talk about the political and personal contexts of what they were studying.

"This is the Middle East, so these sessions are not especially quiet. Sometimes the students end up yelling at each other and storming out," admitted David. Students retreat to their rooms but then realize that they still needed to share milk and coffee and textbooks and decide who will do the dishes in their dorm. "It creates an understanding that we live in too small an area to continue to fight with each other."

Rarely did a school term pass without a flame war or two. "When these kinds of incidents happen, everyone moves to their corner, everybody picks a side, everybody puts on their war paint." A month before my visit, the capture of the *Mavi Marmara* and the shooting deaths of the Turkish activists trying to reach Gaza aboard the ship had ignited debate. Before that, the Operation Cast Lead invasion of Gaza by Israeli forces had begun on a Saturday, after many students had gone home for the weekend. Teachers didn't know if they would return—and yet they all did. That first night back, David and the students sat in a circle. The tension felt electric. He asked if anyone wanted to speak.

"It was like a dam broke," he recalled. The room filled with accusations and rebuttals, tears and anger. Palestinians yelled, "You're creating a Holocaust on *our* people!" Israeli Jews shouted back, "Where were *you* last week when bombs were falling on Sderot?" By evening's end, the anger had burned out. The students, hugging and crying, arranged a vigil to protest the violence. "On the second night of the War of Gaza," David said, "I'm pretty sure this was the only place in the Middle East where Israelis and Palestinians were sitting in the same room and screaming at each other. They weren't throwing rocks or Molotov cocktails at each other or shooting at each other. They were *yelling* at each other. 'Use your words'—that's what we try to teach them. In the Middle East, when a crisis breaks out, the first thing that happens is a disconnect. Immediately, both sides stop talking to each other."

Not at Ketura. Joined by an intellectual passion for solving environmental problems, the students from different sides of the conflict also learned that it's possible to disagree, often in extreme ways, but still work out their strong emotions through dialogue, not violence.

—

It wasn't all work and study at Kibbutz Ketura. On hot afternoons, students, staff, foreign volunteers and kibbutzniks cool off in the swimming pool. Between laps, Khaleid, a garrulous middle-aged summer student from East Jerusalem, held onto the pool's edge, a pair of pink kids' goggles pushed up on his forehead, and chatted with other swimmers. He had a Jordanian passport, studied engineering in Iraq and lived for six years in Orlando, Florida. A scholarship let him research improvements to disposing of organic solid waste in his community. "The kibbutz is very relaxing—the pool, the pretty girls!" he said. He felt welcome, even as an Arab on a Jewish kibbutz. "Jerusalem is stressful. Every day, people are looking at you, stopping you." East Jerusalem was a labyrinth of bureaucratic rules and Arab neighbourhoods lost to Jewish construction. "People blame the Palestinians for the environmental problems," he said. At the Arava Institute, students could talk about these prejudices and work out solutions. "I've been to America," he said. "I know what a civilized country looks like."

Tareq Abu Hamed, the director for the Arava Institute's Center for Renewable Energy and Energy Conservation, was also from East Jerusalem and took a special interest in helping Palestinian and other Arab students negotiate life at Ketura. He studied chemical engineering in Turkey, worked at the Weizmann Institute—Israel's MIT—and the University of Minnesota before moving with his wife and three daughters to the kibbutz. "This is the place where it's possible to have cooperation between Jordanians, Palestinians and Israelis," he said. "Politically, I always believed in talking to the other side. We need trust, and you cannot build the trust sitting with each other for two or three hours. Trust needs time."

His research team was collaborating with international partners on projects that included hydrogen-fuelled car engines, biodiesel production and photovoltaic cleaning and cooling to improve the efficiency of solar panels. They were helping Bedouins in southern Israel and rural villages in northern Jordan to convert animal waste into gas for cooking, so women wouldn't poison their lungs burning untreated animal waste and old plastic in cooking fires.

As a teenager, Tareq had picked fruit on a kibbutz in suburban Jerusalem and improved his English chatting up foreign volunteers.

Every month, he hosted a meeting to help Arab students to adapt to life on a Jewish kibbutz. "It's not easy for Jordanian students to come study in Israel," he said. Their families and friends question why they would want to live and study in a Jewish community. "We know they are brave and special students because they choose the hard way," said Tareq. "These kids—these students—will become teachers or lecturers. Each person will become hundreds in the future. *This* is the change."

—

At the turn of the millennium, Daniel Gavron, a British-born Israeli journalist and former kibbutznik, toured dozens of kibbutzes (including Ketura) and predicted the privatization that would sweep across the kibbutz movement in the decade that followed. "The values of equality and cooperation are eternal," he concludes. Communal life, however, needs an extra ingredient to hold people together—a glue. "In the early communes it was religion; in the case of the kibbutzim it was pioneering and Zionism." For years, the dream of a Jewish homeland unified kibbutzniks and justified their sacrifices. Once Israel was born anew, that glue began to lose its grip.

"I don't think the kibbutz movement has much of a future," said David Lehrer. He had tried to start a "green kibbutz movement" but found few partners in Israel. "Cooperative movements all over the world last for a hundred years and then become privatized—that's what's happening here." The kibbutz once offered solutions to local problems faced by early Jewish immigrants to Palestine: rural settlement, collective education, integration of immigrants, agricultural development, industrialization. Those challenges were past. "Today, you can't look at Israel's problems in a vacuum," he argued. "You have to look at Israel as part of the global world. The question is: What does the kibbutz have to offer to problems like poverty and desertification and climate change?

Do we have something special to say to the Palestinian-Israeli conflict? To poverty in Africa? If we are irrelevant to *these* issues, then we're irrelevant. It may mean that we have a lot fewer kibbutzes, but those left may lead us to a new era of sustainability and community life."

Later that afternoon, students from the institute gathered in a small auditorium to deliver end-of-term presentations. Their research posters explored ecological cooperation between kibbutzniks and Jordanian villagers, water quality in Bedouin communities, Palestinians' opposition to a canal between the Red and Dead Seas, case studies in environmental resistance in Israel. The future graduates—Palestinians and Jews—joked together, in English, as they shared ideas and fielded questions. Like the first drops of rain in a landscape that knew only drought, an annual trickle of young alumni from the two kibbutz schools in the desert might one day grow into a cleansing flood. They would spread their wisdom throughout the Middle East and beyond. That was the dream. One day, these future researchers, inventors, activists and political leaders will cross borders to conquer problems that no single nation can solve. They will build a sustainable future for everyone who shares this hot and fractious corner of our blue planet.

— CHAPTER 15 —

Love and Rockets

After visiting the eco-kibbutzes, I drove north out of the desiccated rift valley and the Arava Desert. Turning west, my car descended into and then rose out of the huge earthen maw of the Ramon Crater, and I continued across the moon prairie of the Negev Desert as the red ball of the sun descended. On the dusky pink horizon, Israeli tanks on maneuvers kicked up veils of dust. Approaching the coast, disoriented by nightfall, I missed a turnoff and nearly drove toward one of the gates to the Gaza Strip. I pulled a panicky U-turn before I reached the army checkpoint.

The next morning, as I headed out from my guest room on Kibbutz Urim, I could see a mammoth satellite dish dominating the skyline of a nearby military base. In the distance hovered what looked like white weather balloons but were more likely surveillance orbs eavesdropping on militants in Gaza. For all the grim headlines, I'd never felt unsafe in Israel, and yet as I reached the outskirts of Sderot, my pulse thrummed. I kept glancing in the rear-view mirror and listening for the shriek of a rocket warning siren. As most Israelis know, Sderot is a good city to get bombed in. It's both praised for its heartland values and the butt of jokes from the rest of the country. Sderot: a nice place to be *from* but you wouldn't want to live there. Or visit. In an episode of *Arab Labor*, a caustic Israeli TV comedy, a Jewish-Israeli photojournalist tries to woo a Palestinian lawyer by promising to follow her anywhere: "For you, I would live in Nazareth, I would live in Nablus . . ." He lists Arab cities few Jewish Israelis would venture, except in an army vehicle, before delivering the punchline: "I would even live in Sderot!"

Sderot was established in the 1950s, a kilometre from the Gaza Strip, as a transit camp for Kurdish and Persian Jews, and grew into a "development town"—a community hastily erected to house waves of new immigrants: at first mostly Moroccan Jews, then Ethiopians and later, Russians from the Caucasus. The city remained out of mind for most Israelis until Palestinian militants began to fire unguided short-range rockets—known as Qassams—at Jewish settlements within Gaza, border kibbutzes and eventually Sderot itself. (The IDF forcibly evacuated the settlers from Gaza in 2005.) A "code red" warning gave residents 15 seconds to sprint to the safety of the nearest bomb shelter. In 2007, after Hamas took political control of Gaza, the Israeli government gave special privileges to Sderot, nearby kibbutzes and towns within seven kilometres of the occupied territory, including preferences for government tenders, funds to fortify daycares and subsidies for families. The area was known as the Gaza Envelope or, more cynically, Qassamland.

As Gaza became the international symbol for the plight of the Palestinians, Israeli politicians pushed Sderot into the role of civic martyr. The prime minister's office tried to rope Justin Bieber, the pop star and evangelical Christian, into meeting fans from Sderot as a goodwill gesture with a political bent. "What about the children of Sderot?" justifies almost any action by the Israeli army. In late 2008, after an uptick in rockets, the IDF launched the Cast Lead assault on Gaza and killed

1,400 Palestinians. In 2011, the Israeli military deployed the "Iron Dome" missile-interception system to protect Sderot and other targets in the south. Meanwhile, the municipal government teetered on the brink of bankruptcy.

And yet Sderot is also home to an ambitious attempt to reboot the ideals of the kibbutz movement. A new commune had broken ground within the city's maze of bomb shelters. I had come to see if it could survive another war.

—

I expected a city under siege. Instead I passed shopping malls and apartment blocks, a community college and grassy boulevards, residents waiting for buses or walking to work. Not the bombed-out shell I'd imagined from newspaper headlines. I spotted a few graffiti-decorated concrete shelters. But that was all. When I parked beside the cobbled sidewalks and tree-shaded crescent of Kibbutz Migvan, I could have been on a suburban lane in Anywhere, USA. I didn't need to lock my car, let alone run for cover.

But appearances can be deceiving. This was, I would learn, a city straining under psychological pressure.

Kibbutz Migvan had no cotton fields, no orchards, no farm equipment, no factories, no barbed wire encircling the grounds. It looked like a "co-housing" development in Copenhagen, Berkeley or Vancouver. Migvan took co-housing one step further. They didn't just live together. They kept a common purse, too. As on the first kibbutzes, everyone pooled their earnings.

Nomika Zion, one of the founders, had been born on a traditional kibbutz and raised among kibbutz aristocracy, political leaders and left-wing artists and intellectuals. Now in her fifties, she still had the fire of her early idealism. Dark hair fell in coils past her shoulders, and her kohl-shadowed eyes pulsed with humour and sadness, outrage and inspiration. Her grandfather, Yaacov Hazan, was a legend in the Labor movement, a founder of Kibbutz Mishmar HaEmek and the Artzi Kibbutz Federation who was elected to the first seven Israeli parliaments. Her mother was a journalist and theatre director; her father career-hopped between socialist politics and avant-garde drama. "I grew up in the kibbutz but also in bohemia with actors and writers," she recalled. "I developed social sensitivity at a very early stage."

As a girl, she saw that kibbutzniks' ideals weren't always reflected in their behaviour. Her own kibbutz was near a development town, like Sderot, populated with poor Jewish immigrants from Morocco, Algeria and Tunisia. There was little communion between the well-educated, well-connected Ashkenazi members of her kibbutz—children of European immigrants—and the darker-skinned Mizrahi arrivals, often refugees, from North Africa. "The kibbutz surrounds itself with a fence—and that fence becomes a wall. I'm talking about an emotional and mental wall," Nomika told me. "And a profound conflict started to develop between the people from the kibbutz and the people from the development town."

One Shabbat, when she was 10, Nomika invited several Mizrahi girls from the town to visit the kibbutz. Boys from her school threw stones and taunted her guests: "Get out, you Moroccans! We're going to call the police!" The girls ran away; Nomika never saw them again.

"It's an emotional wound," she said, four decades later. The pain reminded her that human conflict springs from ignorance and lack of contact. It can't be overcome by well-meaning abstractions. At the kibbutz high school, students came from the same background, cut off from Israel's cultural diversity. "When people don't meet each other, they start to develop stigmas and stereotypes and prejudices toward each other. And this is what happened to us." Kibbutzniks were locked in an echo chamber, a suburb for socialists, in which they never heard opposing points of view. "You build your identity in the reality of conflict," observed Nomika, "much better than in a homogeneous society where people all come from the same ideological roots, the same background, the same mentality."

During a pre-army year of civil service, Nomika worked with high-school dropouts. In her second year in the IDF, she taught in the slums of Netanya, a coastal city north of Tel Aviv. "Very violent young people—teenagers," she recalled. The year was 1981. A national election split Israel into factions: Labor Party supporters versus Likudniks, Ashkenazi versus Mizrahi Jews, secular versus religious, kibbutzes versus development towns. In Netanya, Nomika represented everything the kids from impoverished immigrant families despised. "I remember so much hostility and hatred and violence toward me—not as Nomika, but as a symbol," she said. "I realized I had to make a major change in my life and create a true dialogue with these young people."

Many of her friends left Israel. Nomika stayed home. She took a job as a journalist. She taught in a kibbutz high school. For three years, she worked in the offices of the Hashomer Hatzair youth movement. She convinced parents and school officials to let kibbutz kids study for a year in Tel Aviv or Jerusalem among non-kibbutz peers to expose them to a different reality and different voices, to break down the emotional and mental walls. That project was the seed of Migvan. The idea, however, needed a few years to germinate. Nomika began to talk with friends from college about a new model of living together—neither the lonely crowd of the city nor the isolated collective of the rural kibbutz. Something different. An evolution. An *urban* kibbutz. "It was only a title. An empty word," she admitted. "We had to build the vision."

A nucleus of friends coalesced around the idea of a city commune. Every month they organized cultural evenings and seminars with readings and debates, how to build a new society. People came and people left until, as Nomika recalled with a smile, "after two and a half years, we said, 'Okay—it's time to give birth!'" But to what? And where?

In a poor neighbourhood of Jerusalem there *was* an urban kibbutz named Reishit, founded in 1979 by ex-members of Nomika's home kibbutz. Reishit had been an inspiration. So her group visited Jerusalem as a possible location. They considered an industrial suburb south of Tel Aviv. Nomika suggested Sderot for the short list. They debated the options: *Where could they do the most good?* Then they voted. Sderot won.

Everyone who didn't like the result left the group. A core of six friends remained. "Young, very ideological!" Nomika raised her fist and smiled at the memory. "We decided to come here because we wanted to make some *tikkun*—personal and social *tikkun*, yes?" The rabbinical phrase *tikkun olam*—to heal or repair the world—is Hebrew shorthand for social justice. "The first goal was to repair the damage and build a new relationship with the people from the kibbutzim and the people from the development towns." They would start with Sderot.

The commune grew to 80 residents, half adults, half children. In 2000, Migvan's members bought a plot of land, moved from the slum where they had lived for 14 years, and built two rows of townhouses, workspaces and a common building for their mini-village in the city. Like the founders of Degania, the urban kibbutzniks in Migvan wanted to remain intimate enough to maintain dialogue between individuals— no more than a hundred people or so, not like the mega-kibbutzes many members had left. They didn't know it, but their cap on expansion echoed the work by British anthropologist Robin Dunbar who had calculated the theoretical limit on social relationships humans can manage without overtaxing their neocortexes. "What keeps the community together is a sense of mutual obligation and reciprocity," he concluded, "and that seems to break down once community size exceeds about 150." He had observed the same population figure repeated throughout history: Neolithic villages; the fighting units of the Roman army;

English villages in the census of the *Domesday Book*; Hutterites and Amish, who consciously split into separate groups when they reached that limit. The 150 top-out for community capacity became known as the Dunbar Number.

In 1995, the kibbutz launched a tech company, the first in Sderot, for consulting, database management and website design. Today, it has 14 employees, half from the kibbutz, half outsiders. "You can find Bedouins, Caucasians, Moroccans, Ukrainians," said Nomika. "We have lunch together and we argue about politics. The others like to tease me because I am the leftist!" The employees and the directors earned the same salary, and the management was democratic, not hierarchical. "They feel that they create together—it's something of their own." Programmers weren't expected to stay past midnight or work weekends to meet impossible deadlines. "We don't want that kind of high-tech slave," said Nomika. Every year, kibbutz members debated whether to close the company because it never earned much money—nothing at all in the lean years of the Gaza conflict. The highly educated members who ran it could make four times the salary at bigger firms. "But what happens to you as a human being?" she asked. "At the end of the day, the decision is to go on, because this is ours. It's based on our human values, our social values. So the company still exists—and now it's slowly starting to flourish." It was high-tech capitalism with a human face.

Kibbutz Migvan had inspired smaller groups of young Israelis to found urban kibbutzes in Haifa, Nazareth, Tel Aviv and elsewhere. The goal was not to live as equals and work as equals; the original kibbutz movement had tried that. The greater vision was to improve the lives of the city around each kibbutz. Migvan had accomplished that goal in Sderot. In 1994, six Migvan kibbutzniks started an NGO called Gvanim to offer social services to adults with disabilities; it now oversees 260 employees and runs dozens of projects: early childhood education and health care, teaching Hebrew to new immigrants, an "extreme sports" centre for at-risk youth, a retraining program for young men rejected as unsuitable for army service. Gvanim leverages government and private funding to re-knit the city's frayed social safety net. "This comes from the kibbutz ideology—cooperation between the three sectors," said Nomika. "You have to learn how to work together." Through Gvanim, the members of Migvan accomplished a mission at which the traditional kibbutz often failed: taking care of the less-fortunate *outside* its fences.

"It is a significant dimension of our life," said Nomika.

Her first instinct had been right. They *could* build something beautiful in the streets of a difficult city.

—

A few years after the founding of Kibbutz Migvan, the new mayor opened Sderot to an influx of immigrants from the former republics of the Soviet Union. Almost overnight, the city doubled in population and struggled to find housing for the newcomers. The social services and welfare programs couldn't keep up with demand. By then, the children of Sderot's original Moroccan Diaspora had ascended into the middle class, and the immigrants from the Caucasus became the new targets of discrimination in Sderot's fractious mosaic, which included Ethiopian Jews, ultra-Orthodox Haredim, religious Zionists and an anonymous enclave of Palestinians who once worked as informants for the Israeli secret service and would be shot by Hamas if they returned to Gaza.

"Sderot is a multicultural and multitribal city," said Nomika. "So what do you think we have in common?"

It wasn't politics. It wasn't religion. It wasn't economics or ethnicity. I didn't know.

"The ultimate answer is Qassams—the rockets!" Nomika laughed darkly. "External threats always unite people."

Sderot had enough to worry about with its population boom, its mix of immigrants, its poverty and exclusion from mainstream Israeli life. In 2002, the city added downpours of rockets to its forecast. The Second Palestinian Intifada intensified, with bus bombings and infiltrations and Qassams. Sderot was the closest, densest urban centre to Gaza. And a target.

For eight years, the city lived under Qassams. Thousands of rockets and mortars dropped on the streets and buildings of Sderot. The Israeli army responded with air and ground attacks. Even after Israel's unilateral pullout of nearly 7,000 settlers from Gaza, in 2005, the citizens of Sderot felt anxious, depressed, eager to escape. Rates of crime, substance abuse and divorce rose. A 2007 study revealed that half the middle-school students in the city suffered from symptoms of post-traumatic stress. Nearly two-thirds of residents would flee Sderot if they could afford to; a tenth had already abandoned the city. Residents with a gallows sense of humour posted a banner that read: "I came to Sderot because it enchanted me," punning on *Kassum*— Hebrew for "enchant"—and *Qassam*. Nomika sensed a hardening of attitudes toward the Palestinians in Gaza and elsewhere by the citizens of Sderot, even among her fellow kibbutzniks. In January 2008, the conflict hit a low point. Upwards of 50 rockets a day struck the city for a month. The wail of sirens was the soundtrack to daily routines, as citizens kept an eye out for the nearest bomb shelter when they walked the streets.

Nomika felt helpless under the barrage, without a voice. So she and a fellow Migvan member gathered 20 people from Sderot and nearby communities to discuss their feelings as the tit-for-tat retaliations between the militants in Gaza and the soldiers of the IDF escalated. "They hit, we hit back. Always stronger and stronger. And we were trapped in this vicious violent cycle which never stops." They named their new group Kol Aher, or "Other Voice." The members connected with citizens in Gaza; the two sides couldn't meet in person, so they shared stories via phone and email.

In late December 2008, residents of Sderot cheered as Israeli fighter jets dropped deadly payloads on Gaza. Two families left the kibbutz, Nomika recalled: "Because the relationships are so close here, it's like cutting an organ from your body." Other members would have moved, too, if not for a loyalty to the disadvantaged populations of Sderot they served. Within the kibbutz, political tensions percolated among friends who were once united by progressive beliefs. Members wondered if Migvan would survive.

Staying quiet doesn't come naturally to Nomika, so she wrote an open letter to the government about life as a citizen under siege and her front-row seat to the deadly fireworks of Cast Lead. She acknowledged her own anxiety about the Qassams but argued that the changes she saw in her friends and her neighbours—in her homeland—scared her more. "I am frightened we are losing the human ability to see the other side," she wrote. "To feel, to be horrified, to show empathy. With the code word 'Hamas' the media paints for us a picture of a huge and murky demon that has no face, no body, no voice, a million and a half people without a name."

She did not want anyone to believe the war was for her benefit, as a citizen of Sderot. "Not in my name and not for me did you go into this war," ran a line that became a chorus. "The bloodbath in Gaza is not in my name nor for my security." A newspaper published her letter and used that phrase as the headline. Overnight, her *cri de coeur*, so out of tune with the martial demands for payback from other corners of her country, went viral on the Internet. Her "War Diary from Sderot," as it became known, was translated into more than 20 languages and jumped from website to website, nation to nation. Television crews showed up on her doorstep. She did a half-dozen media interviews—every day. People around the world emailed her to say, "You are our echo—this is the saner and human voice we are afraid to express because everybody supported the war."

She also received threats and accusations of treason. But the positive reaction affirmed her belief that hope might lead her people out of the darkness. Her friends in Other Voice offered a forum for views not always welcome on her own kibbutz. Many of her old friends, the so-called leftists, were not leftists anymore. One of Migvan's founders, a man who had gone to jail for six weeks rather than serve as a soldier in the West Bank, told Nomika: "If they shoot one Qassam from Gaza, we should destroy a whole village."

"What about the women?" she replied. "The children?"

"I don't mind," he said. "Eye for eye, tooth for tooth."

The encounter chilled her. "This is the new game in this region—it has completely changed," she told me. "And this is what happens to people, what the conflict did. It has left a profound mark on their souls."

—

Nomika Zion remains active in Other Voice, a public spokesperson, in Israel and abroad, against military action as the sole option to keep Gaza in check. In January 2013, the *New York Review of Books* published a translation of another letter she wrote, addressed to Prime Minister Netanyahu, to protest yet another military operation against the people of Gaza. "We will continue to raise another voice in the dwindling light, as we wait anxiously for the next bloody round," she promised her country's politicians and an outside world that has grown numb to the endless news cycle of violence in the region.

Few people in Israel today can claim such deep roots in the kibbutz movement as Nomika. Her grandfather Yaacov Hazan had sustained the communal movement as a powerful national institution. Later, Nomika rejected the old kibbutz to create a new model of communal life. Her grandfather had been dead now for nearly 20 years. The kibbutz had changed. Israel had changed. Nomika had changed.

"What would you tell him, if you could?" I asked.

Nomika laughed. "He thought that Israeli society at the time was not ready to accept urban kibbutzim," she recalled. "He thought that we won't manage to keep our identity, our values in the city—that we will become part of the capitalistic society because the influence of the outside would be stronger."

Other leaders in the kibbutz movement shared her grandfather's skepticism. In Hebrew, *kibbutz ironi* means "urban kibbutz" but sounds, as in English, like "kibbutz ironic." Traditionalists used to tease the young pioneers about their ironic kibbutz. And yet Migvan and other urban kibbutzes enjoyed the last laugh. In a new millennium, as the old rural kibbutzes privatize into gated suburbs far from Israel's multiethnic cities, the urban kibbutzes survive and inspire a new generation of young Israelis to start small communes dedicated to social work and political justice.

"I think if he could come here today," said Nomika, conjuring the ghost of her grandfather, "he would say I am the winner! Absolutely. It took 10 years for the kibbutz movement to realize that this is the only chance for the renewal of the kibbutz and its socialist ideals." She liked to think of her intimate urban commune as "soft socialism," a cozier kind of communism. "At the end of the day, we built here a more human model without giving up the social responsibility that was part of the classic kibbutz. We took it, and gave it a new face that was more relevant to Israeli society. Maybe the next generation will found another model of social life in Israel."

The success Kibbutz Migvan carved out amid the storm and stress of life in Sderot was based not on *what* they built but *who* did the building. Relationships mattered more than ideologies. The decision to remain small, intimate, an extended family of friends and neighbours, on a single street, held their community together. "When we realized that the most important thing is who are your partners to this adventure, we started to put much more weight on the emotional relationships and less about intellectual topics," she said. "So, as long as you share your life with the right partners for you, it is worth it."

Pick your partners wisely. Small is beautiful. A shared life is a better life. And don't be shy to extend a hand to neighbours over your back fence—even when they toss rockets at your yard. Simple lessons can be hard to learn in a time of war. But these values make Migvan a beacon of hope.

"As a pioneer, we have what we call the second day of the revolution," said Nomika, reflecting on a quarter-century of life in Migvan. "When you have a vision, when you have a dream, and then when you face the reality—yes, the second day—there are many disappointments, many compromises. It's not what you think when you just wrote your thesis." The disappointment of the day after the revolution caused many idealists to leave the kibbutz system. It makes every attempt at utopia elusive. But it didn't bother Nomika Zion. "After 23 years, for me the reality is better than the dream. How many pioneers can tell you that?"

CHAPTER 16

More Than a House

On a cloudless July afternoon, I took a break to stroll the Mediterranean promenade near Jaffa, the old port south of Tel Aviv. Fishermen cast long rods at the breaking surf. Spandexed roller-skaters and Segway riders zipped down sidewalks thick with selfie-snapping tourists. It was easy to forget the tensions elsewhere in Israel. On the route out of town, a commotion down a side lane caught my eye. Six police cars and ambulances had clustered, lights spinning, sirens off. A crowd coalesced around the entrance to a stone house. Two Arab women in dark *hijabs* stood near the steps, hands outstretched, mouths agape. While I couldn't hear their voices, their body language needed no translation. Two paramedics were hurrying a stretchered body toward the open mouth of an ambulance. Police officers pressed forward, one with an Uzi slung under his arm. Kids in school uniforms jogged toward the scrum of gawkers. A security guard smoked a cigarette next to a locked gate.

"What's going on?" I asked

The guard gave a seen-it-all shrug. "Someone got shot."

Welcome to Ajami, one of the toughest neighbourhoods in Israel.

—

A few hours earlier, I'd been sitting in a courtyard in Old Jaffa, a lit-tle north of Ajami. A horse clopped past, its wagon stacked high with watermelons. My imagination toppled back a century to an era when Jaffa had been the epicentre of trade in Ottoman-ruled Palestine. In 1909, the first foundations of Tel Aviv were being laid by Jewish immi-grants in the sands to the north. Both the notion and the nation of Israel were sentences in a manifesto passed between writers and diplomats in distant Europe.

That was the stuff of nostalgia. The activists of Sadaka-Reut, in their late teens and early twenties, preferred the urgency of youth. The past would always be there, hanging over their shoulders. But the future—well, *that* was worth fighting for. And only by thinking of the future could they keep the past, and the history of Arab Jaffa, from being erased. Sadaka-Reut was founded as an NGO, in 1983, by Jewish and Palestinian university students. They believed partnerships between the two sides could break the stalemate of fear and incrimina-tion. The name joined the Arab word for "charity" with the Hebrew for "friendship." Over the next three decades, Sadaka-Reut organized programs for young adults: summer camps, workshops, art activities, encounter groups, high-school outreach, anything to get Palestinian and Jewish Israelis out of the ideological bubble in which they grew up. I'd come to Jaffa to learn first-hand about Sadaka-Reut's most daring experiment: the Commune.

Every year since 1998, administrators selected eight to ten young volunteers. Half were Palestinian Israelis, half were Jewish, with an equal split between genders, too. The teenagers lived for a year in a Jaffa apartment, collaborated on educational and activist projects—and negotiated the emotional ups and downs of living with the enemy.

Jawad Maekly and Lena Rotenberg were about to graduate from the Commune. Lena was 18, with a round face and blonde hair, and spoke in bursts of outrage and insight. She was born in Russia; her parents moved to Israel when she was two, part of the wave of post-Soviet immigrants in the 1990s that transformed the demographics of Israel. The new arrivals fled the ruins of state socialism, so the idea of joining a kibbutz—a communal farm straight out of Stalinist propaganda—held little appeal. Many Russians moved instead into cheap housing in the Occupied Territories. Lena grew up in Ariel, the largest settlement, a city of nearly 20,000 residents that split the West Bank and any future Palestinian state in half. What to do about Ariel was an elusive puzzle piece to any peace agreement. The city was too big for Israeli politicians to evacuate—or for Palestinians to relinquish.

When she was 15, Lena participated in a Sadaka-Reut youth group and visited the Arab-Christian town of Taybeh in the West Bank, famous for its brewery. The Jewish kids felt enlightened about the Conflict; some wore checkered *keffiyehs* in solidarity. The Palestinians sat in silence. Finally, a young woman from Taybeh spoke. "I can pretend to be your friend," she said. "But two years from now, you will go to the army, you will take a weapon and you will start shooting at my family in the West Bank."

"Before she said that," Lena recalled, "I felt like I'm a good person, meeting Arabs, moving forward peace in the Middle East, opening my hands for co-existing." The young Jewish visitors broke down in tears. Lena felt that no matter what she did, she would still be the "bad Jew." Afterwards, Lena visited Jaffa, where she met Jawad and joined the Commune as alternative service to her mandatory two years in the army. She chose *not* to take up a weapon. Foregoing IDF service—and the social connections it cemented—disappointed Lena's parents. She didn't care. She had nothing to prove; she felt Israeli enough. She intended to make her family's new homeland a better place, even if she diverged from the politics of her parents.

Jawad was slender and handsome, quiet spoken, but with a sly intelligence and an eye for the hypocrisies around him. Now 19, he had grown up in an Arab village in the Galilee. His parents worried that living away from home might affect his preparations for his entrance exams to university, where he planned to study medicine.

Living communally, even for a year, wasn't easy. "The first month, we were all emotional," recalled Lena. "Everything was a big deal. Everything was an issue." Eventually, arguments cooled, and members focused on monthly projects, their studies, the rest of their lives. A romance flourished. Life went on. They try to focus on political activities in Jaffa rather than emotional conflicts within the Commune. "But it's there," admitted Lena. "We just prefer not to talk about it."

"If you were in America," I joked, "they would hide a camera in every room and turn you into a reality TV show." Producers could call it *Big Brother by the Sea* or, even better, *Jaffa Shore*.

"That would be high rated!" said Jawad, with a laugh. "We always suspected our guides put cameras in. There's a weird light in our bathroom that we're not sure about."

The Commune's members reminded me of the pioneers of Kibbutz Degania, who once dreamed of building a binational state. Jawad, however, felt the Jews who devised the kibbutz were different than those who founded the Commune. He pressed a hand to Lena's shoulder, and she smiled. "Because the Jews who came with the idea of the kibbutz came with the intention to build it on another people's land. And you can't come and build something and say to the ones whose land you took, 'Come join me!' It's ridiculous. It's not going to work. And it didn't work."

"I don't see it that way," Lena replied, scrunching her lips. "I don't think the people who came here were aware of taking other people's land. Those people—the 18-year-old boys and girls who came to the kibbutz—I don't think they were aware of the political history they were creating here. Not in the same way that I can say about myself that I'm an Israeli living in Jaffa, so I'm part of 'Jew-ifying' Jaffa." Lena knew Arab residents often considered her an intruder in their city, even if she tried to help Jaffa remain a Palestinian village. The first kibbutzniks, she felt, were more naive about their impact. She couldn't be.

Lena volunteered with Machsom Watch, an activist group that documented incidents between Israeli soldiers and Palestinians at the checkpoints dividing Israel from the occupied West Bank. On her way to a checkpoint in the Jordan Valley, she met an old Arab man, maybe 80 years old, who lived in a refugee camp.

"Where are you from?" he asked.

"I'm from Jaffa," she said.

"You're from Jaffa? I'm from Jaffa, too!"

She didn't know how to react. The old man hadn't been back to Jaffa since his exodus in 1948. As a reminder of that loss, many former residents of the Old City still wore around their necks the thick metal keys to houses they'd abandoned. Lena had only come to Israel in 1993, decades after the old man's exile. Perhaps she was living in his former house. Even as she was doing her political work, she was part of the Conflict, too.

During their time together, Jawad, Lena and the other Commune members produced short films explaining the situation in Gaza—the medical needs, water problems and educational deficits. They screened kids' movies in poor neighbourhoods, such as Ajami, because Disney flicks were only dubbed into Hebrew and shown in Tel Aviv. They scrubbed away anti-Arab graffiti from building walls. Every week, authorities or developers demolished houses from which Palestinian residents had been evicted, and the activists at Sadaka-Reut would rush to the site to protest. Police barricaded the streets and monitored the protesters from helicopters. "In the end, the house is destroyed," said Lena. "You can see the family crying and screaming. It doesn't really help that we're there." The same drama played out daily in various neighbourhoods of East Jerusalem—Sheikh Jarrah, Silwan—where local protesters and international activists tried to block the evictions and demolitions and the Jewish gentrification of Palestinian districts.

"In the beginning of this project, I was full of hope," said Lena, after eight months in the Commune. "Right now, I don't know."

"Now she has a lot of *awareness*," quipped Jawad.

"What moves me to be active and to fight the political situation," Lena continued, "is not hope of what it will be in the future. It's right *now*. I see things that are going wrong. I see people who are being pushed from their houses, killed, hurt, in the name of my security. I feel I can't let it go. It's not that I'm seeing how the future will be brighter then. It's that now I can't just sit and see what's going on. It would be easier if I couldn't see. But now that my eyes are open, I can't go back. Now I see really, *really* wrong things that happen in the name of my security, and I can't stay silent. That's what moves me to act. Not hope."

Jawad agreed. There was a reason the Commune was described as a "partnership" rather than a "co-existence" project. The young Palestinians and Jews lived and worked together, but it wasn't always a peaceable arrangement—and that was fine. They didn't paper over the tensions for the appearance of superficial unity, unlike some other left-wing groups. "Partnership needs to have awareness of the balance of power between Jews and Arabs," said Jawad. Acknowledging the disparity meant looking at personal biases and privileges so embedded that they feel natural.

Lena admitted that talking about Palestinian independence some-times panicked her. "I have something here that's so strong in my mind," she said. "I've spent 12 years in this educational system, which is so political and goes so deep."

"We need to stop scaring people!" said Jawad.

Lena laughed. "Yes, the educational system is one of the most powerful tools for the Occupation—on the Jewish side and also the Palestinian side." In Israel's schools, history lessons focused on the Zionist narrative and fed the fears of young Israelis about the threat of an Arab takeover. Sadaka-Reut offered a counterpoint to that storyline. But they were only a handful of young activists arguing against the vast bureaucracy of the state.

A year after my visit to Jaffa, the Commune was closed down. The board of directors of Sadaka-Reut decided the apartment was too expensive. Traditional Arab families remained reluctant to commit to a child living away from home for a year. Sadaka-Reut still organized encounter groups between Arab and Jewish teenagers but now focused resources on problems faced by the citizens of Jaffa, where house demolitions, street crime and racist graffiti and violence were on the rise.

Like the first kibbutz, the Jaffa Commune began as a brave dream. It held out the promise of joining two sides in this long conflict under one roof, to live and to work, to quarrel and to make up, to wrestle with their messy and mutual histories—and to change, to become better citizens. Perhaps it had been too little, too late. The members of the commune could shout until their throats grew raw. The houses and the memories of old Jaffa were still pulled to dust around their feet.

———

"Sometimes I feel like a *bomb!*"

Muhammed Mugrabi delivered his startling confession in a café in Jaffa's Old City on a mild December evening more than a year after I'd visited Sadaka-Reut. His compact body thrummed while his knee drummed against our patio table. A young musician and athlete, he jumped to his feet to make a point and sat again. He joked and laughed, and then scanned the square for eavesdroppers, as his good humour spun on an axis. Life as an Arab in the city's increasingly Jewish community made him want to explode. Jaffa felt like a ticking bomb, too. If Tel Aviv represented the glossy promise of Start-Up Nation—the go-go hub of high-tech, high-finance, high-life hedonism—then Jaffa was its shadowy unconscious: a Palestinian community, alive and dispersed, present and absent, whose citizens called this stretch of Mediterranean coast home long before Theodor Herzl invented the idea of modern Israel.

Muhammed released his flashes of rage in a band called System Ali—they were the reason I was back in Jaffa. Lena and Jawad had told me about the group, a collective of hip-hop musicians, often 10 or more, that emerged from the Commune and became its most enduring legacy. Around the café table sat three other members of System Ali. Mouhamad Aguani, dark-eyed and brooding, hunched in the shadow of a blue hoodie, looked like a dour Jedi master of political hip hop; he'd grown up in the same sphere of discrimination and diminished opportunities as Muhammed Mugrabi. Big Mouhamad and Little Muhammed—that's how I thought of them, the yin and yang of System Ali. The other two bandmates were Jewish Israelis. Yonatan Kunda was a spoken-word poet and guitarist. He wore wire-rimmed glasses and spoke in a flat, analytical tone, peeling away layers of meaning from his community—his place, his family's place and System Ali's place within it. I thought of him as the Professor. Neta Weiner had angular features and a mane of wiry brown hair, swept back off a tall, pale forehead as though he were leaning into a coastal breeze. He looked and talked like a Russian revolutionary before Stalin's purges, an accordion-wielding and rhyme-rapping Trotsky. I could picture him in the autumn of 1910, cultivating socialism among the cornflowers of Kibbutz Degania. I thought of Neta as the Prophet.

"Why are you here?" he wondered.

I explained how I'd been a volunteer on a kibbutz now listed on the NASDAQ.

He laughed. "Ah, ha! So you can buy it now!" Big Mouhamad asked if he could volunteer on a kibbutz in Canada. I said I'd look into it.

Neta lived in Tel Aviv but had roots in the kibbutz movement. Both sets of his grandparents had been founders of kibbutzes; he grew up on Givat Haim, his father's kibbutz, but his parents moved the family to the city when Neta was only six. I wanted to know if the old kibbutz meant anything to young activists in 21st-century Israel.

Neta admitted the kibbutz's philosophy was in his DNA; it shaped how he saw the world and the possibilities of communal life. The power of the collective was strong in System Ali, too. And yet he felt the kibbutz carried a great burden as a colonial enterprise that had displaced Palestinians from their ancestral homes. He told me about the cowshed on his old kibbutz. He remembered it from his boyhood as a symbol of Givat Haim's rustic ideals. He never knew until recently that the shed stood atop the ruins of a Palestinian village.

"How is System Ali like a kibbutz?" Even as it left my lips, my question sounded ridiculous.

Still, the band members took it seriously. System Ali embraced the revolutionary mission of the original kibbutz, they agreed. "We operate like a family more than like a band," said Big Mouhamad. "There's a mission, an aim, of social revolution. There's a communal theme and revolutionary ethics regarding justice for things not looked at, not covered, silenced. And then there is the *personal* revolution—and it's different for each of us."

Mouhamad's mission, however, differed from that of the original pioneers. "It's not like a kibbutz in the homogeneous combination of people," he said, "because we gather from all around." Mouhamad was of mixed heritage. His mother's family had fled to a refugee camp in

Jenin in the West Bank after Jewish forces dispersed their village near Ramle during the War of 1948. Originally from Afghanistan, his grandfather was detouring through Palestine on his way to Mecca, for the Hajj, when he joined the Turkish army and married a Palestinian. The couple moved to Jerusalem after the War of 1948 and to Jaffa after the War of 1967. In the span of a century, his family history piled exile upon exile. His mission? That was an easy question.

"As a son of the Palestinian nation," said Big Mouhamad, "I want to bring justice to my nation, to my people. And to show that something is wrong. System Ali is about bringing the truth, number one, without any censorship."

—

Six years earlier, Neta and his older brother, who was part of the Sadaka-Reut Commune, started a youth centre for Arabs and Jews in an old bomb shelter. System Ali emerged out of sessions held in the centre for creative writing and music, forged by the social injustices they saw every day in the city streets beyond the walls of the shelter. Their live performances feature a stage packed with instrumentalists and vocalists, men and women, Palestinian Israelis and Jewish Israelis and new immigrants from Russia, hopping like pistons in an engine, taking turns on the microphone. The group's repertoire fused four languages heard on the streets of Tel Aviv and Jerusalem, Haifa and Eilat—Hebrew, Arabic, English, Russian—in a boisterous collage of influences: Israeli folk tunes, old military bands, traditional Russian music, Egyptian poetry, American rock and pop, and global hip hop's politicized call and response. Their songs ranged from upbeat anthems, like "Building the House Anew," to stark apocalyptic dirges. "All that is left is the shock," raps Yonatan, in a song called "War." "Spinning around the block of our souls like a hawk. As our ministers mop up blood with theoretical talk."

The previous week, a notoriously fickle critic from a major Israeli newspaper had attended a show in Tel Aviv. Afterwards, his rave review declared that he had seen "the future of Israeli music, and its name is System Ali."

The band's creative process, however, wasn't a "Kumbaya" session of mutual admiration and artistic conformity. They had musical differences, personal differences, political differences. "We fight a lot—physically sometimes," said Neta. "And we hug a lot as well. When we're in the rehearsal, it's a struggle. Texts come in, texts come out. This body of creation is continuously changing."

In 2006, the eviction of Palestinian renters and the demolition of apartment buildings in Ajami sparked local activists to react against the gentrification of Jaffa. The protests offered an opening shot for System Ali as a band. Their music was more than a soundtrack to the protest movement; it was essential to the revolution they envisioned.

And so was Jaffa. One of the most important ports in the Middle East until the middle of the 19th century, the city was known as both the Bride of Palestine and the Mother of Foreigners, as the junction between Cairo and Damascus, Ramle and Gaza. In 1948, 60,000 citizens lived in Jaffa and surrounding villages. After the war, roughly 4,000 Palestinian residents remained; many Jewish newcomers moved into the abandoned homes. System Ali sang about how Jaffa was being groomed—gentrified and segregated—into a backyard for Tel Aviv.

Every member of System Ali had deep links to Jaffa. Yonatan's father's family immigrated to Jaffa from East Poland in the wake of the Second World War and witnessed the mass displacement of Palestinian residents after 1948. "Family stories and also family shadows accompanied my childhood," he recalled. History was forever being erased in this corner of the world, buried under the dust, covered over by new shops and condos and the perpetual thrust into a gleaming new future. And yet Jaffa symbolized a hope that history could be remembered, too, and the neighbourly trust between Arabs and Jews restored. "Jaffa is a place of partnership," Yonatan said. "It's the only place that could enable System Ali."

Big Mouhamad nodded. "Jaffa is more than a house," he explained. "It's life. All of my struggles are for one thing—to bring back the good life for the people of Jaffa." For System Ali, music and art were the most potent vehicles to carry this message of hope and resistance to the citizens of Jaffa—and beyond. Their revolution might not be televised, but it would be *amplified*: loud and proud and shouting in the polyglot urban *patois* of Israel's complex cultural mosaic.

"You can't have a struggle without art supporting it," said Mouhamad. "This is what fucked up so many of the revolutions in the world. They didn't have the art."

CHAPTER 17

Broken Promises in the Promised Land

In the summer of 2010, members of the International Communal Studies Association gathered at a college near Afula, in the Jezreel Valley. The symposium coincided with the centenary of Israel's kibbutz movement, but the event held an oddly mournful air. Some American and European members had balked at visiting the country in the aftermath of Operation Cast Lead and the Gaza Flotilla deaths. The heyday of the kibbutz had passed. By the end of the conference, the scholars were hungry for inspirational words about our common future rather than bemoaning a tainted present or fixating on a nostalgic past. A panel of experts discussed the communal impulse and why it matters even more today, now that the dogmatists of global capitalism were waving victory flags. A feel-good aura descended on the auditorium.

Then a tall delegate with a shaved head raised a hand. He was in his mid-thirties but dressed younger and had been video-recording talks and Tweeting highlights on a smartphone. "Hi, I'm David," he said, in a North American accent. The moderator asked him to speak up. He talked about the growing divide between the ideals of the kibbutz and the global environmental and social-justice movements. He described how "Zionism" had become a dirty word for a generation of international activists and progressive Jews in the Diaspora. "I've been surprised that 100 years after Zionism, 62 years after the founding of the state, 43 years into the Occupation of the West Bank and Gaza, there wasn't any discussion whatsoever of an Arab-Palestinian narrative. Of how some kibbutzim were built on them. Of how Arabs who tried to join kibbutzim were refused membership. Of how the plan to create an Arab model for a kibbutz was not allowed. All this talk about how we're equal and we want to live together as equals just completely ignores the fact that—"

The room ignited. People clamoured to be heard. Several demanded the microphone. "This will tear the association apart!" shouted a *kippa*-wearing Israeli academic. The moderator tried to regain control. "Stop right there!" he demanded. "I think that's a big area. We could spend a whole session on how the kibbutz has responded to the Occupation. But I would like to bring us back to this room. We are all experts in community . . ."

A few minutes later, in the foyer, several attendees told David he had raised a vital question that tainted the kibbutz: How can an intentional community of equals exist amid a society of oppression? How long can the kibbutz—and Israel—ignore the aspirations of the Palestinian people before cognitive dissonance erodes their higher ideals? And how can an uncompromising seeker of utopia find a home in our broken world?

———

David Sheen seems an unlikely shit disturber, a gentle giant with a restless heart and a buoyant optimism that we can build a better world. That we *should*. Even in a crowd, David stands out. He towers six inches above the average Israeli and eschews beachwear for the radical chic of the urban anarchist. An Arab *keffiyeh* often hangs around his neck, a Mao cap perched on his head.

A few days after the conference, we arranged to meet on the beachfront promenade of Tel Aviv, where he greeted me in a soft voice. Our rendezvous was next to the boarded-up shell of the Dolphinarium, site of a once-thriving nightclub. I asked what happened to it. David told me it was the target of a suicide bombing in June 2001, at the start of the Second Intifada. The bomber had walked into a queue of young Russian immigrants and detonated a belt of explosives. Twenty-one bystanders died; another 120 were injured by shrapnel. The Palestinian Hezbollah claimed responsibility. After the attack, the Israeli army clamped down on the West Bank and Gaza and ordered Arab guest workers to return to the Territories. In 2003, Israel began to erect its security fence. Nine years after the blast, Tel Aviv had sunk back into its days of languor, its nights of forgetting. And yet the Dolphinarium remained derelict, a silent monument to the past.

David suggested we meet his journalist friends at a café on Ben Yehuda Street, so we dodged strollers and talked about his personal quest for the Holy Grail of community. He used the C-word with solemnity, as though "community" was as solid as the gold standard, the only thing of true value in a society that reduced every relationship to a commodity. And yet finding community, for David, had proven elusive.

Talking to this man felt like stepping back in time and meeting a kibbutz pioneer. He had the same intellectual intensity, I imagined, as the young pioneers from Eastern Europe who had built a new society from scratch. Like many of the *chalutzim*, David had grown up in a conservative, middle-class Jewish family that ate kosher and went to synagogue on Shabbat. In David's case, it was Toronto rather than

Tsarist Russia or Poland. He was a bookish child with an artsy bent and a future guided by his bourgeois upbringing: a professional job in the city, big family, bigger house.

His father had been born in Israel; David had visited many times and spoke Hebrew so he moved to Tel Aviv at age 25 to escape Canada's harsh winters and start a career as a graphic designer. But the art of advertising quickly felt barren, and Tel Aviv's relentless entrepreneurialism lost its lustre, too. He longed to be an artist. Instead he found himself shilling for weapons-makers, pornography stores, and—even worse for a vegan—producers of *foie gras*. "How do I get out of this system?" he wondered. "How do I live a life that doesn't involve these moral quandaries?" His instinct was to get his hands dirty to cleanse his soul. "I had a romantic idea of going back to the land," he recalled. "I wanted to work in agriculture or horticulture, something to do with nature."

David was a creature of the city, however, and knew little about farming. He hadn't even joined the Scouts or Jewish youth groups as a kid. In Israel, he approached the Kibbutz Movement, where officials used a battery of psychological tests to gauge his suitability for joining a community. "They weren't able to discover my inherent axe-murdering tendencies!" he joked. He was a young, healthy, well-educated, highly skilled, ideologically motivated immigrant from North America. He began speed-dating for the perfect home and toured a different kibbutz every other weekend. Communities with open doors, however, tended to be in demographic decline or economic crisis and desperate for young blood. David had no interest in a kibbutz that had abandoned its socialist ideals. "I was looking for a place that had not gone through a privatization process—and wasn't planning on it."

He moved to Kibbutz Lotan and marvelled at desert scenery straight out of *Lawrence of Arabia*. At Lotan, David apprenticed with Mike Kaplin, who had co-founded the Center for Creative Ecology, and fell under the spell of a new religion: ecological architecture. "It really moved me," he recalled. "I ended up spending the next decade being obsessed with it."

But not at Lotan. He was to live on the kibbutz for less than six months. One weekend, he caught a bus to Tel Aviv for a wedding. In his absence, the kibbutz secretary posted a notice, called a meeting and oversaw a vote in favour of an issue that troubled David: foreign labour. Other kibbutzes had outsourced their farm labour to Thai guest workers, who were often housed—and treated—like lesser citizens. Guest workers were a major issue on kibbutzes in the Arava Valley. Many members felt the agricultural arm of their kibbutzes couldn't stay profitable without cheap labour. On Lotan, David had argued against this. In a kibbutz democracy, any important decision was usually advertised a week in advance, so members could mull the consequences before the vote. This time, the decision was rushed through in mere days. David felt betrayed.

"Many people's commitment to human rights and against racism ranked lower than economic concerns," he said. "And the way of getting that decision approved was antidemocratic. What depressed me was that even in a community of 150 people there was still political manipulation. I realize that in a system of millions there will be a lot of abuse. That's why I want to live in community, so that we can have human-level interactions with each other and honest dialogue, not bureaucratic interactions. But that wasn't the case here."

After the decision to allow guest workers, he couldn't live on the kibbutz in good conscience. He wrote a long, emotional letter and left copies in every member's mailbox. Then he walked out of the desert Eden.

"At first, I didn't know what the solution was," he admitted. "I wanted there to be a community that was ecological and *really* socialist—not just socialist for the Jews."

Before leaving Lotan, David had articulated his evolving political philosophy to his boss, who gave him a copy of *The Dispossessed* by the science-fiction author Ursula K. Le Guin. In her novel, a tribe of austere anarchists live as colonists on a moon that circles a planet ruled, in stark contrast, by a decadent capitalist society. David felt inspired again. He read everything he could about anarchism and discovered a philosophical tradition deeper than the stereotypes of bomb-tossers and punk-rock anthems. "These are the principles that are important to me," he realized. "This is an accurate description of how the world should be." The self-sufficient cooperative society of equals mirrored ideas in Peter Kropotkin's classic manifesto *Mutual Aid*, the blueprint for the early kibbutz movement. In Israel, a hundred years of compromises had eroded these ideals beyond recognition. David realized he was frustrated living in a society that wasn't as good as it could be—and didn't want to be.

David returned to North America and apprenticed with reclusive eco-building gurus in mud-walled, straw-baled, solar-panelled, compost-toileted off-the-grid lairs. He learned how to handcraft cob houses. He studied biomimicry, the design philosophy inspired by examples from the natural world. A friend donated a video camera, so David recorded interviews as he travelled around the world to the meccas of natural building: the cob mansions of Dorset, England; the millennium-old rock-hewn cities in Ethiopia; the straw-roofed villages and mud mosques of Ghana; the adobe counterculture "earthships" in New Mexico. He edited the footage into a documentary extolling what he called "uncompromising ecological architecture." He had seen the future. And it was made of mud.

In 2006, he returned to Tel Aviv and organized a collective of eco-communards to start an off-the-grid settlement. For a hundred years, Zionist organizations had helped young Jews colonize the Promised Land. But a band of anarchists rejecting corporate capitalism?

No, thanks—not anymore. David's collective of Israeli eco-anarchists faced a dilemma. "We were too politically radical to get funds from the state, nor would some of us have wanted to," he said. "But there wasn't a critical mass of us to start from scratch."

Then David remembered visiting Kibbutz Samar, in the Arava Desert, not far from Lotan and Ketura. He returned to give a talk there about ecological building, stayed for 10 days and asked if he could remain longer. Samar had been founded in 1976 as a rejection of authority and bureaucracy—of the state, of the family, of the old kibbutz hierarchy. Its members were true anarchists. The kibbutz's economy was built on organic date plantations and members had rejected the "need" to recruit cheap Thai labour for the harvesting. It was perhaps the last kibbutz in Israel to hold to the original Zionist ideal of self labour: *Do the work yourself or not at all.*

———

Other communities had embraced a libertarian philosophy of almost total freedom, both in Israel and abroad, but few lasted more than a year or two. "Samar deserves its place in the communal equivalent of the *Guinness Book of World Records*," observed Daniel Gavron, in 2000, after a visit. Not everyone was impressed by Samar's woolly ways. In Tel Aviv, I asked a kibbutz leader and former member of the Israeli parliament about the anarchists in the Arava Valley. "Samar is *not* a kibbutz!" he exclaimed. "They're like Bedouins in the desert!"

Just the idea of Samar divided people. The kibbutz had been founded by young members from traditional kibbutzes disillusioned with the ideological drift of their homes, much like the pioneers of the urban kibbutz in Migvan. Samar's founders declined an offer to settle in the occupied Golan Heights and travelled instead to the desert. Here, away from prying eyes, they could discard their parents' mistakes.

Here, communal living would give people more freedom, not less. What they wanted was a blank slate—both freedom *to* and freedom *from*, in the famous distinction by philosopher Isaiah Berlin. Freedom to express their better selves. Freedom from bureaucratic rules. After retiring from public life to Kibbutz Sde Boker in the Negev Desert, David Ben-Gurion, Israel's founding prime minister, had written: "For those who make the desert bloom there is room for hundreds, thousands and even millions." The pioneers of Samar took him at his word.

It's hard to separate fact from legend in the story of Samar. On the kibbutz, no single authority, no guru set the rules or even said there were no rules. Such *laissez-faire* anarchism had been tried in communes and hippy outposts throughout North America and Europe. It usually imploded after a few years, when finances ran low and emotional tensions ran high. Love might be free; not much else was. Somehow the members of Samar made it work. They did away with the weekly work schedule and job rotation. Members decided when and where they laboured; if a kibbutznik needed help on a job, to milk the cows or pick the dates or scrub the kitchen, he or she made a request, stated the case, and took whomever would come. Usually, the work got done. Samar's financial philosophy was equally radical. In the traditional kibbutz system, every member received a tiny allowance while the kibbutz paid for living expenses. To buy anything extra, a member had to plead to the finance committee; the result of the vote was final. The tense, political and often humiliating experience made adult members feel like preteens asking their parents for a raise in allowance.

Samar said to hell with that. If members couldn't trust each other, their community was doomed, so they agreed to keep an open cash box. If someone needed to take a trip to Tel Aviv or Jerusalem, they could go into the dining room, flip open the lid, and—if enough money was there—remove the bus fare and maybe a few shekels for a falafel. The box was refilled with profits from the date orchards or other enterprises.

If the cash box was bare, everyone made do.

The common purse was a giant middle finger to the tragedy of the commons—the thought experiment that assumes when a resource can be accessed collectively, self-interested people will devour more than their fair share until the resource has been squandered. Conservatives believe that this proves our genes really are selfish and we should accept capitalism as natural law; some environmental activists use the theory to argue for state intervention before we consume all our natural resources. "The Tragedy of the Commons has no real technological solution," observed mathematical biologist Martin Nowak, an expert in the evolution of cooperation, "only one rooted in ethics and behaviour." Samar's experiment in radical trust turned Hardin's controversial theory upside-down by giving its members the freedom to help one another for the greater good of the kibbutz.

—

On Samar, David Sheen found an outlet for his restless energies amid the social, cultural and political life of the desert commune. "That's the way I live," he admitted. He held slideshows and films, talks and concerts. Inspired by his experiences at the Burning Man Festival in Nevada's Black Rock Desert, he tried to organize a similar event on Samar. He made an immediate impression on the kibbutz—and not always a welcome one.

David understood his communal faux pas. "What I did was the equivalent of walking up to your face and screaming. In the city, you have to be loud for anyone to hear you—there are so many competing messages. In a community, they don't have huge billboards, you don't have the same level of intense dialogue and debate. It's quiet. It's the desert. You have to be more measured in your discourse. Some people felt that I had come to the community and started preaching. Some people felt that I was talking too loud. Other people felt I had no right to do it all. They said, 'Only after living here for several years do you have a right to start talking about your opinions.'" Even an anarchist utopia has rules, apparently. "Obviously, I can't abide that," said David. "That's stymying voices. That's not cool. It's imperial to say, 'We'll take your labour but not your personal opinions.'"

When David applied for full membership, residents of Samar debated his suitability, whether his personality felt simpatico with the kibbutz. His friends could not sway the skeptics. The vote failed. David could remain living there as a non-member. But why bother? Who wants to live in a village where the majority of your neighbours don't value your voice and might not even want you around? It was a painful discovery. After a decade of searching, David thought that he had found his personal utopia, an organic Eden in the desert of Israel that was more than a mirage. Samar only had one problem: the kibbutz didn't want David.

—

David still lives in Israel. He copy edited for the left-wing newspaper *Haaretz* and produced documentaries and YouTube exposés. He fights the rightward political tilt in the country. During the "J14" economic protests in summer 2011, when young activists camped out in Tel Aviv and 500,000 people marched through the streets of Israel, David chronicled how even this mass revival of progressive ideals avoided any mention of the Occupation. His country continued to frustrate his ideals.

"Why do you keep being drawn back to Israel?" I asked. He seemed locked in a love-hate relationship that bordered on the codependent. "Do you consider yourself a Zionist? An eco-Zionist?"

"That's a loaded question," he replied. "Today, there is a new parlance. Yes, there is Zionist. There is also anti-Zionist. There is also non-Zionist. There is also post-Zionist."

David professed to be an "ambi-Zionist"—a Jew who has not firmly committed to Zionism, non-Zionism or anti-Zionism. "Someone who is still on the fence," he explained, "because they feel there are some positive elements to the word and some negative elements to it."

David still felt the tug of family and cultural history in Israel. It fuelled his extended argument with the divided nation. "I do feel a connection to the land." He laughed. "Call it education, call it brainwashing."

—

In late 2011, a year and a half after I first met David Sheen, I was back in Israel and curious if he had made any progress in his quest for community. He and his wife had moved from Tel Aviv into a rental unit in Jaffa, so I reunited with him under the clock tower at the entrance to the Old City. David was shooting activist videos about racist incidents against Ethiopian immigrants and the internment of Sudanese refugees. His wife was Jamaican-Canadian and often felt uncomfortable walking the streets of Tel Aviv. "She thinks that people here look at her like she is ugly," said David. "Over time, that wears you down."

The couple was planning to move to Dimona, a town of 33,000 in the Negev Desert. Dimona was also home to Israel's nuclear facilities and a community of so-called "Black Hebrews." In 1969, the 30 original Black Hebrews followed their charismatic leader from Chicago to Israel. They were African-Americans who believed they belonged to the lost tribe of Judah and lobbied for citizenship under Israel's Law of Return. More followed and stayed illegally in the country, where they forged a syncretic religion from Torah laws, African traditions and their own unique holidays. Orthodox rabbis never recognized their claims of ancestry; only a handful of the 3,000 residents ever received citizenship. In 1984, the Speaker of the Israeli parliament threatened to deport them with force; two years later, a standoff with the IDF nearly ended in bloodshed. And yet the Black Hebrews remained in Dimona until they became an accepted, if eccentric, facet of the nation's multicultural mosaic. "Your community is beloved in Israel," said President Shimon Peres on a visit in 2008. "Your destiny is our destiny." Their gospel choir tours Israel and overseas, while the locally grown, organic, vegan diet of the Black Hebrews has become so fashionable that they have opened restaurants in Jerusalem and Tel Aviv. A banner above their gate announces to new arrivals: *Welcome to the Village of Peace.*

"If you're talking utopian communities," David told me, "at least in Israel, I can think of few that are so exemplary."

Well, except for one hitch. According to David, the Black Hebrews remain a patriarchal cult of personality that treats women as second-class citizens. "They're old school," he said. "There are things that we can't accept." He and his wife were considering how to enjoy their company without joining the settlement. "If we move next to them, we could have the advantage of having them as a community—without living by their rules."

The injustices he witnessed on a daily basis in Tel Aviv and Jaffa, his own financial insecurity and awareness of getting older made David philosophical about the receding possibilities of utopia. Can we ever reframe how we live as a society to be more fair and less damaging to our planet?

"I used to think we could change *everywhere*—that we could create a small fractal to change everything. Then I thought, at least we could create something that could be a refuge from all the shit. Now, I'm at the point where I don't think I'm capable of doing that. Not for a community and not even for myself. So I'm willing to accept less shitty. Less cesspool in my life—that's my goal right now."

"That's not exactly a good bumper sticker," I suggested. "*A Life Less Shitty.*"

He laughed. "I shouldn't be a motivational speaker!"

The road from ideal to compromise, from utopia to suburbia, is a well-worn path. I'd seen it repeated on every kibbutz I'd visited; it pulls at every alternative community that dreams of creating a perfect society in an imperfect world. Building community will always be ad hoc and messy. David Sheen's frustrated quest for a flawless city upon the hill to call home was hardly unique. It reflected the century-long plot arc of an entire movement.

He nodded at the suggestion. "It really is the evolution of the kibbutz."

CHAPTER 18

Revival of Faith

"Tell me what you're hearing . . . other than the noise of the car."

I craned an ear out the passenger window. Bird song? A jackal's cry? Jets overhead? I detected nothing. That was the point. That was why Susan Levin and her family—her husband and their three sons— had moved from the suburbs of Washington, D.C., to the rocky hills south of Jerusalem. "It's totally, completely quiet out here."

Quiet—as in far from the car horns and cellphone chatter of Tel Aviv. Quiet—as in the whisper of wind through pine stands and olive groves. Not quiet if you mean free of controversy or conflict. Far from *that* kind of quiet.

We were idling in Gush Etzion, one of Israel's earliest expansions into the Palestinian West Bank. Even in the most optimistic fantasies of a two-state solution, nobody believes Jewish settlers will ever leave this land. A year before my visit, Prime Minister Benjamin Netanyahu planted a tree and promised residents on nearby Kibbutz Kfar Etzion,

"The message is clear—we are here, and we will stay here. We plant and build—this is an inseparable part of the State of Israel forever."

I had travelled to the Etzion Bloc to understand how the Occupation had taken root after the Six-Day War. I wanted to witness how religious Jews had assumed the utopian mantle of secular kibbutzniks as the nation's new pioneers—and perverted that original vision in the eyes of left-wing critics. "Settlers are a fanatical freedom-hating Hezbollah," novelist and former kibbutznik Amos Oz warned in 1989. "They threaten to destroy all that is holy." And yet the possibility for peace, or its opposite, in Israel and Palestine rested largely in their hands.

Levin steered her red Mazda up to the electric gates of Bat Ayin, a religious settlement of 200 families on a promontory that overlooks the coastal plain. Somewhere below us ran the Green Line—the border set by the 1949 armistice that divided Israel and the now-occupied West Bank. The hodgepodge of modular bungalows and mobile homes looked unfinished around the edges. Like the Green Line, I couldn't tell where Bat Ayin began or ended. Unlike other Jewish settlements in the Palestinian territories, residents refused to erect a perimeter fence. It was an ideological choice, even though you could walk to the Arab villages in the valley below. I was struck by how, in Israel and Palestine, dots on a map I'd assumed might take an hour to link by car were only a stone's throw apart—and how neighbours often measured that distance by throwing stones. "It's a small country," Susan chided. "Canada is *not*."

She had a point. Critics of Israel overlook the problem of proximity when they watch the conflict on TVs or laptops. Geographical density complicates any peace settlement. The colonial legacy in Israel and Palestine always lies underfoot. Layers of history hide just a spade's scrape below the surface. And antagonists live within earshot. In North America, we've shunted the dark history of our settler past into textbooks and relocated our First Peoples—the survivors of epidemics and genocides—onto reserves far from our cities. In the hills of the West Bank, the lives of Jews and Arabs still overlap. Fences *can* make good neighbours here. But the settlers of Bat Ayin had no interest in being neighbourly.

"They don't have a perimeter fence," explained Susan, "because their attitude is, 'This is our land, this is our country. If you fence us off, you're saying anything outside the fence isn't ours.' It's totally philosophical. It's part of living here. They don't have fences between neighbours either." Kibbutzes were often fenceless, too. Only after the terrorist attack did Kibbutz Shamir wrap its perimeter in barbed wire. Only after privatization did other kibbutzes set off internal properties with pickets or wire. In Israel and Palestine, *not* putting up a barrier made a statement, too. "If I put up a fence, I say, *That is somebody else's*," Susan told me. "And who's that somebody else? The people who are sworn to kill me! So I should *give* them it? Because they're not nice to me?" She scoffed. "You don't give gifts to people who tell you, from morning to night, they're going to kill you."

The residents of Bat Ayin, I later learned, were notorious troublemakers of their own. Organic-farming Orthodox Jews founded the community in 1989. It has housed members of a Jewish terrorist group known as the Bat Ayin Underground, implicated in drive-by shootings and attempted bombings at Palestinian mosques and schools. In one incident, a terrorist left an explosive-laden baby carriage in front of an Arab girls' academy. The Underground's settlers conducted so-called price tag attacks as a response to Palestinian unrest or the dismantling of illegal Jewish settlements. An eye for an eye. In 2010, after two fatal attacks on residents, including the axe murder of a 13-year-old boy by a Palestinian infiltrator, Bat Ayin residents fired their own security chief rather than submit to the fence he insisted they erect. *This land is our land. All of it.*

We slowed at the yellow metal gate until a bored IDF soldier, reluctantly hired by the settlement, pressed a button to let us through.

Government law required the community without a fence to have a gate. "It reminds me of—what's that movie?—*Blazing Saddles*," said Susan, with a laugh. "They're in the middle of the desert and they stop and put up a tollbooth!"

The residents of Bat Ayin hardly seemed like happy-go-lucky cow-pokes from a Mel Brooks comedy. Many were artists and musicians, into recycling and yoga, opposed to the evils of television—or anything made by Germans. They were also racist ideologues who refused to hire Arab labour or let Palestinians set foot near the community. Youths from Bat Ayin vandalized the orchards and farm equipment of nearby villages. A year earlier, a gang descended upon Beit Ommar, opened fire on villagers in the grape fields and killed a 17-year-old student. After I visited, masked settlers beat the Palestinian driver of a delivery truck and pepper-sprayed two Israeli soldiers manning Bat Ayin's gate. The IDF demanded the attackers be prosecuted and refused to guard the settlement any longer.

The West Bank settlers of Bat Ayin didn't need a fence. They needed a *cage*.

—

A lone pine rises from a hill near Kibbutz Kfar Etzion. Everyone recognizes it. The tree symbolizes the loss and longing and rebirth of Jewish settlement in the area. It's part of the history I watched on a film at the Gush Etzion Visitor Center at the kibbutz—history as written by the victors. The documentary justified the history of Jewish settlement of Gush Etzion. Jewish immigrants had established the first farming community in 1927 but abandoned the site after Arab riots. A second attempt in 1934 was rebuffed by more Palestinian unrest. Finally, pioneers established Kfar Etzion as a religious kibbutz in 1943. "I can still hear the death trains from the execution camps," intoned an actor/

pioneer, urging his comrades to create a home for Holocaust survivors. "Here was the path of the patriarchs. Hills that were familiar to David and the prophets. Here in the mountains the Bible comes to life." From the Old Testament to the Final Solution, the kibbutz joined the highs and lows of the Jewish epic. The Arab villagers in the nearby valleys remained a footnote to this drama.

Black-and-white footage described the War of 1948. Letters from kibbutzniks and transcripts from radio dispatches evoked the siege of the kibbutz by Arab legionnaires and villagers, the evacuation of women and children, and the final battle on May 13, 1948, a day before Israel's official Declaration of Independence. "Our comrades fought until the last bullet . . ." The narrator then catalogued the massacre of 129 Jewish soldiers and kibbutzniks. Women and wounded defenders huddled in a bunker, into which a grenade was tossed. Four survivors were taken prisoner. Arab villagers burned the kibbutz to the ground. The lone tree marked the community's absence—and its sacrifice—for the next two decades. The massacre cast a shadow over the victory of the War of Independence. The fall of Kfar Etzion became the Alamo of the new Jewish state. The abandoned kibbutz remained lost beyond the borders of the Hashemite Kingdom of Jordan for nearly 20 more years.

The projector's beam dimmed, and the screen retracted into the ceiling to reveal a hidden room. The narrator's voice filled the space: "The public is invited to descend to the bunker." And there it was, the scene of the massacre: two square holes in the stone floor, crisscrossed with bent and broken rebar, as though the shock and smoke of the explosion had dispersed only minutes ago. I peered into the depths and felt the same dread I'd experienced, years before, when I walked the ruins and reconstructions of Auschwitz-Birkenau in rural Poland. History released its shadows. I was standing on stones where human blood had spilled.

A new film flickered on. "I know of no campaign more tragic or more heroic than the fight for Gush Etzion . . ." The words of David Ben-Gurion, Israel's woolly haired founding father, echoed in the room. "Isolated, deprived of all hope, the defenders of the Bloc stood their ground knowing they were defending a holy site—the heart of Israel, the eternal city Jerusalem. If a Jewish Jerusalem exists today, Israel owes its gratitude to the defenders of the Etzion Bloc." Colour footage showed the red-tiled rooftops of the modern kibbutz. Children played on the lawns. A kibbutznik struck a hoe into a field. The Hebrew Marlboro Man. I'd seen similar images a hundred times before. "We have returned to our homeland," intoned the narrator. "Today those of Etzion are returning, your defenders have answered the call. Bringing peace, bringing light to the centre. Never more, never more shall we fall . . ."

—

I exited the theatre into the fading light of an early December evening and walked the grounds of Kfar Etzion until I found Yaacov Taube. My guide was a stocky kibbutznik, originally from Montreal, in an olive parka and blue-and-white *kippa*. In Canada, he'd joined the Bnei Akiva religious youth movement and travelled to Israel in 1966 to live on a kibbutz. "I was enthused by the way of life, the simplicity, and the cooperative ideal," he recalled. "At that time, the kibbutz in Israel was a lot more fashionable than it is today."

The Six-Day War erupted—and everything changed. By the cease-fire, the Israeli military had overrun all the land west of the Jordan River, as well as the Golan Heights, the Gaza Strip and the Sinai Peninsula. The Jewish nation no longer formed an awkward geographical barbell, a thin stretch of land along the Mediterranean Coast that linked the Galilee and the Negev Desert. It had room to breathe. And expand.

Secular kibbutzniks, not religious nationalists, were the first to cross the Green Line and settle on Palestinian territory. Members of

United Kibbutz Movement established the first kibbutz in the captured territories on July 14, 1967, on an abandoned Syrian base in the Golan Heights, not far from Kibbutz Shamir. Further south, religious leaders and children of the original kibbutzniks lobbied Prime Minister Levi Eshkol for permission to resettle the Etzion Bloc. He gave his blessing. On September 26, 1967, the orphans of Kfar Etzion returned home and rebuilt the kibbutz. Yaacov Taube arrived with his own young family from Canada four years later. He watched other Jewish settlements spring up in the Etzion Bloc and throughout the West Bank. A network of communities and checkpoints and private roadways, which allow settlers to circumvent Arab villages, now transect the Palestinian Territories—what the settlers call Judea and Samaria.

"Kfar Etzion is a success story. We have this faith that things are moving ahead that still guides me today," said Yaacov, as we strolled in the dusk. He pointed out igloo-shaped concrete dormitories, the synagogue and fields that extended into the gloaming horizon. "It's one of the reasons why I feel that Israel should not give up any part of the Territories."

Advocates for peace on the Israeli Left sometimes argue that, if the status quo persists and a Palestinian state isn't created in the West Bank and Gaza, then Jews will become a minority in their own land. Yaacov had different ideas. In 1948, Ben-Gurion declared independence. The Arab states promised to attack and did. "And we're still around," said Yaacov. "Not only are we still around but we are thriving. And doing a better job of it than the Arab states around us." He noted how the brief Arab Spring was collapsing into a long winter of intrigue and suffering. By contrast, in Jerusalem that afternoon, he saw roads packed with vehicles. "A lot of the cars on the roads are Palestinian cars," said Yaacov. "When I came to Kfar Etzion, there were no Arab cars. Every Arab that you saw on the road was riding a donkey. Today, you don't see donkeys anymore on the road."

The hardline views of Yaacov didn't surprise me. When I lived on Shamir, kibbutzniks organized an educational debate in which volunteers played the roles—and researched viewpoints—of politicians across the ideological spectrum. I got cast as a right-wing member of parliament, along the hawkish lines of Ariel Sharon. "No negotiations with the PLO—they are a terrorist group whose goal is the destruction of Israel!" I argued. "No setting up a Palestinian state in the West Bank and Gaza. They're too near Jerusalem and Tel Aviv, and a Palestinian state will degenerate into civil war, like in Lebanon." I knew all the talking points; they hadn't changed in 20 years.

The sky had darkened. A winter chill settled on the kibbutz. Yaacov Taube wasn't especially interested in my opinion. Even if he hadn't been born here, he maintained the gruff, no-nonsense manner of the Israeli *sabra*. But he didn't fit the caricature of the raving religious nationalist either. He believed in the communal ideal—just not with his Arab neighbours. Any peace plan, I realized, needed to reckon with the opinions of Yaccov Taube and settlers like him: more than 300,000 now lived in the West Bank, nearly 200,000 had moved into Palestinian East Jerusalem and 20,000 Jewish Israelis occupied the Golan Heights. Some were frightening zealots, like the Bat Ayin Underground, committed to overturning any peace process; another radical group of so-called hilltop youth set up an illegal Jewish outpost on Palestinian land and called it Kibbutz Givat Menachem—in the vain hope that Israeli authorities wouldn't tear down a "kibbutz." Many more settlers were rough-edged pragmatists, united by a religious vision of Greater Israel as home to the People of the Book. They looked askance at the blue-sky utopian plans of the Israeli Left and the demands of international activists to roust their families off land they saw as a birthright. Maybe the day would come, as it had in Gaza, when the Israeli military will forcibly remove Jewish settlers from the West Bank in the name of peace. But it was unlikely to happen in the Etzion Bloc. History had given this place roots deeper even than those of the lone pine. Learning to live together, on disputed land, was the future of Kfar Etzion. It had to be.

—

On a five-day trip when I was a volunteer, we visited Masada. At four in the morning, after sleeping under the stars, Itzik Kahana and our other guides from Kibbutz Shamir urged us into boots and sneakers, and we marched up the narrow Snake Trail to the high plateau so we could witness the sun lift over the Jordan Rift from the citadel's flat-topped peak. I knew more about the Siege of Masada and the mass suicide of its defenders in 74 CE than almost any event in Jewish history. I grew up during the great age of the network miniseries—*Roots*, *Shogun*, *The Thornbirds*—but my favourite was *Masada*. It had swords, togas, a desert castle, huge war machines and a tragic ending. Parts of the reconstructed dirt ramp from the set remained; modern movie magic mixed with a nearly 2,000-year-old historical site. We trudged up the steep pathway and tripped on the broken steps. The cliff loomed above us in the dark. I half-expected to find Peter O'Toole, in a polished breastplate and Roman tunic, brooding at the top.

In the first slivers of daylight, the distant mountains of Jordan looked like piles of spilled salt. We saw for the first time the towering vantage on which we now stood, and far below, the false oasis of the Dead Sea. IDF soldiers often climbed the summit at daybreak to celebrate a heritage of Jewish resistance; the army conducted swearing-in ceremonies there, too. "There almost seems to be a sort of mystical presence on the top of the mountain," wrote one historian of the gravity of the "Masada myth."

The morning glow gave way to the glare of a desert sun, and Itzik led us through the remnants of the stone compound and offered his own interpretation. The fortress, he told us, had been built in King

Herod's time and served little military value. Herod had married into the Maccabees; when he died, he left his kingdom to his nephew. "That's because Herod was paranoid," explained Itzik, "and already had his sons and wife killed." The Romans let ambassadors administer the territory of *Palestina*. After Herod's death, they decided to enforce Imperial law directly. The Jews didn't appreciate the move. A faction known as the Zealots incited a Palestine-wide revolt. "Like a successful intifada," suggested Andrew, an older Australian volunteer who had hitchhiked into the occupied West Bank and witnessed the Palestinian uprising up close—too close. Arab villagers helped him escape when Palestinian youths started clashing with Israeli soldiers.

Masada's uprising could hardly be described as a success. The Romans mustered legions and captured Jewish towns. They added to the crucifixion count and stormed Jerusalem. Josephus Flavius, a Jewish historian in the Romans' employ, recorded events. Only through his book, *The Jewish War*, do we know much about how the Romans snuffed the revolt. Even with these facts, not everyone agrees what Masada *means*. In the heroic version, the settlers of Masada were the last free Jews to hold out against insurmountable odds, like the rebels in the Warsaw Ghetto during the Final Solution. When the siege machines of the Roman Tenth Legion bulled down the walls, the selfless defenders of Masada chose death over bondage.

That wasn't the story Itzik told. In his version, the thousand-strong gang who holed up on Masada were more zealous than the Zealots, a splinter off a splinter sect: radical, violent, willing to kidnap or kill moderate rivals or "collaborators." They took their Latin name, the Sicarii, from daggers they concealed under robes to perform assassinations. The Romans might have left the shiv-toting thugs alone in their mountain hideaway, but the Masadans kept plundering nearby villages. In an attack on Ein Gedi, they chased away the men and killed scores of women and children. The visitor centre at Masada left this gory factoid off historical plaques. The Romans decided to mop up the bothersome redoubt of Jewish resistance. They sealed off escape routes, battered down the stone wall and set fire to the wooden reinforcing wall. Masada's leader told his followers that death was the noble option—and his men would execute anyone who didn't agree. Drink the Kool-Aid, or else. The Sicarii killed their fellow Jews and then fell on their swords, with gusto. There was no evidence of any battle at Masada. Hiding in a cavern, two women and five children survived the mass slaughter to tell the story. Hardly the makings of myth.

Two readings of history were etched in the rocks. Remember Masada. Like the Alamo. Or like the Jonestown Massacre. Heroic epic or cautionary tale. Take your pick.

"Some people say that Israel suffers from a Masada Complex," Itzik told us. The Masada myth is a complex complex. Does the isolated fortress represent the collective resolve of a persecuted people surrounded by enemies, a nation under siege? The David-beats-Goliath myth that has held sway from the War of Independence to the present day? Or does the message of Masada foreshadow a darker future? Does it warn that the irrational forces of religion and nationalism might goad the Jewish state into civil war and another suicidal *cul-de-sac*?

—

"It was very cloudy, like in a legend . . ."

Three decades later, Eliaz Cohen could still picture the scene, his first memory of Kibbutz Kfar Etzion. A bride and groom strode beneath a moody sky toward a traditional four-posted wedding tent—trailed by a long retinue of turkeys. An older relative worked in the turkey run, where the birds followed him everywhere, and so they trotted along when he attended the wedding, too. Eliaz, a boy, didn't understand the connection. "I thought that at every Jewish wedding there were turkeys," he recalled, with a laugh, "that followed the bride and the groom to the *chuppah*!"

Kfar Etzion remained for Eliaz a place of wonder, part of what he calls his "pre-biography." Several relatives had been evacuated from the kibbutz during the siege of 1948 and before the massacre of its defenders. "I was born into this story," he told me, as we sat in the library of the *yeshiva*, next to the kibbutz's synagogue. Eliaz, nearly 40, wore a checkered flannel shirt, with shoulder-length coils of rust-coloured hair, topped by a knit *kippa*, like an Orthodox grunge rocker. He spoke with an excitability that peaked in peals of laughter. If Yaacov Taube reflected the settlers' ideological certainty, Eliaz Cohen was the movement's suppressed conscience. He was man of contradictions: a modern poet and a student of the ancient Torah; a right-wing settler and a left-wing peacenik; a believer in the right of the Jewish people to live in Judea and Samaria—the occupied West Bank—and their responsibility to share the land of Israel and Palestine with their neighbours. He offended all sides of the political spectrum.

Eliaz was born in 1972 in the Galilee. When he was seven, his parents moved to the northern West Bank—what religious Jews call Samaria. Growing up, he developed a connection to the landscape of the Hebrew Bible and heard the siren call of the settler movement. "At the age of 15, I fell in love with Hanan Porat," he recalled. An intense religious student and aspiring poet, Eliaz discovered a spiritual mentor in Porat, the charismatic rabbi-politician who resurrected Kibbutz Kfar Etzion in 1967 and opened the gate for thousands of Jewish settlers to move into the West Bank. Eliaz first heard Hanan Porat talk at his *yeshiva*. By then, the rabbi was a legend. A child of Kibbutz Kfar Etzion, Porat had been evacuated to Jerusalem before its fall; his father had arranged the convoys and had survived, too, unlike most of the other male kibbutzniks. Porat matured into a fiery advocate for resettling the entire West Bank. In 1967, he re-established Kfar Etzion on the grounds of the old kibbutz and later helped to settle a Jewish religious community in the heart of Arab Hebron—a source of immediate controversy and future bloodshed. In the early 1970s, he helped to found Gush Emunim ("Bloc of the Faithful"), a religious organization that advocated extending the borders of Greater Israel all the way to the Jordan River, and served as a member of parliament, in various religious parties, for nearly 15 years. He bent the future of Israel to his iron will.

Rabbi Porat overturned the stereotype of a bookish, bespectacled, bearded Torah scholar. The young Porat had the muscular presence of a rock star, with a *kippa*-topped mane of dark hair and a beatific smile. A famous photo reprinted with his obituary—he died of cancer two months before I visited his kibbutz—showed a young Porat, in jeans and an army parka, held aloft by his followers, his arms spread to the heavens, like a football coach carried off the field by adoring fans. To religious settlers, Porat was a holy visionary and a national hero. For secular Israelis, he was the mischief-maker who had detonated the prospects for peace.

"What was it about his personality that was so attractive?" I asked.

"If you could close your eyes and imagine King David," said Eliaz, "beauty, charisma, wisdom, sensitivity, all mixed together in one personality. It was very strong." At the same time, the young poet also discovered socialism and recognized a confluence between his religious studies and political readings. "It captured my soul," Eliaz said. "I understood that the Torah is socialist."

Eliaz moved to Kfar Etzion, at the age of 23, after completing army service and getting married. He found a kibbutz in the hills built around the pillars of spiritual faith and mutual aid. "As a religious Jew, it is the precise echo I hear from the Torah and the prophets." He worked for years as a social worker until one of his poetry collections, depicting his arguments with God, got him fired from a job in an ultra-Orthodox community. He now focused on social activism and teaching creative writing. In the summer of 2011, when social justice protests erupted across the country, Eliaz walked the nation with a Bible in hand and a message on his lips: "The real protesters for social justice are in *this* book," he preached, as he read aloud passages from Isaiah and Josiah, Zachariah and Amos. He reminded listeners that, more than the laws of the Sabbath, the essence of the prophets' message was social justice. "If Isaiah was alive today," said Eliaz, "he would be a member of a religious kibbutz."

As a boy, Eliaz played in a grove of five ancient olive trees near a Palestinian village. He and his friends would wrap their arms around the gnarled and twisted trunks as old as Abraham, or so they'd been told. One huge trunk had a split deep enough that a boy could slide inside its dark skin and feel as though its roots ran up through his sandals. Years later, he returned to show his own children the landscape of his youth. Instead of the olive grove, Eliaz found the Separation Wall dividing the Jewish settlement and the adjacent Arab village.

That wall asserts its presence to any traveller to the West Bank: a blank slate on the Israeli side, a canvas for graffiti and satirical slogans, by Palestinian youth and celebrity artists like Banksy, on its opposite face. The silhouette of a girl floating upwards with a handful of balloons. A protester hurling a bouquet of flowers. *Make Hummus Not Walls.* Or simply: *CTRL + ALT + DELETE.* The poet recognized the symbolic tension between the military barrier and what it concealed. "The two symbols currently fighting over the land: the tree and the wall," Eliaz wrote. "Becoming rooted—and separation. The old and the new. In my mind's eye, I see how, in somewhat different times, we approach hand in hand, a wall of people: Palestinian villagers and the children of the settlements, left-wing activists and the right-wing believers. And in the name of the solitary olive tree that has not yet been uprooted, we defeat the wall."

The Tree versus the Wall. It seemed a fitting image for a poet from a West Bank kibbutz whose famous emblem of resistance and rebirth was a lone pine.

Eliaz knew words held power—and not just as poetry. On reserve duty, he had to guard a checkpoint within the West Bank, one of the many sites of humiliation for Palestinians, where they were often detained and interrogated or delayed for hours by young, tense Israeli soldiers. Eliaz wanted to dispel that mood of perpetual confrontation, so he composed a Hebrew-to-Arabic primer, an etiquette manual for fellow soldiers that rephrased routine orders. "Give me your ID!" became "Good morning, may I please see your ID?" Suspicious Palestinians smiled tentatively and returned the greeting. A small, subtle gesture of humanity lubricated the crude military bureaucracy of the Occupation.

Eliaz believed the fusion of spirituality and socialism in the religious kibbutz movement could bridge his divided nation. The devout in Israel, he lamented, had turned spiritual practice inward. "They are working to be the slaves of God—not to care about the poor, the widows, the non-Jews who are among us." He tried to live by another vision, the artist as sacred seer. "It's from the same basic philosophy that every human being, for me, is the way to meet God," he said. "To see the other eye is the way we have to see the face of God—whether you are religious or secular, or a Jew or Palestinian." It sounded to me like the idea, and ideals, of another poet, the Romantic visionary John Keats, whose notion of "negative capability" suggested an artist's ability to transcend set ways of seeing and thinking about the world.

Most kibbutzniks I had met viewed religion as an obstacle to peace. Theodor Herzl had warned about the dangers of religion in his blueprint for utopia. "Shall we end by having a theocracy? No, indeed. Faith unites us, knowledge gives us freedom," he wrote, in *The Jewish State*. "We shall keep our priests within the confines of their temples in the same way as we shall keep our professional army within the confines of their barracks." In modern Israel, religious parties wielded great power and influence, in part due to proportional representation. They have been rewarded with subsidies for ultra-Orthodox schools, *kosher* laws imposed on secular citizens, and funding to build settlements in the Occupied Territories.

On Kfar Etzion, I met a poet-preacher with an inclusive vision in his faith. When Eliaz Cohen read the Bible, he told me he saw a Promised Land that cannot stand bloodshed, cannot stand social inequity, cannot stand corruption. He understood that his people were here as a privilege. His voice quavered as he described how social justice was written into the Biblical contract between the Jewish people and the land of Israel. "I think that the covenant between God and Abraham includes this because when I open the Bible—" Eliaz crossed the library to locate a bilingual copy and flipped to a passage; he looked up and noticed my raised eyebrows. "In other countries, it's a kind of mysticism what I'm saying, but I believe it!" Eliaz viewed Kibbutz Kfar Etzion not as an immovable obstacle to peace but as a source of inspiration for both sides in the Conflict. After the military victory of 1967, the orphans and refugees of Kfar Etzion were allowed the right to return to their former homes. Jordanians had never settled the abandoned kibbutz; nobody needed to be displaced. "The unique characteristics of the return to Kfar Etzion offer a model for returns yet to come—this time, perhaps, returns by Palestinians," Eliaz wrote. "We must not allow further dispossessions of residents of this land, whether Jewish or Arab, anywhere between the Jordan River and the Mediterranean Sea."

A land haunted by its past didn't need to remain lost in the nightmare of history. A return *could* happen. The Jewish people had returned to their ancestral home. So could the Palestinians. That was the poet's reading—unconventional by most standards—of the holy texts. Eliaz wondered if a collective awakening was on the horizon. He was inspired by the street protests in the summer of 2011: 500,000 people, speaking out against economic injustice. "It's a kind of miracle," he said. Rightwing governments and the rise of capitalist individualism had quashed the social solidarity of the country's early years. "Social activists almost gave up."

Kibbutz Kfar Etzion continued to inspire and to defy optimism. Eliaz had published a collection of poems, with English translations, titled *Hear O Lord: Poems from the Disturbances of 2000–2009*. The poems were soulful, searching, lyrical investigations of his emotional landscape during the violent upheaval of the Second Intifada. They spoke of angst sparked by the removal of the Jewish settlers from Gaza, and the tense relationship between Jews and Palestinians in the West Bank and Israel. Instead of one-sided polemic, Eliaz transformed difficult material into deeply searching verse.

And yet tragedy refused to abandon Kfar Etzion. In 2014, three young yeshiva students—two studying at Kfar Etzion—hitchhiked from an intersection near the kibbutz. They were kidnapped by a pair of Palestinians, killed and their bodies dumped in a shallow grave. By the time they were found, three weeks later, reprisals and revenge attacks had jumped from the West Bank to Gaza and sparked another summer of bombing and bloodshed. Another catastrophe to transfix and perplex the world.

In the midst of the fighting in Gaza, Eliaz and Ali Abu Awwad, a Palestinian activist, organized a group called Choose Life to bring together settlers from Kfar Etzion and nearby Arab villagers. They talked and fasted and demonstrated that religion could unite their peoples, too. "We're all tied to children in one way or another, and it hurts us in the deepest place," Eliaz told a reporter. "It brings us back to our diaphragms, to a place that twists and turns and brings people in. And now there's the larger story of Gaza, and we're in this loop. It's something larger than us, and it feels like a massive earthquake. You feel very small, like there's nothing you can do."

CHAPTER 19

Boxing Hope

I leaned in and stared at a city trapped in a terrarium. The civic diorama within the exhibition case reminded me of Miniature World, a ticky-tacky attraction back home in Canada, where half-bored tourists paid to gawk at scale models of historical scenes encased behind finger-print-smudged Plexiglas: Dickens' grotty London, a colonial timber camp, a travelling circus, the stilted cabana of the Swiss Family Robinson. The Miniature World in front of me now was not a Lilliputian version of the past but rather a vision of the near-future. A horseshoe arrange-ment of Legoland apartment towers spilled down an AstroTurf slope atop a billiards-sized table. Puny windows glowed as though inhabited by yuppie leprechauns. Matchbox cars idled on curving lanes. Artificial trees dotted the promenades and marked the borders of this city caught in a bell jar.

I was looking at Rawabi—or at least an architectural model for the biggest construction project in the history of the Palestinian people.

One day the "green city" in the West Bank would house 40,000 residents in 23 different neighbourhoods.

On a nearby wall, a bank of nine LCD screens brought the model to life. Video-game images swooped into view. A cartoon child tossed a paper airplane that dove through the alleys and arcades, past shopfronts and down broad avenues. It looked like a generic pitch for a mega-development, a sanitized fantasy of domestic perfection, the messy bits of urban life left in the delete bin. And yet Rawabi—Arabic for "The Hills"—promised a better future for the Palestinian people of the occupied West Bank. It was an architectural moon shot. A road out of the limbo they have been locked in for the last half-century. A hundred years after the first kibbutz broke ground, Rawabi was the Palestinians' opportunity to build a new way of life from the ground up.

—

Leaving Jerusalem, the first thing I noticed was the Separation Wall. And soccer balls. First one. Then another. And a third. On the road to Ramallah the minibus skirted the edge of the towering concrete barrier, up to eight metres high, and I counted the grubby, half-deflated playground orbs, caught in a shelf of barbed-wire that ran near the top of the Wall that divided Israel from the occupied West Bank. Perhaps a school playground or soccer pitch was on the far side, but I could only see the lost balls, 10 or more—along with sneakers and shredded plastic bags—caught in the wire screen and fading in the sun and the smog.

As Eliaz Cohen discovered, the Wall is a concrete emblem of the divide between Palestinians and Israeli Jews. If Rawabi represented hope for the future, the 700-kilometre fortification—nearly two-thirds complete—was an attempt to bunker down and accept the Conflict, to keep the two sides apart. What you called the barrier was a political litmus test: the Security or Anti-Terrorist Fence (favoured by most Israelis and their supporters), the Separation or West Bank Barrier (used by journalists and Wikipedia editors), the Segregation or Apartheid Wall (preferred by Palestinians and solidarity activists).

At the Qalandia checkpoint, I expected long lines and military scrutiny and guns and X-ray screens and questions. I had my passport ready. Instead, our bus wheeled through a roundabout, passed an empty guardhouse and shuttled alongside the concrete barrier. Then the Wall retreated in our rear-view mirror, as we headed north, past shops and street stalls and the thick traffic on the road to Ramallah. I disembarked not far from Al-Manara Square, the central traffic circus. A giant's chair, lacquered in the baby-blue of the United Nations, had been erected in anticipation of the Palestinian Authority's bid, in the fall of 2011, for a seat at the UN. That plan set off hand-wringing in Jerusalem, Washington and New York. As Palestinian officials lined up support, diplomats exchanged threats about the potential damage of unilateral action. President Obama wielded a Security Council veto like a sword over the dream of a Palestinian nation. The Israeli press stoked fears of new violence, even a Third Intifada, if the bid for international sympathy failed. Or if it succeeded.

In the end, the UN ploy was much ado about nothing. Mahmoud Abbas, the Palestinian president, submitted a bid that was debated and retracted and put on hold and . . . well, it was hard to follow what happened as the bureaucratic digestive system of the United Nations swallowed the motion. Nobody danced in the streets of Ramallah or Nablus. No bombs detonated either. The low-grade protests against the Wall continued. So did the construction of Jewish settlements in East Jerusalem and the West Bank. The Big Blue Chair, with its UN emblem, sat empty amid the traffic and pedestrian flow of the square. I watched a curious teenager shimmy up a leg to relax on the high perch. A few months later, the chair collapsed in a winter storm.

—

The labyrinthine streets of Ramallah felt like a roller coaster stuck in low gear: San-Francisco-steep rises and drops clogged by L.A.-esque traffic snarls. It was a lively city, the Tel Aviv of the West Bank, but I understood the urge to escape and start from scratch. North of the city, an abandoned Israeli checkpoint stood at the side of the road; a slit-windowed watchtower remained in case the Israeli army decided to return. The uneasy truce between Israel and the Palestinian Authority, which coordinated security and policing throughout the West Bank, made the dream of Rawabi possible. Green banners on lampposts advertised, in stylized Arabic and English, the route to the future city.

George Rafidi, the marketing manager for Rawabi, was a stout and quick-smiling Christian from Ramallah who had worked in Houston, where he had acquired his fluent English and the habit of dreaming big. Near the gates, George pointed across the valley to the high fence and white bungalows of Ateret, a religious settlement of more than 800 Jewish residents, founded in 1981. At first, the settlers had threatened workers at Rawabi. Construction pressed on. Protests dwindled. Did the settlers make peace with their future neighbours? "It's not like they accepted it," he explained. "They have to live with it. Rawabi is all on Palestinian land."

He ushered me into the office of Amir Dajani, the deputy managing director of Rawabi. Amir had worked on development projects for USAID and the European Commission and now oversaw the daily progress of turning a blueprint into reality. I told him I was researching modern utopias, and he dared me to name a more ambitious project anywhere in the world: "Who else is building a city of 40,000?" His refrain: Rawabi would create a modern, sustainable city and demonstrate that the entrepreneurial spirit of his people could never be crushed by the Occupation.

Many people hoped he was right. Many, too, expected Rawabi to fail.

When Amir had joined the project four years earlier, he met with the other managers. The brainstorming session was led by Bashar Masri, the Palestinian-American businessman behind the entire development. As a teenager in Nablus in the late 1980s, Masri had been jailed by the IDF during the First Intifada. He later studied in the U.S. and made his fortune as a real-estate developer in the Arab states. Massar, his holding company, had arranged two-thirds of the $1 billion financing from the state of Qatar, hired an international consulting firm to draft a master plan, and enticed Palestinian architects, managers and engineers home from their jobs in various Gulf states to manage the project. They were all practical men—and many women, too—problem solvers with an eye for detail and a calculator at ready. None was prone to fuzzy predictions. They listed potential pitfalls—political, economic, logistical—of creating a city in the Occupied Territories. The catalogue grew. And the builders of Rawabi knocked off each obstacle.

First, there was the question of the land. Getting a building permit for a renovation was a hassle for most Palestinians. Erecting an entire city? Planners examined the jigsaw puzzle of zoning designations in the West Bank, gerrymandered since the Oslo II Accord of 1995 into a quilt known as Areas A, B and C. They found a 1,556-acre patch north of Ramallah, the second biggest property in Area A, the jurisdiction overseen by the Palestinian Authority rather than the Israeli army. Determining who owned each parcel of land was an administrative odyssey of Kafka-esque proportions. Lawyers and paralegals tracked down deeds and absentee landowners and consolidated patchwork acreages from more than 2,000 families into a single footprint. The process took four years. "It's a pure reflection of the Palestinian question," Amir explained. "There are people who left after the war and could not come back, and so their properties were not properly registered."

Then began the creative part: designing a city. Every architect sustains a childhood fantasy to build a metropolis from scratch; few get the chance. Local planners teamed with university experts and international consultants, and interviewed families curious about Rawabi. They debated how to embed modern infrastructure into a 45-degree slope. They worried about building a walkable, energy-saving "green city" without making it too expensive for middle-class Palestinians. They debated how to integrate traditional Arab motifs into contemporary urban design and build a community that didn't look like the despised Israeli settlements, with their signature white walls and red-tiled roofs. By fusing elements of the modern city with Palestinian culture and tradition, the architects wanted to ensure that the identity of Rawabi didn't feel alien to new residents. They studied the alleys, walkways, arches, windows and overall design of the old cities of Jerusalem, Nablus and Hebron. They noticed how the basic unit of these cities is a neighbourhood—*hai* in Arabic—with a unique entrance and an average of 15 buildings.

The architects envisioned a 5,000-seat open-air amphitheatre and a public park, the first planted in Palestine. They saw a high-tech hub hard-wired with fibre optics and humming with Wi-Fi, fitted out with GSM and AMR and other acronyms. They hoped the city would act as a mini Tel Aviv, a start-up incubator for young entrepreneurs drawn from the universities in Nablus and Ramallah, the Arab Spring's Net Generation of cosmopolitan twentysomethings. They sketched out roads, wastewater facilities, eight schools, several mosques, a church, a medical clinic, a hotel and a conference centre and homeowners associations like any North American suburb. It was a project of pharoah-like ambition.

"This will be a city without borders," promised Amir. "The first city in Palestine that has no fences." I couldn't help but think of fence-less Bat Ayin; sometimes fences weren't such a bad idea. "We are driving away the notion of enclosure and promoting the open approach to urbanized centres." He paused to catch his breath and concluded with an understatement. "It is, no doubt, a challenging exercise."

Travelling through Israel, I'd come across many fences, borders, walls. Even the open society of the most communal kibbutz was bounded by barbed wire. In Rawabi, I could look out the window of Amir's office at the hemmed-in settlement of Ateret on the far hillside. We could stare down the bare slopes and see, in the distance, the horizon and the glistening towers of Tel Aviv and know that Israel's metropolis by the sea was cut off by checkpoints and motion detectors and permits and the ever-lengthening Separation Barrier. We were a few minutes' drive from the village Nabi Salih, where every Friday Palestinians and international activists clashed with Israeli soldiers over land confiscated for another settlement. A few days after I visited Rawabi, an Israeli border policeman shot a Palestinian protester in the face at close range with a tear-gas canister as he threw stones at their jeep and the victim died of his injuries.

When finished, the city would provide affordable housing for middle-class families, act as a destination for visitors from nearby villages, and prove to the world that the Palestinians were ready for their own state. A high-tech suburb near Ramallah and Birzeit University made sense. The region was the heart of secular Palestinian society, propped up by international funding. But it hadn't been Bashar Masri's first choice. Originally, he had imagined Rawabi in Gaza. But the rise to power of Hamas—and the ousting of their political rivals, Fatah— ended those plans. Gaza was now blockaded by the Israeli military, locked in an exchange of rockets and retribution. What if Hamas gained power in the West Bank?

"The project is built for today's politics," Amir admitted. "If the political environment improves, then you are bound to see a magnificent opportunity of Rawabi multiplication: Rawabi One, Rawabi Two and so on . . ." It sounded like the original dream of Kibbutz Degania, a utopia that could be franchised. Amir knew that if the political environment deteriorated in the West Bank, Masri and his backers might reconsider the project's financial exposure. Construction might slow down, downsize or even stop.

For now, Rawabi generated more rumours than revenues. Its PR promised a futuristic vision of what American urban theorist Richard Florida trumpets as the "creative city": clean, walkable, ecological, wired for 21st-century life and at an affordable price for young families. I asked Amir, George and the other employees I met if they planned to live in Rawabi. "Of course," they all replied. The response sounded somewhere between "Who wouldn't want to?" and "What did you expect me to say?"

But Rawabi had its skeptics. A day earlier, at the Ramallah Cultural Centre, Palestinians in their twenties and thirties, students and IT workers and activists, blogged and Tweeted and tapped at smartphones and laptops at a conference organized by the U.S. State Department about the impact of the Arab Spring. The attendees seemed like perfect prospects for the new city: bright, young, well-educated, multilingual global villagers. Suspicion tinged their curiosity about Rawabi.

"Affordable? Hardly!" scoffed a translator. "Maybe affordable if you've got a government job. But not if you're a teacher or anyone else." He imagined the apartments bought up by émigrés, with dual citizenship and foreign incomes, who wanted a second home, or upper-tier apparatchiks in the Palestinian Authority, with cushy salaries underwritten by foreign aid, all fleeing the *hoi polloi* of the West Bank. Palestinian activists had expressed similar concerns and complained that filling apartments—with list prices between $85,000 to $140,000—would require aspiring Palestinian yuppies to take on the same subprime debt that had cratered the American economy and caused financial turmoil around the world. Families would be hog-tied by the Occupation *and* mortgage payments. Most residents in the West Bank, where the per capita annual GDP of roughly $5,000 U.S. ranked between Moldova and Tonga, could only dream of living in Rawabi's hillside suburb.

Another common complaint about Rawabi was that the project mostly profited Israeli businesses and Jewish labour. Activists even argued Rawabi should be boycotted for its collaborations with Israel. Amir Dajani rolled his eyes. "This is absolutely untrue," he insisted. "The Israelis prefer to use Arab workers—they're cheaper. Why would we use Israelis then?" It made no sense. ("Arab labour," in fact, is pejorative Hebrew slang for "cheap labour" in both senses of the phrase.) "We are building the city with Palestinian contractors," he repeated. "There are no Israeli contractors involved *at all*."

Conspiracy theories don't need facts to thrive. "Everything is controversial in this region," admitted Amir. Rawabi *did* rely on Israeli suppliers and consultants. I'd seen stacked bags of cement, labelled in Hebrew, from the port of Ashdod. Amir didn't apologize for that. The West Bank lacked a maritime port and had restricted access to imports. Even with an on-site stone quarry and metalworks, Rawabi depended on Israeli suppliers for raw materials. Project managers bought concrete from Israel proper, but they refused to buy services or material produced in Jewish settlements within the West Bank. "We believe that settlements are illegal," said Amir. "That is part of our policy, and we are committed to enforcing it."

Rawabi's managers asked suppliers in Israel to sign statements promising not to do business with settlements. That tactic got Rawabi into trouble, too. A 2011 civil law in Israel, written by right-wing parliamentarians—and perhaps inspired by Rawabi's actions—penalizes anyone who promotes a boycott of products from Israel or the settlements in the West Bank. Israeli institutions or individuals that break the law can lose public funding, tax exemptions and be liable for financial losses suffered by settlers' businesses. The Israeli Supreme Court upheld the law in 2015.

As Rawabi took fire from both sides, the hilltop construction site felt like a castle under siege. It looked that way, too. Excavators and bulldozers were levelling the tiered ledges on which the buildings would rise and the streets would be paved and lined with trees. A satellite view via Google Earth made the earthworks look like a graffiti tag sprayed into the hillside by an alien vandal. It hardly seemed human-made at all. A few months after my visit, Rawabi finally got some good news. Four years of lobbying earned approval from Israeli authorities to build a vital access road to the main site. "This is a big step in the right direction," Bashar Masri told journalists. "Israelis are invited to come and visit any time. Even though our target audience is Palestinian, if Israelis also want to buy apartments there, they're welcome."

His offer is unlikely to be taken up. Not anytime soon at least. Even the PR animations and diorama of Rawabi didn't indulge that domestic fantasy: Arabs and Jews living together in harmony, under the plastic dome of a sci-fi city. That was a piece of public relations no one was buying.

—

Leaving the West Bank wasn't as easy as getting in. If Rawabi's promoters positioned the gleaming neighbourhoods as a dream factory for a new nation, then the Qalandia checkpoint was where such dreams went to wither. There were worse places, I knew, in the refugee camps of the West Bank and especially Gaza. More dangerous. More destitute. More oppressed. But Qalandia was the key intersection between the northern West Bank and Jerusalem. Thousands of times a day at Qalandia, the Occupation replayed its loop of routine humiliations.

As lanes of cars and trucks slowed and snaked through the inspections, the #18 bus from Ramallah disgorged end-of-the-day commuters, mostly students, at the checkpoint's entrance. We grabbed our bags and crowded into a fenced-in waiting area, blocked off by a wall of bullet-proof glass and a thick metal revolving door, unlocked electronically by guards in a bulletproof booth on the far side. The pace of inspection made airport security feel like the 100-metre dash. The door buzzed, and two or three people would press bodies and baggage into the pie-wedge opening and spin the door a half-turn on its axis until they were spat out on the other side of the bars and Plexiglas. We were all in a terrarium now.

An amplified voice barked in Hebrew. People thrust backpacks and purses and shopping bags and shoes onto an X-ray machine. The herky-jerky moving belt reversed and spilled belongings onto the floor. More barking. People held ID papers to an electronic screen to get waved through. Buzz. Bark. Repeat.

And these were the "good times." The IDF had dismantled some of the internal checkpoints erected during the Second Intifada. The arbitrariness of who got through had diminished, and Palestinians had adjusted to the regime of permits. They had learned patience.

Minutes ticked past. An hour. The line extended behind me, as more buses arrived. We pressed against each other, front to back, shuf-fling a half-foot every few minutes. Edward Said, the Palestinian intel-lectual, once noted that the "truest reality" of his people was "expressed in the way we cross over from one place to another." A semblance of etiquette prevailed amid the crush. A narrow space opened to allow a woman and her baby to squeeze to the front. Anxiety permeated the queue as we inched forward. We could see the cars moving through the vehicle checkpoint. A young IDF soldier, an Ethiopian Jew, stood behind a concrete screen, assault rifle in hand, and stared at the oncom-ing traffic. As I neared the door, a few students took pity on the tall blonde foreigner with too much luggage and gave my daypack a nudge to wedge me like a bent quarter into the exit slot.

An hour and a half after I'd arrived, I was through, bags scanned, passport inspected. Our bus filled and pulled away from the checkpoint. The purple half-light of dusk settled over East Jerusalem as we drove toward the Old City. I glanced back, one more time, at the checkpoint and the Wall. Then I closed my eyes.

I was going home.

—

Israel can be a hard place to leave, too. Once you wander its hills and alleys, its shorelines and *shuks*, its cities and synagogues, its mountains and mosques, once you listen to the stories of the people who call it home, the nation exerts a gravitational tug on your imagination, even for someone without an ethnic or religious or family connection to the land. When I walked away from Shamir, after my 21st birthday, I assumed I had closed a chapter in my history. Here I was again, half a lifetime older, looking for answers to questions seeded in my imagination back on the kibbutz.

Israel can be hard to leave for other reasons, too. Airport security in the country that invented "homeland security" is intense. Ben Gurion International had tightened its protocols in the decades since my first trip: post 9/11, post-Gulf War (I and II), post-Intifada (I and II). Its officials had practically invented profiling. On my first return visit to Israel, I'd been grilled by a customs agent: "Are you visiting any Arab towns? Do you have any Arab friends?" I wondered if she would ask next whether I liked Arab food or used Arabic numerals. Flying home through Ben Gurion, I fielded the standard airport questions: "Did you pack your own bags? Did anyone give you something to carry? Do you have any gifts?" Then the X-ray operator ejected my bags through the cannon of a scanning machine, slapped a sticker on my luggage and waved me toward the next stage. On a stainless steel table, I opened my luggage for a bored young security officer who fondled my unwashed clothes with plastic gloves. "Where did you visit on your trip?" she asked.

Honesty, I figured, was the best policy. "A few days near Nahariya. Kibbutz Shamir. Tel Aviv. Jerusalem. Ramallah. Haifa—"

"Ramallah?"

Her ennui vanished. She extracted a map of the West Bank city from my luggage and examined it with a colleague. Then she called her supervisor. He was stocky, bald, light-skinned, six inches taller, a decade older and 40 pounds heftier than the crew of twenty-something baggage inspectors. I could tell he was the Grand Inquisitor of the airport. He stared at my passport and inquired about the "Achzivland" stamp. I said I'd been married on the beach by Eli Avivi, and he smiled.

"How long did you stay at Shamir?" he asked, casually.

I told him.

"How long at Tel Aviv?"

Ditto.

"And Jerusalem?"

Two nights.

"How long in Ramallah?"

Same.

"And how long were you in Nablus?"

"I wasn't in Nablus."

"How many days in Hebron?"

"I wasn't in Hebron either."

His smile was gone. I waited for him to say, "Who is Massoud Falsometer?" Instead my interrogator asked, "Did anybody give you anything?"

I had a pot of honey from Kibbutz Shamir, knick-knacks bought in the Jerusalem market and two bottles of craft beer from the West Bank; one was from a Christian Arab brewery in Taybeh, the other from a Jewish settler operation near Kfar Etzion. And then I noticed, nestled in my underwear, the Rawabi Cube. *Oh, shit.* At the end of my site visit, Amir Dajani had handed me a keychain and a green-and-blue cardboard box, with a glossy finish, covered in English and Arabic text. *Palestine*, it read. *A gift for you.*

The Bald Inquisitor glared and handed the offending box to an underling.

The box itself was simply a vessel for . . . well, I wasn't quite sure. A paperweight perhaps. A puzzle. A public-relations *boîte*. The Rawabi Cube was the size of its Rubik's cousin, with a two-by-two-by-two configuration of squares. It folded outward on cardboard hinges to display the city's name, its trademark heart-shaped leaf and its motto: *Live. Work. Grow.* The cube turned inside-out to reveal illustrations of tiny people ascending urban staircases, a close-up of a white-stoned arcade, a photo panorama of the scrub-topped hills that gave Rawabi its name, the white-turning-deep-blue sky above and the faintest hint of a settlement along its acropolis. Utopia in the palm of your hand. I knew my kids would love it.

The airport interrogator ordered my belongings through the X-ray scanner again, and I was sent to a windowless back room with a blasé young agent who asked me to loosen my belt so he could pat down my waist inside my pants. Afterwards, as I redid the buckle, he groomed his hair in a full-length mirror. Back at security, I assumed a bomb-unit robot had detonated my Rawabi Cube in a basement bunker. I was wrong. Despite its provenance, my gift from Palestine proved to be made only of ink and paper. A harmless token. I could take it home. The Bald Inquisitor still looked unimpressed.

"Why did you say, 'No' when they asked if you were given anything to carry? What if it was a bomb? Why would you put all these people in danger?"

He was right. What better deception than to insert a box of

explosives as a souvenir in the luggage of a gullible visitor from Canada? The inspector waved me along with contempt for my naiveté. I tucked the cube in my bag and hurried to catch my flight.

I had come to Israel to look for the legacy of the original dreamers, the kibbutzniks, the ones who believed that a rough and beautiful land could be both settled and shared. To these pioneers, Palestine felt like a gift. I'd wanted to find out, a hundred years later, what had become of their version of the good place. Why had it withered? Where did it survive? I witnessed the faded dreams of the kibbutz, hundreds of socialist communes turned into country suburbs or bankrupt retirement homes. Still, I want to believe their collective vision of utopia was rising again, despite the odds, in communities like Rawabi and Nes Ammim, the Oasis of Peace and Kibbutz Migvan, in the eco-villages of the Arava Valley, on the hilltops of the Galilee, among the activists and artists of Givat Haviva and Zochrot and System Ali, in the voices of resistance like those of David Sheen and Nomika Zion and Eliaz Cohen. I want to believe these new experiments in radical sharing, co-existence and political dissent will take root and grow broad and strong, as the kibbutz once did. I want to believe the concatenation of unique communities can shade a path for the peoples of Israel and Palestine to walk together into the future. I want to believe they can make the desert bloom, and the cities thrive, this time for all the peoples of the Promised Land.

Utopia, I know, only ever exists in our imagination. In the pages of historians and philosophers and poets. In the blueprints of architects and the rhetoric of politicians. In rosy guidebooks for starry-eyed tourists oblivious to the shadowy corners of the countries they hurry through. Perhaps utopia is a disposable paperweight, a Pandora's takeaway box. Shiny and colourful on the surface. Lift its lid and look inside, however, and you will find its vessel contains nothing more substantial than that most helium-light and elusive and all-too-human of elements: *hope*.

And maybe that's enough.

Sources

General

During the five years of researching and writing (and rewriting) this book, I often described the loose-and-baggy manuscript as an "investigative travel memoir" rather than a conventional academic study of the region's history, sociology or political science. Re-reading the two volumes of diaries I kept as a volunteer made me cringe at times, but my confessional record rekindled memories and allowed me to recreate my experiences on Kibbutz Shamir and original travels through Israel. Along with personal memories and observations, the portraits of the people and places chasing utopia in Israel, the Golan Heights and the West Bank derive from on-site and in-person interviews, mostly in English, during three extended research trips.

To provide cultural and historical context, I consulted a variety of books, newspapers, journals, websites and films, which I have listed by chapter below. My first step was to re-read microfiched issues of the

Jerusalem Post, from autumn of 1988 through spring of 1989, to recall the articles I'd skimmed over lunch in the dining hall as a volunteer and to reconstruct the media frame that shaped my early opinions about Israel. For current affairs, I turned to the excellent English-language reporting from *Haaretz*, especially Eli Ashkenazi's extensive coverage of kibbutz-related news. The Israel-based, English-language alternative news site 972mag.com also offered critical viewpoints on contemporary issues in Israel and the Occupied Territories. The essential guide to Israel's kibbutzim remains Henry Near's two-volume chronicle *The Kibbutz Movement: A History, Volume 1: Origins and Growth 1909–1939* (Oxford University Press, 1992) and *Volume 2: Crisis and Achievement 1939–1995* (Oxford University Press, 1997). I used Martin Gilbert's *Israel: A History* (Key Porter, 2008) to trace the general plot arc of the Jewish state in the 20th century.

Prologue: It Is Dangerous to Read Facebook
The excerpt from "Volunteers" is from *The Hands in Exile* (Random House, 1983), the debut collection by American poet Susan Tichy and reprinted with her permission; many of the poems describe her experiences as a volunteer on Kibbutz Shamir in the 1970s. The excerpt from "It is Dangerous to Read Newspapers" comes from Margaret Atwood's *Selected Poems: 1965–1975* (Oxford University Press, 1976).

The bloody outcome of the West Bank slayings and the ensuing Operation Protective Edge in Gaza was documented by Israeli and international media. Data scientist Gilad Lotan published a fascinating analysis on Medium.com titled "Israel, Gaza, War & Data: Social Networks and the Art of Personalizing Propaganda" that visualizes the network connections of pro-Palestinian and pro-Israeli postings on Instagram and Twitter. The left-leaning Israeli newspaper *Haaretz* was one of the few online sites where both sides of the conflict escaped their respective filter bubbles and read the same news and commentary.

"Compared to all other nodes on the graph," Lotan concluded, *Haaretz* "has the most potential for bridging across biases and political barriers." I hope that my book, in its own small way, can do the same.

Part One: Who Killed the Kibbutz?

The epigraph is spoken by a kibbutznik character in the detective novel *Murder on a Kibbutz: A Communal Case* by Batya Gur (HarperCollins, 1994).

Chapter 1: Ghetto Life in the Finger of Galilee

The works of Lewis Mumford influenced my style as a young writer and sparked my interest in utopias and urban planning; his quote comes from *The Story of Utopias* (Boni and Liveright, 1922). The correct wording for Winston Churchill's famous line about architectural determinism was confirmed in *Never Give In!: The Best of Winston Churchill's Speeches* (Hyperion, 2003). The latest data on kibbutz populations can be found on the website for the Kibbutz Program Center in Tel Aviv. While it's no *Breakfast Club*, Lewis Gilbert's 1985 romantic-comedy *Not Quite Paradise* (titled *Not Quite Jerusalem* in Europe) will evoke memories for any kibbutz volunteer from the 1980s. Bruno Bettelheim's *The Children of the Dream* (Macmillan, 1969) remains the best-known—and most controversial—study of the practice and impact of the kibbutz movement's communal child-rearing.

Details from interviews about the terrorist attack on Kibbutz Shamir were confirmed in "Four Terrorists Slay Three Women in Kibbutz; All Killed" (Jewish Telegraphic Agency, June 14, 1974) and "Middle East: Cease-Fire Strains" (*Time*, June 24, 1974). The Vanderbilt Television News Archive provided archival footage of the CBS news report on the incident by veteran Vietnam War correspondent John Laurence. I also discovered transcripts of an alternative version of the attack, allegedly broadcast by the Voice of Palestine radio service, in which the four members of the Popular Front for the Liberation of Palestine — General Command captured (and killed) 31 hostages in the kibbutz dining hall and killed or wounded "more than 15 Zionist soldiers" before the "group of heroes" martyred themselves; it was yet another case of two competing narratives with few overlapping threads. See also: Joel Brinkley, "4 Israelis Killed in Attack on Bus" (*New York Times*, October 31, 1988).

The psychological impact of the Golden City was studied by Yair Bar-El et al. in "Jerusalem Syndrome" (*The British Journal of Psychiatry*, January 2000). Arthur Koestler's "Jerusalem sadness" quote comes from Michael Scammell's excellent biography, *Koestler: The Literary and Political Odyssey of a Twentieth-Century Skeptic* (Random House, 2009). Amos Oz recorded his own memorable description of his hometown in his memoir, *A Tale of Love and Darkness*, translated by Nicholas de Lange (Harcourt, 2005).

Chapter 2: Between the Hammer and the Anvil

The Yossi Schneiberg incident and its aftermath were reported by several Israeli news sources, including Yuval Goren, "Disgruntled Kibbutznik Kills Self After Shooting Community Director" (*Haaretz*, May 27, 2009) and Eli Ashkenazi, "Kibbutz Leaders Fear Backlash Against Privatization" (*Haaretz*, June 3, 2009). On the PR battle over Israel's gay-positive reputation, see Aron Heller, "Tel Aviv Emerges as Top Gay Tourist Destination" (*Huffington Post*, January 24, 2012) and Morten Berthelsen, "'Stop Using Palestinian Gays to Whitewash Israel's Image'" (*Haaretz*, January 10, 2009). The account of Arthur Koestler's abortive experience as a kibbutznik comes from Michael Scammell's biography; Noam Chomsky discussed his experiences on Kibbutz HaZorea in "Reflections on a Lifetime of Engagement with Zionism, the Palestine Question, and American Empire," an interview with Mouin Rabbani (*Journal of Palestine Studies*, April 1, 2012) and his general thoughts about Israel's communal movement in "Eight Questions on Kibbutzim" (*Z Commentaries*, August 24, 1999).

For details about other famous kibbutz volunteers, see Judy Maltz, "Mission Impossible? Finding Bernie Sanders' Kibbutz" (*Haaretz*, September 3, 2015); Michael Morain, "Sigourney Weaver's Roles Spark Interest" (*Des Moines Register*, May 13, 2011); "Bob Hoskins Tells It Like It Is, Mate" (Reuters, April 11, 1998); Ellis Shuman, "Seinfeld's Kibbutz Days" (*The Times of Israel*, December 9, 2013); Simon Le Bon discussed his formative kibbutz experiences with Mary Griffin (*Birmingham Mail*, June 19, 2015). Also: Eli Ashkenazi, "Kibbutz Movement Planning Reunion for Thousands of Foreign Volunteers" (*Haaretz*, June 28, 2010).

Chapter 3: A Few Grams of Courage

Esti Ahronovitz, "Socialist Paradise" (*Haaretz*, March 31, 2005) offers a detailed portrait of Kibbutz Shamir after its NASDAQ listing, as well as the contrasting debt of nearby Kibbutz Amir. Ber Dov Borochov, "Eretz Yisrael in Our Program and Tactics," an excerpt from a speech delivered in September 1917, is reproduced in the Jewish Virtual Library, which also offers biographies of Borochov, Hannah Senesh and Haviva Reik; "Jewish Parachutists from Palestine" (*Holocaust Encyclopedia*, updated August 18, 2015); the excerpt from Senesh's poem "Eli, Eli," written in 1942, was reprinted in the *Jewish Week* (December 22, 2010); Eli Ashkenazi, "Sarah Braverman, Pioneering Jewish Parachutist in WWII, Dies at 94" (*Haaretz*, February 11, 2013).

Israel's hyperinflation in the 1980s is summarized in "The Rise & Fall of Inflation," the Jewish Virtual Library (updated 2011). Daniel Gavron discusses kibbutzniks' ill-advised dabbling in "grey market" investments in *The Kibbutz: Awakening from Utopia* (Rowman & Littlefield, 2000). The economic turmoil and socio-political changes on the kibbutz movement were studied by Uri Leviatan, Hugh Oliver and Jack Quarter, *Crisis in the Israeli Kibbutz: Meeting the Challenge of Changing Times* (Greenwood, 1998). An academic overview of evolving kibbutz economies can be found in Raymond Russell, Robert Hanneman and Shlomo Getz, *The Renewal of the Kibbutz: From Reform to Transformation* (Rutgers University Press, 2013), as well as Christopher Warhurst, *Between Market, State and Kibbutz: The Management and Transformation of Socialist Industry* (Mansell, 1999). The anecdotes about Kibbutz Hulata are from *Kibbutz* (Seventh Art, 2005), Racheli Schwartz's documentary about her post-privatization home.

Chapter 4: A Village Under Siege
The story of the founding of Israel and the early history of Kibbutz Degania comes largely from Martin Gilbert's *Israel: A History* and Joseph Baratz's memoir, *A Village by the Jordan: The Story of Degania* (Harville Press, 1954), supplemented by Henry Near's *The Kibbutz Movement: A History*. The Amos Oz quote is taken from his introduction to *Until Daybreak: Stories from the Kibbutz*, edited by Richard Flantz (Hakibbutz Hameuchad Publishing House and the Institute for the Translation of Hebrew Literature, 1984). Martin Buber's famous claim about the kibbutz as "the experiment that did not fail" appears in *Paths in Utopia*, translated by R.F.C. Hull (Beacon Press, 1949). For more on Degania's philosophical guru, see Herbert H. Rose, *The Life and Thought of A.D. Gordon: Pioneer, Philosopher and Prophet of Modern Israel* (Bloch, 1964).

Yitzhak Rubin's works as a documentary director and producer include *Degania: The World's First Kibbutz Fights Its Last Battle* (Teknews Media, 2008) and *Udi Adiv: A Broken Israeli Myth* (Teknews Media, 2010). Yossi Klein Halevi's superb work of narrative nonfiction *Like Dreamers: The Story of the Israeli Paratroopers Who Reunited Jerusalem and Divided a Nation* (HarperCollins, 2013) offers a complex portrait of the hero-turned-traitor/activist Udi Adiv. Facts and quotes from Degania's centennial celebrations come from Eli Ashkenazi, "100 Years On, the Kibbutz Movement Is Alive and Kicking" (*Haaretz*, January 4, 2010).

Chapter 5: The Final Solution

Statistics on kibbutzniks' representation in Israel's parliament come from Yossi Sarid, "Israel's First Kibbutz-free Knesset" (*Haaretz*, December 25, 2012). John Hersey described his travels through Israel's communal settlements in "The Kibbutz" (*The New Yorker*, April 19, 1952). Menachem Begin's gibe about kibbutzniks as millionaires with swimming pools has assumed various permutations over the decades; the most accurate seems to come from "Begin Assailed for Disparaging Kibbutz Members" (Jewish Telegraphic Agency, October 2, 1981). Daniel Gavron discusses the Metapelet Complex in *The Kibbutz: Awakening from Utopia*. For kibbutz statistics, see Michal Palgi and Shlomo Getz, "Varieties in Developing Sustainability: The Case of the Israeli Kibbutz" (*International Review of Sociology*, 24:1, 2014) and Harriet Sherwood, "Israel's Kibbutz Movement Makes a Comeback" (*The Guardian*, July 23, 2012). Eli Avrahami's monograph *The Changing Kibbutz: An Examination of Values and Structure* (Yad Tabenkin, 2000) offers an accessible overview.

The story of the founding of Hanita is derived from the kibbutz's homepage, as well as "Founding of Kibbutz Hanita" (Isracast website, March 21, 2015) and "Hanita Forest & Kibbutz Hanita" (Keren Kayemeth Lesrael Jewish National Fund website, n.d.).

My account of the bureaucratic division of "kibbutz" into three separate legal categories comes from an interview in Tel Aviv with Dr. Eliezer Ben-Rafael, who headed the committee; he published a summation of the kibbutz movement's challenges in *Crisis and Transformation: The Kibbutz at Century's End* (State University of New York Press, 1997) and a description of the Ben-Rafael Committee's decision-making process in "Kibbutz: Survival at Risk" (*Israel Studies*, Summer 2011). For contemporary reporting of the Kibbutz Agreement, see "Israel Bails Out Kibbutzim; Plan Is Attacked by the Likud" (Jewish Telegraphic Agency, April 6, 1995). Readers who want a deeper dive into the literature of kibbutz studies should begin with the following anthologies: Yosef Gorni, Yaacov Oved and Idit Paz, editors, *Communal Life: An International Perspective* (Yad Tabenkin, 1987); David Leichman and Idit Paz, editors, *Kibbutz: An Alternative Lifestyle* (Yad Tabenkin, 1994); and Michal Palgi and Shulamit Reinharz, editors, *One Hundred Years of Kibbutz Life: A Century of Crises and Reinvention* (Transaction, 2011).

Chapter 6: Stories from the Ass

For information about conscientious objectors in Israel, see "Country Report and Updates: Israel" (War Resisters' International website, April 21, 1998). Daniel Bernstein, "Calling Artists 'Tight-asses,' Minister Escalates Culture Clash" (*The Times of Israel*, June 19, 2015). Dana Olmert, "Rahel Bluwstein: 1890–1931," and Nathan Shahar, "Naomi Shemer: 1930–2004" (both on the Jewish Women's Archive website, n.d.). Lawrence Joffe, "Moshe Shamir" (*The Guardian*, August 27, 2004). Amos Oz, *A Tale of Love and Darkness*, translated by Nicholas de Lange (Harcourt, 2005).

The right-wing protests of the Haifa Theater's production of Joshua Sobol's *The Jewish Syndrome* are described in Linda Ben-Zvi's *Theater in Israel* (University of Michigan Press, 1996). Sobol gave a memorable quote to an interviewer in the fall/winter 1998 issue of *Kibbutz Trends*: "Of all that happened in our time, only one thing will remain in our collective memory: the kibbutz. Not the yeshivas, nor the towns, nor the 'build your own house' neighbourhoods, nor the shopping centres. All these, along with the materialism, privatization, property sales, exist all over the world and are of no interest to anyone. The kibbutz is the most original creation, not only in Israel, but in the whole twentieth century. It will become more and more significant as time passes."

And, of course, Yoav Eilat, *Stories from the Ass* (Yaron Golan, 1989).

Chapter 7: Moving the State

Sources for the First Lebanon War, the helicopter disaster and the impact of the Four Mothers include Matthew M. Hurley, "The Bekaa Valley Air Battle, June 1982: Lessons Mislearned?" (*Airpower Journal*, Winter 1989); Glenn Frankel, "Israel Cites Army Blunder in Raid on Base" (*The Washington Post*, November 27, 1987); Patrick Cockburn, "Israel Buries Helicopter Crash Dead" (*Independent*, February 5, 1997); Gal Luft, "Israel's Security Zone in Lebanon: A Tragedy?" (*Middle East Quarterly*, September 2000); and Leora Eren Fracht, "The Movement That Shaped the Lebanon Pullout" (*The Jerusalem Post*, June 7, 2000). While Hezbollah's kidnapping of two IDF soldiers was used as a pretext for the Second Lebanon War, Prime Minister Ehud Barak later admitted that plans were being devised months before that incident: Conal Urquhart, "Israel Planned for Lebanon War Months in Advance, PM Says" (*The Guardian*, March 9, 2007).

Betty Friedan's quote about feminism and the kibbutz comes from her preface to the anthology *Sexual Equality: The Israeli Kibbutz Tests the Theories* (Norwood Editions, 1983). Avraham Balaban's memoir, *Mourning a Father Lost: A Kibbutz Childhood Remembered* (Rowman & Littlefield, 2004), is a lyrical and moving indictment of the kibbutz movement's extended experiment in communal child-raising.

Chapter 8: The Shouting Fence

The research publications produced at Al-Marsad include: Jonathan Molony, Michelle Stewart, and Nancy Tuohy, *From Settlement to Self: The Economic Occupation of the Syrian Golan* (Al-Marsad, 2009) and Ray Murphy and Declan Gannon, *Changing the Landscape: Israel's*

Gross Violations of the International Law in the Occupied Syrian Golan (Al-Marsad, 2008). Eran Riklis is the director of *The Syrian Bride* (Eran Riklis Productions *et al.*, 2004). Amos Oz's memories of the Yom Kippur War come from David Remnick's detailed profile of the author, "The Spirit Level: Amos Oz Writes the Story of Israel" (*The New Yorker*, November 8, 2004).

For more about the Druze General Strike, see "Israel Seals Off Villages of Striking Druse in Golan" (*The New York Times*, February 28, 1982); Mark A. Tessler, *A History of the Israeli-Palestinian Conflict* (Indiana University Press, 1994); and Roger S. Powers, *Protest, Power, and Change: An Encyclopedia of Nonviolent Action from ACT-UP to Women's Suffrage* (Routledge, 2012).

Chapter 9: The Architecture of Hope

More background on the architectural history of the kibbutz movement can be found in Michael and Bracha Chyutin, *Architecture and Utopia: The Israeli Experiment* (Ashgate, 2007); Galia Bar-Or and Yuval Yaski, editors, *Kibbutz: Architecture Without Precedents* (Museum of Art, Ein Harod, 2010); and Esther Zandberg, "A Kibbutz Grows in Venice" (*Haaretz*, December 3, 2009). Ray Oldenburg's ideas about the democratic importance of communal "third places" are explored in *The Great Good Place* (Da Capo Press, 1999). Amos Oz discusses the potential revival of the communal ideal in the documentary *Amos Oz*, directed by Stelios Charampopouls (ERT Films, 2008).

Part Two: Look Back to Galilee

The epigraph is taken from Arthur Koestler's *Thieves in the Night: Chronicle of an Experiment* (Macmillan, 1946), a heroic novel about kibbutz pioneers in pre-state Israel.

Chapter 10: Born This Way

Roger Waters' reaction to boycott pressure is reconstructed from Donald Macintyre, "Palestinians Urge Roger Waters to Boycott Israel" (*Independent*, March 8, 2006) and Ruth Eglash, "Bridge Over Troubled Waters" (*The Jerusalem Post*, June 18, 2006). A decade later, Gideon Levy followed up with the musician about his activism: "Roger Waters Sets the Record Straight: I Hate Apartheid, Not Israel" (*Haaretz*, August 2, 2015).

The account of Father Bruno Hussar and the founding of the Oasis of Peace comes from his memoir *When the Cloud Lifted: The Testimony of an Israeli Priest* (Ignatius, 1989); Patra Dounoukos, "Father Bruno's Dream Alive in Israel" (*Peace Magazine*, December/January 1988/89); Wolfgang Saxon, "Father Bruno Hussar, 84, Dies; A Font of Jewish-Arab Amity" (*The New York Times*, February 16, 1996); Joseph V. Montville, "Neve Shalom: A Model of Arab-Israeli Coexistence?" *The Middle East Quarterly* (December 1998); and Daniel Gavron, *Holy Land Mosaic: Stories of Cooperation and Coexistence between Israelis and Palestinians* (Rowman & Littlefield, 2008). Director/producer Yoram Honig's *First Lesson in Peace* (Yoram Honig, 2006) is a touching documentary that looks inside Neve Shalom's School for Peace. Joe Freeman depicts the complexity of life in the community in "The Arab Named Voltaire" (*Tablet Magazine*, August 5, 2015). More about Contact Theory can be found in T. DeAngelis, "All You Need Is Contact" (*Monitor on Psychology*, November 2001). Also: Rick Westhead, "Jerusalem's Mount of Olives Cemetery Running Out of Room," (*Toronto Star*, December 16, 2012).

Chapter 11: Buried History

The standard history of Canada Park can be found on the Keren Kayemeth LeIsrael Jewish National Fund website, "Ayalon Canada Park—Biblical and Modern Israel." Critiques of the park's status include Carmelle Wolfson, "Planting over Palestine" (*Maisonneuve*, September 21, 2011); Yves Engler, "Canada and the Jewish National Fund" (CounterPunch.org, November 2, 2010); and Eitan Bronstein, "Restless Park: On the Latrun Villages and Zochrot" (Zochrot.org). Bronstein's account of the disappearance of the village of Qaqun is confirmed by Noga Kadman, *Erased from Space and Consciousness: Israel and the Depopulated Palestinian Villages of 1948* (Indiana University Press, 2015).

The story of Kafr Bir'im is told by Nihad Boqai in *Returning to Kafr Bir'im* (BADIL Resource Center for Palestinian Residency and Refugee Rights, 2006) and in Joseph Algazy, "A Promise That's Never Been Kept" (*Haaretz*, November 10, 2001). The blueprint for an Israel-spanning bridge between the Palestinian Territories is described by Noam Dvir in "Bridging the Gap Between the West Bank and Gaza with a Dream" (*Haaretz*, March 13, 2012). More on the legal attempts to stop NGOs from teaching the Nakba: Roni Schocken, "Chilling Effect of the Nakba Law on Israel's Human Rights" (*Haaretz*, May 17, 2012).

Chapter 12: Buying Cat Food with the King of Achziv

The history of Achzivland is based on my interviews with Eli and Rina Avivi; the documentary *Achziv: A Place of Love*, directed by Etty Wieseltier and Guy Michael (Wieseltier-Goldfinger Productions, 2009) and Raffi Berg, "One-man Rule in Israel's Hippy Micro-state" (*BBC News Magazine*, March 10, 2015). I can only dream of one day visiting all the other oddball republics listed in John Ryan's *Micronations: The Lonely Planet Guide to Home-Made Nations* (Lonely Planet, 2006). Yehuda Amichai's poem "Return to Achziv" was translated from the Hebrew by Bernard Horn and published in *The New Yorker* (September 30, 2002). An account of the Palestinian village of Al-Zeeb, before and after the 1948 War, can be found at Zochrot.org.

Chapter 13: Living in Glass Houses

The history of Nes Ammim comes from my interviews with Frans van der Sar; the community's website (NesAmmim.org); "Behind the Headlines Nes Ammim: Zionism, Christian Style" (Jewish Telegraphic Agency, August 17, 1977); and Lawrence Jeffrey Epstein's *A Treasury of Jewish Inspirational Stories* (Jason Aronson, 1993). Prime Minister Benjamin Netanyahu cited Theodor Herzl's quote about Galilee during a tour of the region: "PM Netanyahu's Speech at the Convention for the Galilee, Kfar Blum" (Prime Minister's Office, October 13, 2009). The membership of the first Arab kibbutznik was reported in "Kibbutz Welcomes Bedouin Into Fold" (*The Washington Times*, December 1, 2009).

Chapter 14: A Dry Season in the Garden of Eden

Rainfall data for Kibbutz Lotan comes from Climate-Data.org. For background on the Global Eco-village Network, see Jonathan Dawson, *Eco-villages: New Frontiers for Sustainability* (Green Books, 2006). Information about Arava Power is taken from the company's website and Sharon Udasin, "Shyne Launches 'Solar Energy' Song" (*The Jerusalem Post*, June 6, 2011). Daniel Gavron's quote about the need for communal "glue" comes from *The Kibbutz: Awakening from Utopia*.

Chapter 15: Love and Rockets

Arab Labor, written by the brilliant Sayed Kashua, is a binge-worthy Israeli TV comedy (Keshet, 2007). For a biography of Nomika Zion's grandfather, see Joseph Finklestone, "Obituary: Yaacov Hazan" (*Independent*, July 28, 1992). A full explanation of the Dunbar Number can be found in Robin Dunbar, *How Many Friends Does One Person Need?: Dunbar's Number and Other Evolutionary Quirks* (Harvard University Press, 2010).

On the psychological and physical damage of the rocket attacks, see Judy Siegel-Itzkovich, "Report: Missiles on Sderot Increase

Miscarriages" (*The Jerusalem Post*, February 24, 2013); Dan Even, "Israeli Survey: Almost Half of Sderot Preteens Show Symptoms of PTSD" (*Haaretz*, November 20, 2012); Isabel Kershner, "Sderot Residents Evacuate to Escape Rocket Attacks" (*The New York Times*, May 17, 2007); director Laura Bialis's documentary *Rock in the Red Zone* (The Foundation for Documentary Projects, 2015). Gideon Levy offers a harrowing collection of reports of Palestinian casualties in *The Punishment of Gaza* (Verso, 2010). Also: Nomika Zion, "War Diary from Sderot" (*The Huffington Post*, February 13, 2009) and "It's Not Just About Fear, Bibi, It's About Hopelessness" (*The New York Review of Books*, January 10, 2013).

Chapter 16: More Than a House

For more on the Jewish gentrification of Palestinian neighbourhoods and the history of Jaffa, see Anna Lekas Miller, "Israel's Land Grab in East Jerusalem" (*The Nation*, April 17, 2013); Nur Masalha, *The Zionist Bible: Biblical Precedent, Colonialism and the Erasure of Memory* (Routledge, 2014); Yigal Hai, "Protesters Rally in Jaffa Against Move to Evict Local Arab Families" (*Haaretz*, April 27, 2007); Daniel Monterescu, *Jaffa Shared and Shattered: Contrived Coexistence in Israel/Palestine* (Indiana University Press, 2015). The film *Ajami* (2009) by directors Scandar Copti and Yaron Shani is a gripping dramatization of tensions between Jews and Palestinians in Jaffa. System Ali got a shout-out from Ben Shalev in "Jaffa Rappers System Ali Should Be Part of the Future of Israeli Music" (*Haaretz*, December 2, 2011).

Chapter 17: Broken Promises in the Promised Land

Background on the terrorist attack in Tel Aviv can be found in Noam Dvir, "Tel Aviv Postpones Demolition of Abandoned Dolphinarium (*Haaretz*, March 8, 2012). René Backmann gives a history of the Separation Barrier in *A Wall in Palestine* (Picador, 2010). Peter

Kropotkin's *Mutual Aid: A Factor of Evolution* (William Henemann, 1902) influenced early kibbutz philosophy. Daniel Gavron's quote about Kibbutz Samar comes from *The Kibbutz: Awakening from Utopia*. James Horrox's *A Living Revolution: Anarchism in the Kibbutz Movement* (AK Press, 2009) explores the influence of anarchism on the early kibbutz. For background to Isaiah Berlin's philosophy of liberty, see Ian Carter, "Positive and Negative Liberty" (*Stanford Encyclopedia of Philosophy*, March 21, 2002). David Ben-Gurion's legendary "make the deserts bloom" quotation comes from "Why I Retired to the Desert" (*The New York Times Magazine*, March 28, 1954). In *SuperCooperators: Altruism, Evolution, and Why We Need Each Other to Succeed* (Free Press, 2011) Martin A. Nowak offers a fascinating overview of the evolutionary science behind different forms of cooperative altruism.

David Sheen's critique of the J14 protests is supported by Talia Gorodess, "'The People Demand Social Justice': How the Israeli Social Protests Ignored the Palestinian Issue, and the Road Ahead" (The Atkin Paper Series, July 2013). For more on the complex history of the Black Hebrews, see Mya Guarnieri, "40 Years On, Black Hebrews Struggle to Find Acceptance in Israel" (*The National*, March 27, 2010); Andrew Esensten, "Once Reviled, Black Hebrews Now Fêted" (*Forward*, March 18, 2009); and John Torode, "The Black Vegan Cult Finally Loved by Israel" (*The Jewish Chronicle Online*, July 23, 2009).

Chapter 18: Revival of Faith

Prime Minister Netanyahu's visit to Kfar Etzion was reported by Efrat Weiss, "Netanyahu: Settlement Blocs Forever Israeli" (YNetNews.com, January 24, 2010) and Marcy Oster, "Netanyahu Plants Tree in Settlement" (Jewish Telegraphic Agency, January 24, 2010). The excerpt from Amos Oz's speech comes from Andy Goldberg, "Labour Joins Peace Now in Mass Rally" (*The Jerusalem Post*, June 4, 1989).

On the incidents at Bat Ayin and the "price-tag" attacks of the Bat Ayin Underground, see Gideon Levy, "Both Sides of Prisoner Release" (*Haaretz*, August 14, 2013); Yuval Yoaz, "Supreme Court Rejects Appeal of the 'Bat Ayin Underground'" (*Haaretz*, December 11, 2006); and Itamar Fleishman, "Settlers Pepper-spray Soldiers, IDF Leaves Bat Ayin" (YNetNews.com, October 3, 2013). For more about how West Bank settlers (such as the founders of "Kibbutz Givat Mechachem") have assumed the mantle of the original kibbutz pioneers, see Carmelle Wolfson, "Organic Occupation: Redeeming Land from Kibbutz to Outpost" (The Media Co-op, January 21, 2010) and "The World of Yesterday," an episode from the documentary TV series *Did Herzl Really Say That?* (Spiegel Productions, 2006).

Nachman Ben-Yehuda, *The Masada Myth: Collective Memory and Mythmaking in Israel* (The University of Wisconsin Press, 1995). Jonathan Lis and Chaim Levinson, "Hanan Porat, 1943–2011: Pioneer of Settler Movement" (*Haaretz*, October 5, 2011); Porat is also one of the central figures of post-1967 Israel described by Yossi Klein Halevi in *Like Dreamers: The Story of the Israeli Paratroopers Who Reunited Jerusalem and Divided a Nation* (HarperCollins, 2013). The complete text and translation of Theodor Herzl's *The Jewish State* (1896), including his quote about religion, can be found at JewishVirtualLibrary.org.

Further quotes from Eliaz Cohen and extra background on his life, activism and poetry come from his writing in "Don't Uproot My Olive Tree" (*The Jerusalem Post*, May 6, 2005); "A Settler's Argument for the Right of Return" (972mag.com, February 20, 2011); *Hear O Lord: Poems From the Disturbances of 2000–2009* (The Toby Press, 2011); as well as Lonoy Bar-Gefen and Meron Rapoport, "Not All Settlers and Palestinians Want Each Other to Disappear" (*Haaretz*, January 21, 2010) and Jessica Steinberg, "Aided by Calendar, Jews and Arabs Unite in Joint Fast" (*The Times of Israel*, July 14, 2014).

Chapter 19: Boxing Hope

The extended construction of Rawabi has been covered by many media outlets, including Ilene R. Prusher, "Architect Eyes Tony Palestinian City with Eco-Mindset and Fast Internet" (*The Christian Science Monitor*, May 14, 2010) and Armin Rosen, "A Middle-Class Paradise in Palestine?" (*The Atlantic*, February 11, 2013). I took information about the Separation Barrier at the time of my visit from Btselem.org (July 16, 2012) and Ramallah's Al-Manara Square from Adania Shibli, "Al-Manara Square: Monumental Architecture and Power" (*Jerusalem Quarterly*, Spring 2006). On the protests in Nabi Saleh, see Omar H. Rahman, "Nabi Saleh Protester Hit by Tear Gas Canister Dies of His Wounds" (972mag.com, December 9, 2011).

Richard Florida outlines his concept of the "creative city" in *Cities and the Creative Class* (Routledge, 2005). Comparative data and the annual per capita GDP in the West Bank is from the 2014 *CIA World Factbook*. For an update on the legal attempt to suppress settlement boycotts, see Revital Hovel, "High Court Largely Upholds Controversial 'Anti-Boycott Law'" (*Haaretz*, April 16, 2015). Basher Masri's quote comes from Tani Goldstein, "'Big Step' for New Palestinian City" (YNetNews.com, January 26, 2012). The line from Edward Said is taken from *The Politics of Dispossession: The Struggle for Palestinian Self-Determination, 1969–1994* (Vintage, 1994).

Recommended Reading

Other books and movies were sources of inspiration rather than information—equally valuable on the long journey of authorship. Around the time I first lived in Israel, Erna Paris wrote *The Garden and the Gun: A Journey Inside Israel* (Lester & Orpen Dennys, 1988); her book remains a model of the deeply curious and self-questioning investigative travel memoir. *This Heated Place: Encounters in the Promised Land* (Douglas & McIntyre, 2002) by Deborah Campbell is a similarly wide-ranging and critical tour through the troubled corners of Israel and the Occupied Territories, with more emphasis on the Palestinian narrative. *Israel vs. Utopia* (Akashic, 2009) collects Joel Schalit's provocative essays about the political tug-of-war over Israel as a symbol that often obscures the complex reality of life on the ground. Yossi Klein Halevi's *Like Dreamers: The Story of the Israeli Paratroopers Who Reunited Jerusalem and Divided a Nation* (HarperCollins, 2013) is a masterful work of narrative nonfiction in which the cast of influential historical figures includes several kibbutzniks and ex-kibbutzniks. Ranen Omer-Sherman provides an authoritative academic history and analysis of representations of the kibbutz in *Imagining the Kibbutz: Visions of Utopia in Literature and Film* (Pennsylvania State University Press, 2015), published just as I was readying my own book for press. I watched many excellent films about the kibbutz experience; the best primer to the history of the movement and its recent changes is *Inventing Our Life: The Kibbutz Experiment* (2010) by Toby Perl Freilich. Finally, I relied heavily for inspiration and direction from the work of Daniel Gavron, especially *The Kibbutz: Awakening from Utopia* (Rowman & Littlefield, 2000) and *Holy Land Mosaic: Stories of Cooperation and Coexistence between Israelis and Palestinians* (Rowman & Littlefield, 2008). After reading his books, I had the pleasure of meeting Gavron in his home outside of Jerusalem and discussing our mutual fascination with his country's utopian communities.

Acknowledgements

My eight-month tour of duty on Kibbutz Shamir shadowed my imagination for the next 20 years. In 2009, I returned for the first of three trips to investigate what the kibbutz meant to Israel—and to me. Over the next five years, I interviewed hundreds of kibbutzniks and experts, who shared their personal stories and general insights about the 100-year history of Israel's communal movement. Many of the people who opened their lives to my questioning do not appear by name in the final manuscript; all were essential guides on my winding road of discovery.

A lively Facebook group of ex-volunteers prompted memories of life on Shamir; I also reconnected with friends and former volunteers Amanda Cadden, Philipa Bobite Capes, Elenka Alexandrov Todarov and Grant Robertson. My return visits to Kibbutz Shamir—part research, much pleasure—were enabled by Kari Lunder, Danny Tyszler, Zohar and Jo Kadmon, Itzik Kahana, Dagan Avishai, Uzi Tzur, Shaul Kimhi, Emilia Gotliv, Jerry Kurlandski and the staff of the

Kibbutz Shamir archives. Former Shamir members Assaf Razin, Joshua Sobol and Yoav and Avraham Eilat shared memories of the kibbutz. I feel lucky to have spoken with founder Surika Braverman before her death, at age 94, in 2013. In the fall of 2010, management sold a 50 per cent stake of Shamir Optical to French optical giant Essilor, and the company was delisted from the NASDAQ stock exchange; kibbutz members still receive an annual dividend from the thriving business.

Scholars and experts throughout Israel offered insights into the social and political history of the country's kibbutz movement. *Toda raba* to members of the Institution for the Research of the Kibbutz and the Cooperative Ideal at the University of Haifa, including Shlomo Getz, Michal Palgi, Uri Leviatan and Yuval Achouch; staff and researchers associated with Yad Tabenkin, the Research and Documentation Centre of the Kibbutz Movement, including Yaacov Oved, Eliezer Ben-Rafael, Menachem Topol and the tireless Ruth Sobol; staff at the Givat Haviva Center for a Shared Society and the Yad Yaari Archives of the Hashomer Hatzair Movement, including David Amitai, Lydia Aisenberg, Myriam Dagan Brenner and Eli Tzur; economist Ran Abramitzky of Stanford University; Galia Bar-Or, director of the Kibbutz Ein Harod Museum; architects and historians Michael and Bracha Chyutin; Ranen Omer-Sherman at the University of Miami; Oded Lowenheim of Hebrew University; ex-kibbutznik and journalist Daniel Gavron; Aviv Leshem, spokesperson for the Kibbutz Movement; Nehemia Hen of the Kibbutz Industries Association; Avshalom Vilan and Haim Oron, both kibbutzniks and former members of the Israeli Knesset; privatization consultant Israel Oz; and Marie Kushni-Harari, who taught me about cooperative law in Israel.

Kibbutzniks from every corner of the country opened their gates so I could learn more about their communities: Shay Shoshany of Kibbutz Degania; Miri Sela of Kibbutz Mahanayim; David Lehrer, Taal Goldman, Tamar Norkin, Uri Gordon and Tareq Abu Hamed (who went on to become Israel's deputy chief scientist) at the Arava Institute for Environmental Studies at Kibbutz Ketura; Neta Sukenik, Alex Cicelsky, Mark Naveh, Mike Kaplin and Daphna Berger at Kibbutz Lotan; Sofie Berzon of Kibbutz Kfar Aza; Musa Menachem and Yanai Shlomi at Kibbutz Samar; Jonny Whine of Kibbutz Hannaton; Maya Shafir of Kibbutz Yotvata; Tanya Ronen from Kibbutz Lohamei HaGeta'ot; Shlomit Flexer and Uri Pinkerfeld at Kibbutz Revadim; Marc Marcus and Julia Chaitin at Kibbutz Urim; historian Henry Near, whom I interviewed at his home on Kibbutz Beit HaEmek before his death in late 2011; Reuven Shaliv of Kibbutz Harduf; Ehud Satt, an economist on Kibbutz Yagur; Adi Sha'al and Tali Einav-Sapir of the Vertigo Eco-Art Village on Kibbutz Netiv Halamed-Hey; Yehuda Maor, Yoni Avital, Rami Be'er and the dancers of the Kibbutz Contemporary Dance Company at the Galilee Dance Village on Kibbutz Ga'aton—I will never forget the KCDC's mesmerizing performance of "Holy Sand" in Tel Aviv; Eliaz Cohen, Yochanan Ben Yaacov, Yaacov Taube and Myron Joseph at Kibbutz Kfar Etzion in the West Bank. I wish I had space to include more voices from Israel's urban kibbutzim, but Israel's city-based communal movement is evolving faster than anyone can chronicle it. Thanks to Nomika Zion of Kibbutz Migvan; Yiftah Goldman of Kibbutz Tamuz; James Grant-Rosenhead, Anton Marks and Robin Merkel of Kibbutz Yovel; the members of Kibbutz Mishol and Kibbutz Eshbol; and residents of the now-disbanded Ravenna Kibbutz, a Jewish cooperative in Seattle.

I was welcomed (and educated) by founders and members of many other utopian experiments and communities, as well as activists, artists and critics of both the kibbutz movement and the political status quo in Israel. Technically, I am now a bigamist in Achzivland, thanks to Eli and Rina Avivi, the aging rulers and marriage officiants of the break-away state on the Mediterranean coast. Salman Fakhiraldeen, at the Al-Marsad Center in Majdal Shams, opened a window into the complex society of the Druze in the Golan Heights, as did Wael Toraby of the Majdal Shams Cultural Centre and storyteller Denise Assad. Thanks to Rita and Daoud Boulos of Neve Shalom/Wahat-al-Salaam, and co-founder Abdessalam Najjar, whose sudden death, at age 60, less than a year after I interviewed him, sent a shock through the community and beyond; I met nobody else who matched his irrepressible vision of peace. Activist and ex-kibbutznik Eitan Bronstein left Zochrot to found De-Colonizer, a "research/art laboratory for social change," where he continues to teach the history of the Palestinian Nakba. The Sadaka-Reut Commune shut down not long after my visit, but the NGO continues to promote cooperation between Jewish and Palestinian youth; thanks to Fadi Shbeita for coordinating my interviews with Jawad Maekly and Lena Rotenberg. The members of System Ali, including Muhammed Mugrabi, Mouhamad Aguani, Yonatan Kunda and Neta Weiner, continue to perform their multilingual political hip hop. Frans van der Sar returned to Europe from Nes Ammim, where Davi and Asueli Windholz, Yoseph Mubarki and other Jewish and Palestinian residents now guide the "Christian kibbutz" in a new direction; I learned about the unique gravity of Nes Ammim from its young European volunteers, including Marisa Unger, Jennie van de Lagemoat and Lara-Elena Grefen, many of whose parents had once worked there. Shuki Levinger arranged my visit to Kishorit, on a former kibbutz in the Galilee, where Dan Schreier and Israel Eshel showed me the inspiring "home for life" for adults with disabilities. Peace activist Stephen Fulder hosted me at his off-the-grid eco-homestead in Klil. Anva and Nathan Ohn-Bar provided hospitality in the vegetarian village of Amirim. Robert Weinberg gave me a tour of the Bahá'í World Centre in Haifa. Susan Levin of the Lone Pine Brewery showed off her corner of the Etzion Bloc. David Sheen, the frustrated utopian, moved to Dimona with his wife to live near the Black Hebrews; he lectures internationally and produces YouTube exposés about racism in Israel. During my visit to Rawabi,

George Rafidi and Amir Dajani gave me extensive access to the construction site and its employees; after two years' delay getting water access from Israeli authorities and the Palestinian Authority's reneging on promised infrastructure funds, the city of Rawabi welcomed its first 640 families in September 2015. Bashar Masri, the developer, hopes to build a similar project in East Jerusalem.

Colleagues at the International Communal Studies Association offered mentorship through publications, presentations and conversations. Thanks especially to Jan Bang, Bill Metcalf, Graham Meltzer, Michael Livni, Raymond Russell, Esther Vince and my entire cohort (especially roommate Mike Gilsenan) from the Experience Findhorn workshop at the 2013 ICSA conference in Scotland. Yitzhak Rubin, Ran Tal, Jonathan Paz, Ulrikke Pfaff, Lavi Ben-Gal, Toby Perl-Freilich and Tessa Moran shared their superb films about different facets of the changing kibbutz movement; Cara Saposnik of Ruth Diskin Films supplied DVDs of Israeli documentaries; Ian Merkel invited me to talk about kibbutz history at the Vancouver Jewish Film Festival.

My three extended research trips to Israel and the West Bank were made possible by generous financial support from the Canada Council for the Arts and its literary arts program, the B.C. Arts Council and an internal research grant from the University of Victoria. A separate IRG helped to underwrite *Kibbutz: The Settlers of Palestine*, an interactive online narrative, which allows "players" to navigate the ethical dilemmas of a kibbutz founder and Israel's communal movement; Ashley Blacquiere, game designer extraordinaire, helped to create this "choose your own history" experience, which you can play at www.kibbutzgame.com.

Undergraduate research assistants Tyler Laing and Holly Romanow transcribed and indexed audio interviews and video footage. Editorial feedback from MFA students in the Department of Writing helped to refine drafts; thanks to JoAnn Dionne, Danielle Janess and especially Annabel Howard. Online and offline debates with Sid Tafler and Kitty

Hoffman sharpened my thinking about Israel and the kibbutz. Ana-Maria Peredo, the staff and other fellows at the (alas, now defunct) Centre for Cooperative and Community-Based Economy provided a second home for my early research efforts. Dylan Wilks and Carol-Lynne Michaels allowed me to explore what North American neighbourhoods can learn from kibbutz architecture at the first TEDxVictoria event. Chris Roth at *Communities Magazine* also gave me a forum to discuss these ideas in print. My colleagues and students in the Department of Writing at the University of Victoria heard excerpts from the manuscript at our annual faculty readings; their feedback, and the supportive culture of the department, rekindled my creativity when I felt lost in a thicket of revisions. A big *l'chaim* to Richard Pickard and other members of my monthly Beer & Books group, who introduced me to new authors and reminded me to write for a broad and curious readership.

Jerry Flexer, my main research assistant, was a co-pilot on this project from take-off until landing. On my second trip to Israel, he acted as driver, translator, videographer, fixer and road companion. He transcribed many of the recorded interviews, provided tips on research sources and saved my final draft from embarrassing errors with a thorough fact-checking. His personal kibbutz experiences and globe-crossing quest for utopia deserve their own book. I hope he writes it soon.

My manuscript would never have become the book you now hold without the faith and persistence of my agent Sam Hiyate, founder of The Rights Factory. I am also deeply grateful to Jack David, publisher of ECW Press, who saw the promise and importance of this story; editor Susan Renouf, who reined in my runaway paragraphs; creative director Crissy Calhoun and designer David Gee for the book's sumptuous cover design; Jen Knoch for keen-eyed copyediting and curing my overfondness for hyphens; publicist Sarah Dunn, who got the book into more readers' hands; and the whole team at ECW, for their tireless support of all the authors on their roster.

When I announced that I wanted to drop out of university to live on a commune in Israel, my parents bought me a backpack and delivered me to the airport—and I am eternally grateful for that encouragement.

At the core of my fascination with the kibbutz is the early pioneers' belief that we can build a better world for ourselves and, more importantly, for future generations. The abstract ideal I encountered on Kibbutz Shamir as a self-absorbed young bachelor in his twenties feels far more real and urgent today as a husband and a father in his forties. Thank you so very much to Jenny, my wife, and our kids, A.J. and Briar, for their patience and support while I was on my various journeys—and for inspiring my own hope that we can build a just and equal society for all the children of the dream.

More About the Book

To read more about the making of *Chasing Utopia* and the history of the kibbutz, including blog posts, photographs, videos, questions for book groups and contact information for the author, please go to DavidLeach.ca.

Kibbutz: The Settlers of Palestine is an interactive historical simulation designed to supplement the book. Online players assume the role of a kibbutz leader and guide a virtual kibbutz from its origins as a socialist utopia into the current era of privatization. To start your own kibbutz, go to www.KibbutzGame.com.

Photo by Helene Cyr

DAVID LEACH is the author of *Fatal Tide: When the Race of a Lifetime Goes Wrong*. A former magazine editor, he is now the chair of the Department of Writing at the University of Victoria. He lives with his wife and two children in Victoria, British Columbia.

Published by ECW Press
665 Gerrard Street East
Toronto, ON M4M 1Y2
416-694-3348 / info@ecwpress.com

To the best of his abilities, the author has related experiences, places, people, and organizations from his memories of them.

Editor for the press: Susan Renouf
Cover design: David Gee
Cover image courtesy of the author
Interior images: Israel map a modification of derivative work by Mapeh in the creative commons.
Author photo: Helene Cyr
Type: Rachel Ironstone

"It Is Dangerous to Read Newspapers" used with permission of Oxford University Press.

Library and Archives Canada Cataloguing in Publication

Leach, David, 1968-, author
Chasing utopia : the future of the kibbutz in a divided Israel / David Leach.

Issued in print and electronic formats.
ISBN 978-1-77041-340-5 (paperback); ISBN 978-1-77090-939-7 (pdf); ISBN 978-1-77090-938-0 (epub)

1. Kibbutzim. 2. Israel—Social conditions—21st century. 3. Israel—Social life and customs—21st century. 4. Arab-Israeli conflict—1993–. 5. Leach, David, 1968- —Travel—Israel. I. Title.

HX742.2.A3L4 2016   307.77'6095694   C2016-902360-5
C2016-902361-3

The publication of *Chasing Utopia* has been generously supported by the Canada Council for the Arts, which last year invested $153 million to bring the arts to Canadians throughout the country, and by the Government of Canada through the Canada Book Fund. *Nous remercions le Conseil des arts du Canada de son soutien. L'an dernier, le Conseil a investi 153 millions de dollars pour mettre de l'art dans la vie des Canadiennes et des Canadiens de tout le pays. Ce livre est financé en partie par le gouvernement du Canada.* We also acknowledge the support of the Ontario Arts Council (OAC), an agency of the Government of Ontario, which last year funded 1,737 individual artists and 1,095 organizations in 223 communities across Ontario for a total of $52.1 million, and the contribution of the Government of Ontario through the Ontario Book Publishing Tax Credit and the Ontario Media Development Corporation.

Printed and bound in Canada   Printing: Marquis   1   2   3   4   5

Get the eBook FREE!

At ECW Press, we want you to enjoy this book in whatever format you like, whenever you like. Leave your print book at home and take the eBook to go! Purchase the print edition and receive the eBook free. Just send an e-mail to ebook@ecwpress.com and include:
- the book title
- the name of the store where you purchased it
- your receipt number
- your preference of file type: PDF or ePub?

A real person will respond to your e-mail with your eBook attached. Thank you for supporting an independently owned Canadian publisher with your purchase!